# An Unacknowledged Harmony

Recent Titles in
**Contributions in Ethnic Studies**

*Series Editor:* Leonard Doob

# An Unacknowledged Harmony

## PHILO-SEMITISM AND THE SURVIVAL OF EUROPEAN JEWRY

## Alan Edelstein

Contributions in Ethnic Studies, No. 4

GREENWOOD PRESS

WESTPORT, CONNECTICUT • LONDON, ENGLAND

**Library of Congress Cataloging in Publication Data**

Edelstein, Alan.
    An unacknowledged harmony.

    (Contributions in ethnic studies, ISSN 0196-7088;
no. 4)
      Bibliography: p.
      Includes index.
      1. Philosemitism—History.  2. Jews—History—70-  .
I. Title.  II. Title: Philo-Semitism and the survival of
European Jewry.  III. Series.
DS141.E35      909'.04924      81-1563
ISBN 0-313-22754-3 (lib. bdg.)      AACR2

Library of Congress Catalog Card Number: 81-1563
ISBN: 0-313-22754-3
ISSN: 0196-7088

First published in 1982

Greenwood Press
A division of Congressional Information Service, Inc.
88 Post Road West
Westport, Connecticut 06881

Printed in the United States of America

10 9 8 7 6 5 4 3 2 1

FOR MY PARENTS AND MY SISTER

"Who taught you tender Bible tales
Of honey-lands, of milk and wine?
Of happy, peaceful Palestine?
Of Jordan's holy harvest vales?
Who gave the patient Christ? I say
Who gave your Christian creed?
   Yea, yea.
Who gave your very God to you?
Your Jew! Your Jew! Your hated Jew!
Cincinnatus Heine ("Joaquin") Miller, "To Russia"

Yes, I am a Jew, and when the ancestors of the right honourable gentleman were brutal savages in an unknown island, mine were priests in the temple of Solomon.

Benjamin Disraeli

No doubt but ye are the people, and wisdom shall die with you.

Job: XII:2

# CONTENTS

# FOREWORD

"Contributions in Ethnic Studies" focuses upon the problems that arise when people with different cultures and goals come together and interact productively or tragically. The modes of adjustment or conflict are various, but usually one group dominates or tries to dominate the other. Eventually some accomodation is reached: the process is likely to be long and, for the weaker group, painful. No one scholarly discipline contains all the research necessary to comprehend these intergroup relations. The merging analysis, consequently, is inevitably of interest to historians, social scientists, psychologists, and psychiatrists.

This scholarly volume convincingly demonstrates, in the author's words toward the end of the final chapter, that "although anti-Semitism exists and has extracted a monstrous cost from Jews, it has not been ubiquitous, all-powerful, or without Christian opponents." The emphasis, therefore, is not upon anti-Semitism but upon the thoughts and deeds of Christians (with passing references to actions in China, Turkey, and India) who have protected or welcomed Jews and who therefore at the very least have diminished discrimination, injustice, and cruelty. The demonstration is achieved through a historico-sociological analysis that begins in the early Christian era; places great emphasis upon the Middle Ages; describes in some detail the political "emancipation" of Jews, particularly in England and France during the nineteenth century; and reports briefly but adequately the ways in which many Jews were rescued before they became victims of Nazi camps and ovens. The analysis not only provides copious references and anecdotes to sustain the principal thesis but also delineates the societal background in which philo-Semitism has operated. The volume, therefore, is a study in ethnicity: it depicts the relations between superordinate groups and a subordinate group in varying social contexts over time.

Why have Christians—the clergy, philosophers, political leaders, simple people—been friendly and hospitable to Jews? The very question perhaps reveals a prejudice, since it may presume that the relations were destined to be otherwise. At any rate, Professor Edelstein eschews a monistic explanation but reviews the varying historical, economic, theological, and ethical "connections between Christianity and Judaism" as well as the intellectual, political, and humanistic philosophies of leaders, writers, and ordinary men and women who have praised or defended Jews. Oliver Cromwell, for example, is quoted as saying, "Great is my sympathy with this poor people whom God chose, and to whom he gave His law"; in our era C. P. Snow has written that "in almost every sphere of human activity Jews have made contributions utterly out of proportion of their numbers."

The other and complementary theme of this analysis involves the effect of philo-Semitism upon the Jews themselves. A challenging problem for historians and sociologists is to account for the more or less unique survival of Jews as a distinctive ethnic group. The author appraises the various theories now current and presents evidence to show that the friendliness and respect of Christians have played not a minor but a major role.

Identified in this book, in short, are the progenitors of silver linings and the good their efforts have accomplished. Mankind, however, knows or should know perfectly well—and Professor Edelstein agrees—that there are far better ways to promote good than by first creating evil dark clouds.

Leonard W. Doob

# ACKNOWLEDGMENTS

I had the support of many people throughout my work on this study. Edward Falick, Nathan Liebowitz, Elyse Nissim, Goldie Satt Arrow, and Jan Zyniewski provided me with consistent friendship and encouragement and regularly allowed me to use them as sounding boards. Jacqueline A. Lofaro read large portions of the manuscript when it was in its initial stages and offered sound advice and criticism.

Ginny Busch not only translated my own peculiar hieroglyphics into English but was an unfailing one-woman typing and editing service. She also pointed out inconsistencies in the text and offered suggestions that helped clarify it.

Portions of the manuscript were read by Irwin Goldberg, Victor Fisher, Donald S. Frank, A. Justine Jones, M. Barbara Leons, R. Guy Sedlack, Robert Smith, Jay Stanley, and John Toland, all from Towson State University in Maryland. They were generous with their time and made useful suggestions concerning the manuscript. The work is better for their efforts, insights, and wisdom.

My debt to Joseph Bensman and Norman W. Storer of the Graduate Center of the City University of New York can hardly be explained, much less repaid. Their contributions to this book are, literally, on every page. Their contributions to me were of inestimable worth; for the rest of my life I will enjoy the benefits of having had their guidance.

Preparation for the book was supported, in part, by the Memorial Foundation for Jewish Culture. I would like to thank the members of the foundation for their generosity.

# An
# Unacknowledged
# Harmony

# INTRODUCTION  | 1

Almost eight hundred years ago, during the papal reign of Innocent III, the Fourth Lateran Council declared that nonbelievers must wear, in Cecil Roth's phrase, a "Badge of Shame" to announce to the world their failure to adhere to the religion of the majority. This ruling, followed with various degrees of enthusiasm and in varied forms throughout Europe, stigmatized Jews, enhanced differences between them and Gentiles, and presented barriers to social intercourse between the two groups. The Jew became officially different. When, during the Enlightenment, the physical stigma was discarded in most countries, the Jew as different was an established part of European culture. One clear indication of this is the Jewish stereotype. Stereotypes continue to set the Jew apart and contribute to his being perceived as different; historically stereotypes have given rise to incidents ranging from discrimination to pogroms to genocide.

The Jewish stereotype is considered to be a negative one, and because of the traditionally negative stereotype, Jews and many non-Jews conceive of a simple dichotomy in considering Christians' attitudes toward Jews: those who hold stereotypes about Jews are anti-Semitic; those who reject the stereotypes are neutral and unconcerned with an individual's Jewishness.

What has rarely been considered, however, is the fact that Jewish distinctiveness, both real and perceived, has been a source not only of opprobrium but also of approbation. In addition to the more publicized negative stereotypes of Jews, there have been positive ones; and in addition to the more publicized anti-Semitism, there has been philo-Semitism, that is, a belief that regards Jews in neither a negative nor a neutral light, but rather in a positive one. Just as anti-Semitism has traditionally seen the Jew as unique and therefore malevolent, philo-Semitism has traditionally seen the Jew as possessing qualities that are unique but either personally attractive or socially good. This book is an investigation of the phenomenon of philo-Semitism.

The perspective used here to examine philo-Semitism is social history. The mechanism for this analysis is to focus on two specific phenomena: Jewish survival and Jewish emancipation in Europe. Specifically, the study argues (1) that the survival of European Jewry as a salient group and European Jews as

individuals is due in a large degree to philo-Semites; and (2) that the emancipation of European Jewry was due, in the main, to the efforts of philo-
Semites. In sum, medieval philo-Semites secured the right of presence for
Jews in Christendom; modern philo-Semites secured the right of membership for Jews in nineteenth-century Europe.

In general the image of the world as presented by most students of Jewish
history is that of Jews as victims, Christians as persecutors; Jews as passive
recipients of religious and ethnic discrimination, Christians as active pursuers
of Jewish annihilation; Judaism, the father religion, suffering martyrdom at
the hands of Christianity, its theological offspring. All told, numerous students of Jewish history—both Jews and Christians, let it be said—tend to find
Christians, not to say Christianity itself, guilty of persecution, prejudice, and
discrimination; in a word, Christians are deemed guilty of inhumanity.
Moreover, this discriminatory universalism is taken to exist as a particularistic phenomenon in every part of Christendom.

Because of this view, the overwhelming emphasis of studies of Jewish-
Christian relations and Jewish history is on manifestations of anti-Semitism.
Histories, essays, and analyses detail expulsions, massacres, and forced
conversions of Jews as well as the endless forms of physical hardship they
suffered. They cite the periodic and systematic attacks directed at Judaism as
a religion and the social, political, and economic disadvantages to which Jews
have been subjected. Many scholars emphasize that since the rise of Christianity ( and Mohammedanism), Jews have been viewed with opprobrium by,
and have suffered the frustrations, psychoses, and rages of, the adherents of
politically, economically, and socially dominant religions, even though those
faiths originated in Judaism. Tolerance, even in the negative sense of that
term, is the best Jews can hope for. Indeed, tolerance is a welcome reprieve
from the perpetual persecution and repetitive horrors of injustice that Jews
have suffered. In sum, the "wailing-wall" school of Jewish history, as Roth
termed it, is prevalent in studies of the Jews in Christendom.

Perhaps the reason for this is to be found in Gordon Allport's comment
that Jews are obsessed with anti-Semitism.[1] That obsession, however, is not
unjustified. The attacks on, and massacres of, Jews that scholars document
were not the products of their imagination. Nor were the expulsions, forced
conversions, or social, political, and economic restrictions scholarly crea-
tions. Nonetheless, this image of the world is not without consequences for
Jewish studies.

One consequence is that any act by a Christian that could be regarded as
being favorable to Jews is viewed with skepticism. Further, considerable
effort is made to demonstrate a "primary" motive for such an action—that is,
a recondite, nonbeneficent one. It is almost axiomatic in Jewish historiography that Christian beneficence is not what it seems. The majority of these

scholars refrain from documenting philo-Semitism and its concomitant acts, and either disregard or do not consider evidence of its existence. Events that might lead one to suspect the existence of philo-Semitism are usually explained without recourse to that phenomenon. If this tendency is compared with the willingness of the same scholars to accept virtually all hostile acts toward Jews as manifesting anti-Semitism, the contrast makes the reluctance to recognize philo-Semitism all the more visible. While it is true that scholars generally tend toward skepticism, that skepticism is often selective.[2] Some events and their causes are rarely questioned; other events always are.

A second consequence for Jewish history of the emphasis on anti-Semitism is also of significance. In Jewish studies, Jewry is not usually viewed as one of many groups but as a singularly unique entity. Indeed, studies of Jewish history often give the impression that the Jews were the only group outside the mainstream of society, the only group to suffer discrimination.

Although it is justifiable for scholars to regard Jewish history from a Jewish perspective, it is not justifiable, no matter how understandable it may be, for them to ignore other groups or to discount, or at least not consider, all the rest of the events that occupied the minds of men during the periods under consideration. Jewish history must be seen in the larger context of world history as well as within the parochial limitations of Jewish concerns.

A third factor must also be noted. Although most scholars rarely consider it, both logic and empirical data attest to the fact that the persecutions, expulsions, and social and political disabilities the Jews suffered have not been completely destructive—if they were Jewish survival would have been impossible.[3] Further, reason and documentation also attest to the fact that anti-Jewish hostility has not been (and is not) constant and ubiquitous. If it had been, the same conclusion is obvious: Jews could not have survived, individually or collectively, religiously or ethnically. In fact, one might take the opposite tack. Not only have some "disabilities" been beneficial to Jews, but there have been frequent pauses in religious hostilities. Moreover, numerous friendly relations with Christians have punctuated Jewish European history. Even if Jews have not been the favorite people of much of Christian Europe, they have been tolerated not because it has been convenient to do so, but because toleration of Jews was a recognized principle within Christendom.[4] Indeed, the very fact of Jewish presence in Christendom and their transformation from an allegedly pariah status to one of citizenry reflects, in some degree, their acceptance by a portion of European society. Otherwise that presence and transformation would have been impossible.

None of this should imply that the all-too-frequent horrors of Jewish history should be discounted; nor is this intended to cast doubts on earlier scholars' intellectual abilities or on the validity of their writings. The argument is rather that a broader approach to the interpretation of Jewish history is not only possible but necessary, that philo-Semitism must be considered. The intent here is to add a missing dimension to Jewish history, not to substitute one for another. A multitude of students of Jewish history must be applauded for their knowledge and scholarship; yet it is necessary to suggest the fruitfulness of a second perspective, one that is complementary to, not in conflict with, the perspective offered by other scholars.

In placing emphasis on the existence, manifestations, and effects of anti-Semitism, many students of Jewish history document anti-Semitic acts almost exclusively and ignore philo-Semitic ones. As a result of this their descriptions of Jewish-Christian relations and Jewish history are, in effect, studies of the history, significance, and causes of anti-Semitism. In consequence, one doing a secondary analysis of Jewish history that neither focuses on anti-Semitism nor accepts this perspective is faced with methodological problems. Underlying these problems is the difficulty of discerning amicable attitudes and actions on the part of Christians toward Jews when the overall historical tenor is given as rancorous. In order to do so it is necessary to follow a step-by-step procedure of historical analysis.

The first step is to attempt an overall understanding of the place of Jews in Europe over the past two thousand years. The point of this is to determine not only the social, political, and economic situations that directly focused on and affected Jews but also, because the arena of investigation is Christendom itself, to keep in mind the general changes that occurred in Europe. A study of philo-Semitism as a sociohistorical phenomenon involves a preliminary examination of European history on a broad scale. Included in this step is an examination of the history of Jewry in Europe and, concurrently, determinations of "hard data," that is, information about specific historical events.

A wealth of material is available to students of Jewish history. Every epoch of that history has been investigated repeatedly and in depth by a multitude of scholars. The writings of various scholars must be juxtaposed to determine points of consensus and points of contention. The hard data can be accepted through consensus and through use of primary sources. Explanations of those data, however, are subject to interpretation and reinterpretation.

For example, one can accept that Jews were invited into Speyer in 1084, were readmitted to England in the mid-seventeenth century, and were emancipated in Europe in the nineteenth century. But to assert that these events took place is not to suggest causes for them. It is assumed by most scholars that Jews were invited into Speyer and readmitted to England because of the supposed economic advantages Christians would gain by their presence. However, the hard data here are simply the invitation and readmission. Causes are not suggested nor motives implied by those data. The fact of Jewish emancipation can also be separated from interpretations. That Jews struggled to be emancipated is true. That Jews were the catalysts that brought about that emancipation, as many scholars suggest, is open to question. The fact of Jewish emancipation is clearly documented, but reasons for Jewish emancipation are not.

The second step, then, is to determine where the data leave off and interpretation begins. This is perhaps the most difficult aspect of a historical investigation of this kind, because data and interpretations of data have often become inseparable through consensus. This is particularly evident when many scholars share the same perspective, such as that of Jews as victims and Christians as persecutors. Reinterpretation of data is facilitated when a variety of interpretations already exists.

The most effective mechanism for reinterpreting data is to ask questions that differ from, and indeed are often the converse of, those usually asked, in this case about European Jewry, Christendom's attitudes toward European Jewry, and Jewish-Christian relations. The direction of inquiry is controlled by the questions that are posed.

Because scholars are concerned with anti-Semitism, questions about Jewish-Christian relations are posed from this perspective. When anti-Semitic causes are absent and economic causes seem unlikely, scholars tend to ignore the causal issue altogether. Leon Poliakov, for example, points out that attacks on medieval Jewry took the form of "asylums or fortresses taken by assault; mass suicides,"[5] but he does not mention how the Jews obtained these asylums or fortresses. Surely someone granted Jews permission to enter these shelters, and those who did offer them shelter may have been concerned with their survival. It is reasonable to question who these people were and whether and why they were concerned. Similarly, Max L. Margolis and Alexander Marx point out that during the Rindfleisch Massacres two communities in Bavaria escaped injury "thanks to the protection of the magistrates."[6] They do not explain why such protection was offered.

These two examples suggest that clues to possible instances of philo-Semitism are hidden by simple statements that appear in various histories and that point to Christians assisting Jews. Because these statements are often unexplained or explained only by economics, that is, by Christian avarice, questions can be raised about specific events; further, the possibility of philo-Semitism may be raised. By the same reasoning, other events should be investigated. Why did Bernard of Clairvaux try to help and protect Jews? Why did the revolutionary government in France enfranchise French Jewry? Why were Jews welcomed into Turkey after the Spanish expulsion?

More than these, broader questions can be asked. If it is true, for example, as Howard Morley Sachar argues, that "the Catholic hierarchy, and later the Protestant clergy continually besought the sovereigns of Europe to exile their Jewish populations altogether,"[7] then one must wonder why the Jews were never banished from the Papal States and why Jews were accepted into Protestant Holland. These questions may lead to suggestions about the reason for continuance of Jews in Christendom. It may be asked, for example, why no systematic attempt at Jewish annihilation by religious and lay leaders is in evidence, why there were instances of Christians coming to the aid of Jews, and why various Gentiles struggled for Jewish emancipation.

If enough recondite clues become known, that is, if suggestions of Christians supporting Jews and Jewish causes are regularly found buried within histories and primary sources, one is justified in examining these occurrences. Thus the third step is an examination of instances of Christian tolerance, rather than instances of Christian persecution. Just as one can seek out historically consistent causes for anti-Semitic acts, one can seek out historically consistent causes for philo-Semitic acts.

When Oliver Cromwell argues for religious toleration and struggles to ensure the readmission of Jews into England, the possibility of humanistic/ religious philo-Semitism is suggested and should be examined. If similar motives were voiced by other Christians who helped Jews, the possibility that this form of philo-Semitism exists is strengthened. Because the writings of Pope Gregory I (the Great) argue for toleration of Jews for reasons similar to those voiced by Cromwell, and because numerous popes have accepted and endorsed Gregory's doctrines regarding Jews, one is justified in asserting the existence of humanistic/religious philo-Semitism. Similar analyses reveal other historically consistent causes of philo-Semitism.

The underlying premise of this book, then, is that one cannot simply define Christianity (or Islam) as an anti-Semitic faith nor define all Christians (or Moslems) as anti-Semites. Similarly, one cannot define Jewish-Christian (or Jewish-Islamic) relations as consistently manifesting hostility, and only hostility. It is legitimate to examine and, where possible, reevaluate commonly accepted points in Jewish history and to examine the harmonious aspects of Jewish-Christian relations and determine the significance of those aspects for Jews.

There are scholars who do not conform to the lachrymose school of Jewish history and who are willing to consider the possible existence of philo-Semitism. Their works have been invaluable in the writing of this book and as such deserve special mention here.

While virtually every study by Cecil Roth is an intellectual feast, of special value here is his *Essays and Portraits in Anglo-Jewish History*. In this collection of articles Roth asserts the existence of and suggests causes for English philo-Semitism. Jacob Katz's works, too, were of immeasurable importance for this book. His *Out of the Ghetto* provides insights into the significance of non-Jews in Jewish emancipation. An excellent survey of Christians coming to the aid of Jews during World War II is found in Philip Friedman's *Their Brother's Keeper*. Unique essays about Jews, anti-Semitism, and Jewish-Christian relations are available in *Jews in a Gentile*

*World*, edited by Isacque Graeber and Stewart Henderson Britt; of particular importance, given the confusion surrounding the issue of Jews and finance, is the article by Miriam Beard. Salo W. Baron's marvelous *Ancient and Medieval Jewish History* is of special significance because Baron does not hesitate to question Jewish historiography, especially the issue of the alleged social distance between medieval Jews and Christians. Finally, Frederick M. Schweitzer's *A History of the Jews Since the First Century A.D.* is among the best of the briefer studies of Jewish history. Moreover, Schweitzer considers the possible existence of philo-Semitism in Christian Europe; he does not, however, suggest causes for it.

## NOTES

1. Allport (1958), pp. 140-41.
2. Bensman and Lilienfeld (1973), p. 125.
3. Marcus (1965), p. xiii.
4. Cecil Roth, "The European Age in Jewish History," in Finkelstein (1974), p. 226.
5. Poliakov (1965), p. 50.
6. Margolis and Marx (1969), p. 403.
7. H. M. Sachar (1958), p. 28.

# TOWARD A DEFINITION OF PHILO-SEMITISM | 2

It has long been recognized by social scientists that prejudice has two facets. Virtually every theory dealing with this topic notes that there are positive as well as negative aspects of prejudice, or that there exist feelings of attraction for a specific group (or groups) by outsiders as well as feelings of repulsion. Perhaps because the negative component of prejudice is more intellectually interesting, perhaps because the effects of the negative component provide more fruitful research possibilities, perhaps because the negative component lets scholars define themselves in terms of their grievances and provides specific goals for countermeasures, the positive component of prejudice appears to be considered unworthy of study. "Positive prejudice" is rarely examined; usually it is accorded little more than a brief nod, a reluctant recognition of its theoretically necessary existence.

Nowhere is this more obvious than in studies of Jewish-Gentile relations. Although social scientists accept the existence of philo-Semitism, their interest has been overwhelmingly concentrated on the examination, discussion, and analysis of anti-Semitism, to such an extent that consideration of the positive component of these relations is virtually ignored. The term "philo-Semitism" rarely appears in sociological discussions of the interactions between Jews and non-Jews. It does occur in the works of scholars of Jewish history, albeit infrequently, but in these works a definition of philo-Semitism is rarely offered and there is no explication of the term. It is not surprising that this is the case; histories of Jews generally focus on the negative, as do social scientists' analyses of Jewish-Gentile relations. Of course, this is understandable in the light of the history of pogroms, the Holocaust, and other attempts at genocide. Moreover, the work involved in defining and analyzing "philo-Semitism" holds little attraction.

Definitional problems are usually quite difficult; in areas dealing with Jewish studies they take on the appearance of insolubility. This is readily discernible in the seemingly futile attempt to decide what is here the most basic of questions: Who and what is a Jew? Scholars point out that there is no satisfactory definition of Jews or Judaism, that Jewish as well as Christian thinkers fail to agree on proper meanings of these terms and, worse, that attempts to define the Jews are almost necessarily doomed to futility because the Jews are indefinable.[1]

If there are problems in defining the term "Jew," it should not be surprising that there are just as many problems in defining "anti-Semitism." Rudolph M. Loewenstein correctly points out that there is not only no exact definition of anti-Semitism, but no agreement about its symptoms.[2] Still, because it is advantageous to adopt some definition of anti-Semitism that indicates the method that will be used to define philo-Semitism, the one offered by Melvin Tumin will be used here. Anti-Semitism is "that sentiment or action which maligns or discriminates against persons called Jewish on the ground that, being Jewish, they possess certain undesirable traits.[3]

This definition has failings and is somewhat limited in its application; most definitions treat prejudice, including anti-Semitism, as an attitude containing a behavioral component. Tumin's definition fails to discuss degrees of "sentiment" or "action" or consider the emotive aspect of anti-Semitism. Nonetheless, it does offer some advantages. The definition is ahistorical; does not preclude religious, racial, or nationalistic anti-Semitism or any combination of these; and deals with both the attitudinal and behavioral components, albeit independently. Moreover, Tumin's definition does not depend upon a precise understanding of the term "Jewish" but assumes a sociological perspective and allows for several manifestations of anti-Semitism. Despite its limitations, then, it is better—more operative—than most, and it will provide the point of departure here for a definition of philo-Semitism.

## PHILO-SEMITISM AND ANTI-SEMITISM

Social scientists tend to agree that prejudice exists not as a single unit but in components.[4] Generally, and allowing for slight variations, scholars present prejudice as consisting of three components: the conceptions or ideas an individual has, the sensations that grow from those conceptions, and the actions that may or may not result. Scholars further agree that there are degrees or levels of prejudice. In saying that an individual is prejudiced, one does not offer an empirical prediction unless an accompanying discussion examines the likelihood that the prejudiced individual will, if anti-Semitic, "malign or discriminate" against Jews. That prediction depends upon the intensity of the prejudice.[5] Moreover, just as the sentimental component of prejudice is divisible, the action component may also be subdivided, for actions as well as attitudes vary.[6]

In examinations of Gentiles' perceptions of Jews, prejudice may be represented by a continuum:

anti-Semitic ⟶ tolerant

The continuum is shaded; the transition from anti-Semitic to tolerant is taken to be linear, if not absolutely then at least theoretically.

In these discussions (and in all others), analysts stop at the "tolerant" individual. This, of course, is in keeping with the prevailing concern with the negative aspect of prejudice. It is suggested here that the continuum be extended to include the positive component of prejudice, philo-Semitism. The revised continuum then becomes:

anti-Semitic ⟶ tolerant ⟶ philo-Semitic

The spectrum of Gentile views of Jews now ranges from the actively anti-Semitic through the tolerant, or for purposes of this analysis a-Semitic,[7] to the actively philo-Semitic. The anti-Semitic to tolerant to philo-Semitic continuum is more realistic in empirical terms and offers greater theoretical latitude in understanding Jewish-Gentile relations. The full range of Gentile attitudes toward Jews is encompassed by this continuum, and as anti-Semitism is viewed by analysts as having shadings, this continuum allows philo-Semitism to be similarly considered.

Degrees of philo-Semitism are manifest in a way that parallels the degrees of anti-Semitism. The philo-Semite may hold an intense devotion to, a mild (but real) concern for, or a generally sympathetic perspective on Jews. Moreover, combinations of these may, and usually do, exist, depending upon the situation. Actions that result from philo-Semitic attitudes range from those entailing considerable sacrifice, such as risk of life, through those that are less demanding, to those that consist of mild support on various issues of importance to Jews. Just as there are vociferous anti-Semites, individuals who hold somewhat negative images of Jews, and "light grey" anti-Semites,[8] so there are vociferous philo-Semites, individuals who hold somewhat positive images of Jews, and "pearl grey" philo-Semites.

Strong philo-Semitism entails a "historical identification" or sense of "interdependence of fate" with Jews.[9] In its weakest form philo-Semitism is anti-anti-Semitism. "Weak" philo-Semitism can be manifested by resistance to, or perhaps intellectual, social, or political attacks on, anti-Semitism; "strong" philo-Semitism is shown by specific pro-Jewish actions. For philo-Semitism to exist, its attitudes or actions must be directed toward Jews as a group, and not merely toward one or two specific Jews that the individual finds attractive. That is, philo-Semitism must be universalistic, not particularistic. This should not be taken to mean that philo-Semites must regard all Jews equally. Philo-Semitism can be directed toward specific subgroups of Jews, such as Jewish intellectuals or religiously orthodox Jews, so long as other Jewish subgroups or other Jews generally are not negatively treated or regarded.

Perhaps the most practicable way of defining philo-Semitism is to offer the converse of a definition of anti-Semitism. One might, for example, paraphrase

Tumin and suggest that philo-Semitism is that sentiment or action which supports or discriminates in favor of persons called Jewish on the grounds that, being Jewish, they possess certain desirable traits. This provides some indication of the way in which the problem of defining philo-Semitism may be handled, but it is unacceptable as a definition. The philosophic point is that the opposite of anti-Semitism would be a-Semitism, not philo-Semitism—just as the opposite of hate is apathy, not love.[10] Thus the two attitudes are not simply the converse of one another. For example, both anti-Semitism and philo-Semitism have appeared at moments of social unrest and economic chaos, such as the French Revolution. One reason they tend to appear at the same time is that philo-Semitism is often manifested in response to anti-Semitism. If one were the converse of the other, however, each would appear when the other did not, or at least when the other was minimized. Clearly, opposing or converse effects cannot have the same cause.

Further, anti-Semitism almost always endorses elimination of Jews through conversions, expulsions, or physical extermination. Some philo-Semitism was (and is) premised on assimilation of Jews into the larger society; yet in many forms it supports the continued existence of Jews as Jews and the continuance of a specific Jewish culture, although without necessarily endorsing a growth in Jewish culture or population. In addition, it is important that although the reaction of Jews to anti-Semitism has always been negative, the reaction of Jews to philo-Semitism has not always been positive. For example, not all Jews welcomed emancipation.

Finally, defining philo-Semitism as the converse of anti-Semitism could be misleading, given the various interpretations of the latter concept. There have, of course, been occasions in which philo-Semitism has appeared to be the converse of anti-Semitism, and in numerous instances such a definition would be sufficient. Yet one cannot justifiably define philo-Semitism simply as the converse of anti-Semitism and leave it at that.

There are, however, insights to be gained by examining and applying various conceptions of anti-Semitism to the definition of philo-Semitism, and a good deal to be learned from the way in which scholars use the former concept. Actions associated with, and interpretations of, anti-Semitism (as well as examinations of the reasoning of known anti-Semites) provide guides that can facilitate the determination of what philo-Semitism is, how it works, and why. Numerous studies, histories, and analyses of anti-Semitism can provide the *form*, not the substance, of the definition and explication of philo-Semitism.

## THE DIMENSIONS OF PHILO-SEMITISM

For two millenia Jews have lived in virtually every land and have been found in every walk of life. It is not surprising, then, that as Tumin notes, "expressions of anti-Semitism ... vary with time and place.[11] It is reasonable to assume that expressions of philo-Semitism, too, vary with time and place; that the form, tenor, and degree of manifest philo-Semitism depends on era and location; and that these in turn are contingent on factors found in social histories. If theories of socialization are not to be totally discredited, individuals' attitudes are shaped by their times, physical environment, and most significantly, by prevailing ideologies and beliefs. Further, the influence, positive or negative, of the particular Jews with whom the philo-Semite comes into contact cannot be ignored. Because it is probable that Jews constitute one of the most diverse groups of ethnic peoples, Gentiles can and do come into contact only with specific subgroups of Jews. In different geographic areas and in different epochs, Jews have varied widely in their interests, activities, occupations, life styles, and social positions; such diversity has also obtained within the Jewish community. It is not surprising, then, that in each era, in each area, and among different peoples, perceptions of Jews have varied widely.[12]

It is apparent from the above that there must be numerous sources of philo-Semitism. One can suggest economic, political, personal (that is, psychological), religious, and ideological causes for the phenomenon of philo-Semitism, just as scholars offer these as causes for the existence of anti-Semitism.[13] It seems reasonable, given the history and variability of Jews, that there are several possible expressions of philo-Semitism, each having an application in, at minimum, one location and during one era. Each of these several expressions of philo-Semitism may have numerous applications and a variety of permutations, and in each case there are complexities. All of these must be considered in formulating a definition of philo-Semitism. While it might satisfy a user of Occam's Razor to state that philo-Semitism is, more often than not, "pure" and only minimally affected by the vagaries of the world, this would be a hopelessly naïve position.

There are varied forms of philo-Semitism. For instance, an anti-Jewish attitude, based on religion, evolved into an anti-Semitic attitude, based on race; concomittantly, philo-Semitism evolved from a pro-Jewish (or Judeo-philic) attitude, based on religion, to a philo-Semitic attitude, based on ethnicity. The turning point in both cases was the French Revolution. In practical terms this means that for much of history the goal of those who held attitudes detrimental to Jews was the latter's conversion: when and if Jews became Christians they were usually (but not always) accepted. In modern times, that is, since the French Revolution, conversion has not been a criterion for sociopolitical acceptance in most cases.

Before the Revolution, anti-Jewish movements and actions attacked the religion of the Jews and not the people—although, of course, the people were necessarily the focus of the attacks on Judaism.[14] Similarly, affection for Jews was initially Judeophilic, an admiration of and respect for the religion of the Jewish people; for Jewish traditions; and, especially in some Protestant denominations, for the connection between Judaism and Christianity. Those who were philo-Semitic in the Middle Ages often were so because of a religiously-based regard for Judaism, and not necessarily for Jews as people.[15] Judeophilia as such focused on the beliefs of the people and not on the people themselves. Often protection of Jews by Christians was protection of the Jewish religion with, again, the people as beneficiaries of that protection.[16] Since religion was the greatest single institution in Europe at that time, philo-Semitism quite naturally manifested itself ecclesiastically.

An incipient change in the perception of Jews was first discernible with the successful establishment of Protestantism in many European countries. Although much of Protestantism was not especially favorable to Jews, individual sects such as the Puritans tended to admire Biblical Jews and Jewish tradition.[17] Moreover, the Protestant regard for individualism in both personal responsibility and religious commitment tended to benefit Jews.

A greater change in the Christian perception of Jews came with the rise of the nation-state and the spread of the ideology of the Enlightenment. Organized, state-affiliated religion diminished in importance. Concurrently, humanism and the influence of the secular state grew, and changes in the Christian perception of Jews became increasingly apparent. Negatively, Jews were viewed not only as religious outsiders but as national outsiders; anti-Judaism had changed to anti-Semitism.[18] But as anti-Judaism changed to anti-Semitism, Judeophilia had changed to philo-Semitism. Those individuals who now were pro-Jewish were so not because of the ancient traditions and beliefs of Judaism, nor because Judaism was needed to document Christianity—although undoubtedly these reasons were important to some individuals—but for secular reasons.

The assertion by Eckhardt that anti-Jewishness is part of anti-Semitism, which logically follows from his religiously oriented conceptions of Jews and Jewishness, must be qualified, as must any suggestion that pro-Jewishness is a part of philo-Semitism. Although these may be correlated in some instances, it cannot be said to be always the case. Important distinctions exist between philo-Semitism and Judeophilia, and between anti-Semitism and anti-Jewishness. "Semitism," as the term is used today, is a modern concept (post-French Revolution) that implies race or ethnicity. It is historically true, however, that much that was Judeophilic manifested itself as, had effects on, or directly resulted in philo-Semitism. Because of this, and for other reasons that will become apparent during the development of the central theme of this study, the two will not be considered as separate entities here; both will be included under the rubric of "philo-Semitism."

Before this discussion of philo-Semitism is continued, a word of caution must be offered. Because Jewish-Gentile relations have generally been unhappy, and because the history of Jews in Christendom has been essentially bleak, it is necessary to guard against overreaction. Care must be taken to eschew "cheap" philo-Semitism and "patronizing attitudes,"[19] and one must be wary of seeing philo-Semitism in every act that involves Jews but is not detrimental to them. Yet a greater error, both intellectually and morally, is to apologize for anti-Semitic acts because, appearances notwithstanding, it is assumed that an individual had the interests of Jews in mind even when he acted in a manner that was detrimental to them. Great restraint must be exercised in analyses and discussions of philo-Semitism, and it is imperative not to interpret every nonhostile act concerning Jews as an act of philo-Semitism. Similarly, it is necessary to refrain from making (or at least to minimize) conclusive assertions about individual philo-Semites; nor can one make sweeping statements involving generalities of beneficence.[20]

## DEFINING PHILO-SEMITISM

If the concept of "pure," ahistorical philo-Semitism is discounted, as indeed it should be, it becomes apparent, first, that a definition of the term cannot be limited only to an affection for (some) Jews to the exclusion of other peoples (including, perhaps, other Jews). One cannot demand that an individual who endorses a philo-Semitic attitude restrict his affection to Jews alone in order to qualify as philo-Semitic. If the times call for enlightened individuals to speak out for oppressed peoples, one cannot reasonably require that a philo-Semite be someone who speaks out only for Jews (if they are oppressed) while ignoring others who are similarly persecuted. The only requirement here is that Jews, as a group, be distinguished from others, that is, that Jews be regarded as Jews and not simply as one of the many groups who ought to be helped.

It is important to point out that in European history Jews *have always* been identified as a special group. This will be demonstrated throughout this study. Several contingent points should be noted. Because of their unique status, Jews have been viewed as a legitimate focus of attitude and action. More than this, Jews have often been singled out for consideration, sometimes in regard to actions that were directed toward other groups as well, but still as a unique and special entity. The significance of this for philo-Semitism becomes apparent if one considers analyses of anti-Semitism.

It has been documented repeatedly that individuals who hold an anti-Semitic attitude are often also anti-Catholic, anti-Protestant, anti-Black, and so on, although they seldom hold all these prejudices with uniform intensity or for the same reasons. Clearly these other prejudices do not make those individuals any less anti-Semitic. No one would suggest that Adolph Hitler was not (or less) anti-Semitic because he was also anti-Slavic. The circumstances that form one attitude often contribute to the formation of other, similar attitudes. If conditions and circumstances bring an individual to adopt a philo-Semitic position, it is reasonable to assume that those same conditions and circumstances will lead that individual to adopt other enlightened views. Support for non-Jews does not negate the fact, efficacy, or depth of the philo-Semitism—indeed, one often feeds the other. This is not to imply that philo-Semitism *necessarily* follows upon other enlightened views; it is only to suggest that it does not preclude them.

A second point to be considered is that of Christians giving benefits to Jews for economic gain. Although the issue of Christians "using" Jews to enhance their own financial positions will be discussed throughout the book, a brief comment seems warranted here because of the consistently negative interpretations it has received.

It is generally accepted by scholars that during the Middle Ages Jews were invited into (or, after their expulsion, invited to return to) lands because their entry would enhance the economic status of these areas. Scholars are quick to point out that the interests of Jews were not the prime concern of those who asked them into these lands, that the main concern of the Christians was their own economic advantage, and that the Christians showed little hesitation in ordering the expulsion of those same Jews when the fortunes of their lands fell, for whatever reason. Scholars further point out that numerous restrictions would be laid on the Jews along with the invitation to settle in the land in question. Those same scholars, however, do not hesitate to term "anti-Semitic" those acts that, while hurting Jews, proved beneficial to the instigators of the acts.

There have been numerous instances of anti-Semitism for profit. For example, many tradespeople and guild members during the Middle Ages endorsed the expulsion of Jews from their communities because the Jews were unwanted competition; Jews as Jews were not the issue. Here, anticipating a discussion that will occur later in the book, it should be noted that during the Middle Ages, and indeed until September 1791, Jews were not officially members of any nation in Europe. They were there only through the grace of the rulers. Thus it was possible for their economic competitors to work for the Jews' expulsion, an impossibility where native Christian competitors were concerned.[21] Yet these actions are not considered by scholars as less than anti-Semitic, despite the fact that there was an ulterior motive; nor should they be so considered. By the same token, however, one cannot automatically dismiss as *non*-philo-Semitic actions that, although beneficial to Jews, provide benefits to those who instigate the actions. This is not to suggest that such actions should be automatically taken to be philo-Semitic; but they cannot be dismissed out of hand either. If the phenomenon of "economic anti-Semitism" (anti-Semitism for profit) is acceptable, it is also acceptable to assume the possibility of economic philo-Semitism.

A similar problem exists in determinations of political philo-Semitism. It has often happened that Jews and Jewish causes were supported by individuals and groups who had as their primary goals factors other than the welfare of

Jews. But all too often there have been situations in which Jews were attacked, not because they were Jews, but because political advantages were to be gained by attacking Jews.[22] Even though Jews were not the primary concern, and in some cases not even the secondary concern, of those who instigated attacks on them, there has been little hesitation in considering the protagonists to be anti-Semitic. While no doubt caution must be used in determining the various forms of philo-Semitism, this caution necessarily includes a warning against automatically dismissing the existence of philo-Semitism simply because the welfare of Jews was not the primary concern of the actors.[23]

The possibility must be considered that the actions of those people who benefited both themselves and Jews is a manifestation of enlightened self-interest. As there is no quarrel in seeing anti-Semitism while Gentiles attack Jews because of self-interest, so there can be little argument in seeing philo-Semitism when Gentiles defend Jews for that same self-interest. To suggest that philo-Semitism be limited to those who did not, or could not, derive benefits from philo-Semitic actions—including at a minimum, one must suppose, self-satisfaction—is to reduce the number of philo-Semites to the saintedly unselfish. One cannot argue that gaining an advantage from a friendship nullifies that friendship.

The same reasoning applies in discussions of religiously motivated preju-dices about Jews. If one accepts the idea of a religiously based anti-Semitism, as most scholars do, it would be at best narrowly one-sided to discount the possibility of a religiously oriented philo-Semitism. Here, of course, one must be wary of hidden conversionist motives; but this caution in itself cannot negate the possibility and consequent examination of religious philo-Semitism.

Finally, as scholars have long recognized, people's attitudes are not always consistent. Just as the "forms and degrees" in which anti-Semitism manifests itself vary greatly, the same must hold true for the forms and degrees of philo-Semitism.[24] It is unrealistic to demand that philo-Semitism be attributed only to those who are fully committed on every issue involving Jews; it is not reasonable to demand the same support or dedication on all topics. What is reasonable to expect is that an individual who exhibits a philo-Semitic attitude will not malign or discriminate against Jews even on those occasions when he cannot actively support Jews.

In general, philo-Semitism occasions some sympathy with or affection for Jews and entails viewing Jews, but not necessarily all Jews or only Jews, as having at least potentially intrinsic social value. Again, it is not necessary that Jews alone be so viewed. The only requisites here are that Jews be consid-ered a separate and unique entity and that actions taken be directed at Jews as Jews and not at several groups, one of which happens to be Jews, without regard to ethnic or religious distinctions.

More specifically, philo-Semitism is a belief system that

1. sees Jews in a positive light. The term "Jew" here is determined by the philo-Semite and may be specifically limited to a particular sub-group of Jews, but must include at minimum a "tolerant" attitude toward other groups of Jews.

2. may take a multitude of forms, depending on the time, place, and situation—the historical period, national location, immediate reason for its manifestation, and current universalisms and ideologies.

3. has attitudinal and behavioral components. These may be manifested in various ways and may exist in various strengths.[25]

4. in its weakest sense entails anti-anti-Semitism; that is, philo-Semitism necessarily implies a rejection of anti-Semitism in *all* of the latter's forms.

5. may or may not lead to overt actions in various forms and degrees.[26]

6. may or may not be consistent, depending on historical, social, political, or economic conditions, but cannot under any circumstances be detrimental to Jews as a group or to any subgroup of Jews.

7. may exist for numerous reasons—self-interested, religious, political, economic, or humanistic motives.

At minimum, the interests of Jews cannot be discounted; that is, philo-Semitism implies knowledge of the *consequence of an action for Jews*. For philo-Semitism to exist there must be concern for Jews as Jews. Unless one recognizes that his actions will have favorable repercussions for Jews and unless these repercussions are, in part, a basis for his actions, the situations, problems, and lives of Jews must be regarded as irrelevant to the actor. Without the understanding that Jews will benefit from the actor's decisions (and their implementation), philo-Semitism cannot be considered to exist.

This is not to suggest that only Jews benefit from philo-Semitic actions, or that the actor does not derive advantages from them. The crucial issue is that philo-Semitism necessarily signifies recognition of the positive consequences of actions for Jews.

The core of philo-Semitism is a favorable attitude toward Jews. This does not imply that an individual philo-Semite will not be an assimilationist,[27] devoutly Christian or Moslem, or supportive of Israel.[28]

An individual philo-Semite may or may not hold a positive image of the Jewish religion in its various forms—to insist that one does would be to define both Jews and philo-Semitism religiously. However, philo-Semitism does necessarily include positive perspectives toward or actions consciously supporting Jews, and not merely the absence of negative perspectives or actions. Neutral views and refusals to act negatively toward Jews in and of themselves signal "a-Semitism," not philo-Semitism.

Philo-Semitism implies not only recognition of Jews as a specific group, but also a respect for the Jewish people. Respect, while a necessary condition in determinations of what is and is not philo-Semitic and who is and who is not a philo-Semite, is not a sufficient condition, however. Anti-Semites often express respect for Jews. The difference is that while the respect manifested in anti-Semitism is often coupled with fear, the respect manifested in philo-Semitism is coupled with some attitudes of benignity for the Jewish people. This respect and benignity result in an identification with at least some Jews and admiration of at least some things Jewish or a high regard for at least some values attributed to Jews.

## DETERMINING PHILO-SEMITISM

For purposes of clarity there should be some distinction made between philo-Semitism and its behavioral component, the philo-Semitic act.[29] How does one determine what is and is not a philo-Semitic act, and implicitly, who is and who is not a philo-Semite? At first glance there would seem to be a ready criterion: Does the act benefit Jews? An action that favors Jews is positive discrimination. But even when accounting for the time, place, and circumstances, the issue is not nearly so simple. Problems exist first because, as Tumin notes, "intergroup hostilities have unconscious as well as conscious dimensions and unintended as well as positive components.[30] These same unconscious dimensions and unintended components surely exist in inter-group harmony. This makes the determination of philo-Semitic actions difficult. A more fundamental problem is in the very determination of whether or not a specific action is beneficial to Jews.

There are relatively few problems in recognizing benefits to Jews in life saving situations, although even here there are some problems. During attacks on Jews in the Middle Ages, Jews were usually given the choice of conversion to Christianity or death. Many chose to die. In the light of this it would seem presumptuous to assume that in life saving situations all people would at all times accept survival and its consequences.

Situations that do not involve a choice between life and death are still more complex. If an action helped to emancipate Western Jewry but simultaneously diminished the religiosity of Jews, can it be considered philo-Semitic? For example, most Jews chose emancipation when it was granted; yet others feared that emancipation would result in a loss to Judaism and for that reason eschewed sociopolitical "freedom."

Again, in determining whether an action is beneficial to Jews, how is one to consider the temporal aspect? If, for example, an act is initially injurious (or beneficial) to Jews but becomes beneficial (or injurious) at a later time, should one consider only the initial consequences of the act?

Individuals will answer these questions differently, according to their definitions of "Jew," their religiosity, their historical perspectives, and their views regarding assimilation, among other things. It would seem that ultimately one must know the unconscious dimension of the philo-Semite's mind. But to make this the central issue can only result at best in ineffective psychologisms and at worst in misleading speculations. Any attempt to ascribe motives to an actor whose motives are unknowable does more to obfuscate than to illuminate. There is rarely any hesitation in considering an anti-Semitic act to be the work of an anti-Semite. It is thus not unreasonable to use the same criterion, if perhaps more cautiously, in considering philo-Semitic acts.

The best solution would be a determination of the apparent intent of the actor; that is, there must be some viable justification for terming an actor a philo-Semite. One cannot accept the idea, for example, that every anti-Nazi was philo-Semitic. If Jews benefit from an action but the initiator of that action did not concern himself with Jews, it would be folly to consider him a philo-Semite. To do so would make the term useless. This agrees with Hubert M. Blalock's assertion that "definitions of discrimination usually . . . involve some notion of *intent* and require causal inferences."[31] But while Blalock's assertion is reasonable, it assumes that the intent is known or knowable, and this is not always the case. However, this book draws primarily on data that *do* reveal the intent of the actor to benefit Jews.

It is also possible that an action by a supposed philo-Semite was in fact intended to harm Jews, or that the "Jewish problem" was fully irrelevant in determining the action, even though for one reason or another the action had beneficial results for Jews. When intent is not known, it seems obvious that the nature of an action vis-à-vis Jews can only be judged by the reaction of the Jews of the period—by those Jews, that is, who were affected by the action.[32] If, for example, most Jews accepted the emancipation offered to them at the cost of religiousness, one must define that offer as in some sense philo-Semitic.

Caution, of course, must be exercised. It is not impossible that Jews in any given period may have wrongly regarded individuals as philo-Semites because they believed them to have favorable intentions that did not actually exist. Nonetheless, in the final analysis the determination of an individual's actions as philo-Semitic must be made on evidence provided by Jews who were involved in the situation at the time it occurred. If the responses of a very limited number of Jews are the only ones available, one must either withhold judgment or consider the action from a historical perspective; that is, one must characterize the action in the light of resulting events or subsequent evidence. In this book, two historical circumstances will provide criteria for such considerations: the right of presence granted Jews in medieval Europe and the right of membership granted them in nineteenth-century Europe.

## NOTES

1. See Robb (1954), p. 11; Anita Libman Lebeson, "The American Jewish Chronicle," in Finkelstein (1974), p. 517; A. Roy Eckhardt (1973), p. 33; Carl Mayer, "The

Religious Aspects of Anti-Judaism," in Graeber and Britt (1942), p. 312. For various definitions of Jews, see Jacob Katz (1962), p. 3; Nathan Glazer (1957), p. 4; Max Weber (1958b), pp. 173-74; Michael R. Marrus (1971), p. 3; J. O. Hertzler, "The Sociology of Anti-Semitism through History," in Graeber and Britt (1942), p. 83; James Parkes (1962), p. vii; Hannah Arendt (1958), p. 6; Gordon Allport (1958), pp. 88, 117-18; Arthur A. Cohen, cited in A. Roy Eckhardt (1973), pp. 35, 42; Morris Kertzler, cited in Joseph E. Faulkner (1972), p. 72; and Frederick Schweitzer (1971), p. 257.

Ernest van den Haag (1969, p. 31) notes that "the question of what is a Jew has puzzled Jews and Gentiles alike." He also notes (ibid., p. 27) that Jews are ambiguous about their "own great men" as well as their own existence. This is not an exaggeration. Heinrich Heine, for example, is said to have remarked: "I was baptized, not converted," implying that he remained a Jew regardless of the Christianizing ceremony. Pulzer (1969, p. 6) is probably correct in arguing that "both Marx and Disraeli were baptized in infancy, yet most anti-Semites would claim them as Jews. So would most Jews."

Anti-Semites do not seem to have this definitional problem. During Hitler's reign in Germany, the question of who was and who was not a Jew was determined by governmental and technical considerations. There was a marked lack of ambiguity there.

It should also be noted that this definitional problem is a modern one. Frank Talmage (1975) points out that medieval Jewry had no "identity crisis," and Parkes (1962, p. 175) comments that "the medieval Latin *Judaismus* made no distinction" between the several possible definitions. Jews were simultaneously and unambiguously a people, religion, race, etc.

2. Loewenstein (1951), p. 14. J. F. Brown, in "The Origins of the Anti-Semitic Attitude" (in Graeber and Britt, 1942, p. 124) comments that "anti-Semitism means very different things to different people." One possible reason for the confusion is suggested by James H. Robb (1954, p. 173), who views anti-Semitism as a "unique phenomenon," different from all other forms of prejudice. For various definitions of anti-Semitism see James H. Robb (1954), p. 11; Robert F. Byrnes (1969), p. vii; and A. Roy Eckhardt (1973), pp. 3-4. Maurice Samuels considers anti-Judaism a dislike of Jews and anti-Semitism as a sign of someone suffering from hallucinations and delusions (noted in Carl J. Friedrich, "Anti-Semitism: Challenge to Christian Understanding," in Graeber and Britt, 1942). Carl Mayer (in Graeber and Britt, 1942, pp. 317-18) holds a view similar to Eckhardt's, that anti-Semitism "should more precisely be called 'anti-Judaism'." See also *Encyclopedia Judaica*, vol. 3, p. 88; and *The Universal Jewish Encyclopedia*, vol. 1. p. 341.

3. Tumin (1971), p. 309.

4. See, for example, Hubert M. Blalock (1967), p. 7; Robin M. Williams (1964), p. 28; Paul F. Secord and Carl W. Backman (1964), pp. 97, 446; Charles Y. Glock and Rodney Stark (1966), p. 103.

5. See Robin Williams (1964), p. 103; Bruno Bettleheim and Morris Janowitz (1964), p. 117; Glock and Stark (1966), pp. 124-25.

6. Allport (1958), p. 28.

7. See Morton Keller, "Jews and the Character of American Life Since 1930," in Stember et al. (1961). He considers a-Semitism to be "indifference to or unawareness of" identification of Jews (pp. 270-71). Also see Teller (1968), p. 288. A-Semitism

suggests that Jews will not be considered differently than anyone else. This may be an ethically admirable position; it is not philo-Semitism.

8. This term is used by Stark and Steinberg (1967).

9. These phrases are used by Milton Gordon and Kurt Lewin, respectively. Both are noted in Gordon (1964), pp. 42-44. Although these criteria were originally used to express membership in an ethnic group, when applied to Christian perceptions of Jews they can be taken as indicative of a strong philo-Semitism.

10. The *contradiction* of hate is love—and vice-versa.

11. Tumin (1961), p. 2.

12. For examinations of the effects of economics, religion, social status, and other sociological variables on prejudice, see, for example, Glock and Stark (1966), Selznick and Steinberg (1969), and Allport (1958).

13. Loewenstein (1951, pp. 64-65) argues that motives for anti-Semitism are political, xenophobic, economic, and religious.

14. Katz (1962, p. 4) tends to agree with this interpretation.

15. This point must be qualified. Jews were respected for their intellectual contributions, abilities as physicians, and financial talents, as well as for religious reasons. See Marcus (1965), p. 28, and Schweitzer (1971), p. 73.

16. One example of this involved Johann Reuchlin (1455-1522), whose defense of Jews caused considerable debate. Dubnov (1971, vol. 4, p. 159) reports that Germany was divided into two camps, Reuchlinists and anti-Reuchlinists. He also notes that the ensuing debates were as volatile and nearly as far reaching as the Dreyfus Affair would be in France. Yet Dubnov, along with numerous other scholars, argues that Reuchlin was in no way philo-Semitic. He was, the scholars agree, interested in Jewish culture alone; the people meant little to him. Dubnov, in fact, feels that Reuchlin was an anti-Semite (ibid., p. 159). See also Margolis and Marx (1969), p. 483; Schweitzer (1971), pp. 127-28; and Roth (1970), p. 244.

17. Roth (1970), p. 246; Schweitzer (1971), pp. 260-61.

18. Religious-nationalistic alienation existed in the Roman Empire and, more recently but still within the Middle Ages, in Spain in the fifteenth century. However, its greatest manifestations began after the French Revolution.

19. Arendt (1958), p. 23.

20. Dubnov (1971, vol. 4, pp. 555-56, 761-62) points out cases of this that, while extreme, illustrate the point. See his analysis of the speech of Isaac Avigdor and the writings of Isaac Jost.

21. Simon Dubnov (1971, vol. 4, p. 181) points out that as soon as Jews began to settle in Berlin and other parts of Brandenburg, the landed classes started to complain, especially about the Jews' right to engage in trade. Nor were rulers above practicing anti-Semitism for profit. Jacob Marcus (1965, p. 24) notes that in 1182 Jews in France were expelled so that the king, Philip Augustus, could confiscate their goods. For other instances of economic anti-Semitism (or anti-Semitism for profit) see Baron (1965a), vol. 10, p. 30, vol. 4, p. 126; A. L. Sachar (1965), p. 224; Poliakov (1965), pp. 62, 76, 106, 119, 272; Dubnov (1971), vol. 4, pp. 270, 528; Ettinger (1961), pp. 214-15; Pulzer (1969), pp. 144-47; and Grayzel (1966), p. 79. Of course, Jews were not the only ones who suffered from prejudice for profit. Italians and Huguenots were expelled from France for economic reasons, and the same factors caused Germans in Novgorod to wall themselves in for protection from Russian mobs.

22. Dubnov (1971, vol. 4, p. 178) argues that while the Jewish policy in Austria was religiously motivated, in Germany unsentimental, nonreligious reasoning dictated policy. On non-anti-Semitic political anti-Semitism see Pulzer (1969), pp. 97-98; Poliakov (1965), p. 111; Schweitzer (1971), p. 209; and Blalock (1967), p. 83. Jacques Godechot (1971, p. 95) notes that De Maistre attacked rationalistic philosophies and all those he considered its allies, among whom were Protestants and Jews.

23. Joseph Pilsudski, for example, assisted Jews, but by no stretch of the imagination could he be considered a philo-Semite. See H. M. Sachar (1958), p. 358.

24. Mayer, in Graeber and Britt (1942), p. 318. Also see Williams (1964), p. 82. There is a considerable body of work dealing with attitude change; see, for example, Bettleheim and Janowitz (1964); Secord and Backman (1964); Insko (1967).

25. This contrasts with Roth's concept of philo-Semitism. Roth (1962, p. 10) terms philo-Semitism a "psychological and political attitude." Yet it would seem crucial to include, not to say emphasize, the behavioral component of this prejudice, especially if one considers it in a historical context.

26. Rose (1974, p. 105) calls attention to the "timid bigot," a prejudiced individual who is not an activist. This should be kept in mind when philo-Semites are considered. Mayer (in Graeber and Britt, 1942, p. 318) points out that anti-Semitism "may be either active or dormant." It is reasonable to argue that philo-Semitism will also have its activists and its dormant supporters. Allport (1958, p. 402) notes that "some tolerant people are fighters. They will not put up with any infringement of the rights of others. They are intolerant of intolerance." But if some tolerant people are "fighters," then some are not. Nor should "fighting" be considered the sine qua non of tolerance or of philo-Semitism.

27. This is unlikely, however, as assimilation is a cause of the diminution of Jewishness. Still, such a position is not impossible and would depend upon one's definition of "Jew."

28. This challenges the position of Bermant (1971, p. 246), who equates philo-Semitism with Zionism. See Veblen (1919); also see Coser (1971), p. 287.

29. According to Allport (1958, p. 50), discrimination "comes about only when we deny to individuals or groups of people equality of treatment which they may wish." But discrimination, like all prejudicial components, may be positive as well as negative. One may discriminate in favor of a group, granting that group's members considerations over and above that of equality or striving to achieve equality for members of that group when it is denied to them by the larger society.

30. Tumin (1971), p. 307.

31. Blalock (1967), p. 15. Emphasis in the original.

32. Stember (1961, p. 38) notes that "attitudes cannot be measured directly but must be inferred from behavior, either overt or verbal." But who is to pass judgment on the behavior? Such difficulties can be illustrated by comparing the actions vis-à-vis Jews of two U.S. presidents, Ulysses S. Grant and Harry S. Truman. Grant was a good friend of several prominent Jews (Birmingham, 1967, pp. 128-29, 308-9). Truman maintained a social distance from Jews. For instance, his business partner, Eddie Jacobson, never visited Truman at his home because "the Trumans couldn't afford to have Jews at their house" (Miller, 1974, p. 106). Truman, however, is praised by Jews for his actions concerning Israel. (See Teller, 1968, pp. 203, 211, 216.) Grant is damned for his anti-Semitism: in 1862 Grant "curtly ordered every Jew expelled from his

military jurisdiction" (Higham, 1973, p. 13). The difficulty will be resolved by accepting the position that the interests of the many are of greater significance than the privileges of the few. If one is to judge the more pro-Jewish of the two presidents, one must necessarily choose Truman. This is not, however, to term Truman a philo-Semite.

# PHILO-SEMITISM IN THE MIDDLE AGES I

## 3

## THE ROMAN LEGACY

Because Judaism is older than Christianity—indeed, the latter was derived from the former—and because a multitude of peoples inhabited Europe before either religion developed, Jews and non-Jews were in contact before Jews and Christians were in contact. These contacts existed even prior to the reigns of the kings of Judea, although they increased in scope and depth when Israel was dispersed. For want of an absolute date, one can take it that the great interweaving of Jews with various cultures began when Jews became a people without a nation, when they lived with a "portable homeland" in lieu of a geographical one. Thus it is convenient to point to the rise of the varied and ubiquitous Jewish communities throughout the world from A.D. 70, the traditional beginning of the Diaspora, the Scattering, although scholars report that Jews were dispersed throughout the Roman Empire well before that date.[1] These scattered Jewish communities were by no means limited to Europe and the Middle East; indeed, by the first century A.D. Jews lived in virtually every part of the world.

The most obvious effect of this "scattering" was that Jews were settled in lands other than their own. Always a minority, they tenaciously retained their own traditions and often maintained a degree of social distance from the citizens of the host countries. Moreover, Jews often regarded their culture as superior to those of their non-Jewish neighbors.[2] In two respects, then, since the time of the Diaspora Jews have held a unique position: they have been found in virtually every known society and, despite a minority status, they have retained their own values and traditions.

Perhaps the most significant aspect of this uniqueness, especially manifest under the aegis of the Roman Eagle, was the degree of toleration the Jews were granted—and here "toleration" should not be taken with its usual negative connotation. They were allowed to retain their identity; they were accepted as unique. This acceptance of Jews, Judaism, and specifically Jewish social practices is traceable as far back as the Persian conquest of

Judea under Cyrus the Great (558-529 B.C.) and existed during the growth of the Greek hegemony under Alexander.

A pattern seems to have been established by the conquerors of Judea that continued, albeit with some vicissitudes, through the establishment of Christianity and Islam: Jews were allowed both religious freedom and, in varying degrees, sociopolitical autonomy. It was within the Roman Empire, however, that the toleration of Jews was most significant for western Jewry. There is a historical continuity between that Empire, the rise of Christianity, and the latter's domination of Europe. That continuity is manifest in at least two of the legacies bequeathed to Christianity by the Roman Empire: philo-Semitism and universalism.

It is true that polytheistic religions are often receptive to new forms of worship and that permission to continue religious practices and various other freedoms is often granted to conquered nations as a technique to reduce discontent and rebelliousness. Rome, however, demanded some type of obeisance to its religion from virtually every defeated nation. Nevertheless, the Jews were tolerated. In fact, the Jews were the *only* religious group in the Empire that had the approval of the government in spite of their refusal to worship the Roman ruler. Moreover, that toleration continued despite the frequent and often internecine Jewish revolts against Roman rule in Palestine. Cecil Roth correctly notes that "even after the Jewish War [A.D.70], Judaism continued to be regarded as a cult—the only cult, indeed, legally recognized—in addition to the official one."[3] More than being legally exempted from involvement in Rome's state religion, a universal obligation, many Jews in Rome were officially *libertini* (freedmen), *before* the edict of Caracalla (c. A.D. 212) made all the free inhabitants of the Empire Roman citizens.[4] And the Jews were a conquered people, after all.

Jewish contact with Rome was initially political. In 161 B.C., at the instigation of Judah Maccabeus, an alliance with Rome was signed and the Republic recognized the independent Jewish state.[5] That alliance did not last. Beginning in 63 B.C. Rome increasingly controlled Palestine, and by A.D. 6 that control was complete; Judea was incorporated into the Roman Empire.[6] The Jews were not harassed, however. Max Radin is incorrect when he suggests that, in general, "the Roman attitude to the Jews, as to all other peoples, was that of a master."[7] That attitude is more accurately described as a regard for a (frequently reluctant) ally. At the very least the Jews were treated differently—better—than other conquered peoples.

Some scholars dispute the claim that "Roman policy displayed a clear philo-Semitic tendency,"[8] and it seems certain that Leon Poliakov is enthusiastic in arguing that pagan Rome "knew no 'state anti-Semitism.'"[9] Still, there can be no doubt that specific privileges were allowed Jews by numerous emperors and that they did fare well under the aegis of the Roman Eagle.

Beginning with the Great Charter of Julius Caesar, which granted Jews both religious freedom and the same rights as other Roman citizens, and continuing through the early Roman bishops, who treated Jews liberally and tolerantly, Jews enjoyed an officially sanctioned position in the Roman Empire.[10]

It is of considerable importance that Rome accepted this dissenting sect endowed with a particularistic sociopolitical status, even though the acceptance contradicted Rome's universalism. What is significant is not that Caesar granted the Jews privileges or that the Great Charter and the privileged position of the Jews in the Roman Empire were continued and even enhanced under Augustus. The significance lies in the fact that in addition to religious freedom and citizenship Jews were granted a considerable degree of self-determination: for example, they were not subject to Roman law in civil suits involving Jews. This established a precedent that would be followed, with some inconsistencies, for over 1,800 years. Given their minority status and their refusal to adopt the mores of the majority, it is clear that Jews could not have survived the power and weight of Rome, much less have been accepted within it, without support, protection, and official sanction.[11] It is taken here that the granting of unique privileges to Jews, and only to Jews, by the powers in Rome constitutes a discernible philo-Semitism.

The cause of Rome's philo-Semitism is obscure. It was probably based on and sustained by several factors, one of which may simply have been that Judaism itself was attractive to the Romans. Proselytism was not at all unknown in the Empire, and it is possible that at least some Romans regarded both Jews and Judaism with admiration.[12] In addition, the fact that the first serious contact between Romans and Jews was as political allies may have played a part in Rome's regard for the Jews. Further, because from the time of Caesar a tradition of active benevolence had marked Roman-Jewish relations (as long as the Jews were not politically rebellious), it is probable that the unique history of the Roman-Jewish association and the long-established harmony between them influenced the perspectives of later Roman rulers. Other factors, too, must be regarded as credible.[13] The favorable attitude of Julian (the Apostate, A.D. 361-63) toward Jews, for example, may have been motivated by humanitarian concerns.[14]

Whatever the causes of Roman philo-Semitism, the privileged position of Jews in the Roman Empire was the starting point of their privileged status in Christian Europe. Just as Judaism was the only legally recognized dissenting religion in the Roman Empire, it became the only legally recognized dissenting religion in Christendom, despite Christianity's universalistic claim, which was both religious and political. A continuity is apparent: Jews in Europe continued to benefit from the unique privilege of toleration after Christianity was established.

The official (the Church) position regarding Jews in Christendom was set down at the beginning of the seventh century by Pope Gregory I (the Great,

590-604). Virtually every subsequent edict issued by a pope would either quote or paraphrase Gregory's statement regarding Jews. In June 598, in a letter to the Bishop of Palermo, Gregory stated, "Just as one ought not to grant any freedom to the Jews in their synagogues beyond that permitted by law, so should the Jews in no way suffer in those things already conceded to them."[15] It is important to recognize that Gregory was consciously adhering to the traditions established by the Roman Empire, traditions codified in the Roman laws, which had defined the status of the Jews.[16]

There were two specific reasons for Gregory's adoption of Roman traditions regarding Jews and his acceptance, toleration, and protection of them. The first was humanitarianism, which was a direct part of the Roman legacy. And this humanitarian treatment was extended only to Jews; Gregory was quite harsh in his dealings with pagans and heretics. The second was theological, based on the need to preserve Jewry to demonstrate the validity of Christianity. As Jacob Marcus notes, "the Hebrew Bible of the Jews 'foretold' the coming of Jesus; the sufferings of the Jews were reputedly their punishment for the rejection of Jesus."[17] Both of these would be repeatedly reaffirmed throughout the Middle Ages.

Gregory decreed that the Church must not only tolerate Jews but protect them, but this is not to argue that Jews were everywhere fully and absolutely tolerated or effectively protected. Indeed, one might question why protection was needed or why the decree was repeated so often. Nevertheless, the singular position of Jewry within Christendom was a legacy from the Empire of the Romans, and Gregory recognized and endorsed this legacy. He sustained the status of Jews because they "are allowed to live in accordance with the Roman laws."[18]

A philo-Semitic tendency, then, was manifest prior to the inception and growth of Christianity. This tendency became a legacy of the Roman Empire to Christian Europe and then to the modern world.

## THE UNIVERSAL CHURCH

An analysis of European Jewry and the manifestation of philo-Semitism during the Middle Ages must begin with two specific points: (1) Christianity's claim of universalism and power and the effects of these on the legal status of Jews and (2) the vulnerable position of medieval European Jewry.

The term "universalism" suggests human unity. In the theological sense, all men should be members of a single church and show obedience to that church. As noted earlier in this chapter, universalism existed as a fundamental part of the Roman Empire in a political sense, and it was Rome's universalism that "prepared the soil for the universalism of Christianity."[19] Initially the claims of the Church did not conflict with those of the Roman Empire. This was possible because the former seemed to be only spiritual, the latter only political.[20] This mutually acceptable dichotomy did not last; during the last centuries of the Empire and the concurrent growth of Christianity, the two did battle, and as Kohn has it, the Church "emerged victorious over the Empire," claiming for itself the right to unite mankind.[21]

It might be more accurate, however, to say that the Empire crumbled and that the Church filled the resultant void.[22] The Church had to struggle to maintain that position. For perhaps the first millennium of its existence, Christianity labored to become a monolithic religion; it was unsuccessful. The apparently limitless number of heretical sects and the schism between Byzantium and Rome precluded Christian unity.[23]

However, in both the east and the west the major religious organizations grew in power. Eastern Caesaropapism and western Catholicism increasingly dominated a divided Europe, the former segment almost from its inception in the fourth century.[24] In the west, Catholic ascendancy was slower. The rise and spread of Islam, the Moorish conquest of Spain, and the existence of numerous "pagan" peoples delayed the growth of the Church. In time, however, Islam was contained in the west, the Moors driven from Iberia, and the pagans Christianized. By the early twelfth century Catholic domination of the west was effectively complete. Thus in 1123, when Pope Calixtus II called an ecumenical council, the first Lateran Synod, he could claim the same authority as the Roman Emperor, that is, absolute power.[25] In western Europe, then, more than a thousand years after the birth of Christianity, the term "Christendom" was applicable, schisms and heretics notwithstanding.[26]

At the heart of western European Christianity—of Christendom—was the merging of political and religious universalisms. Mankind would be uniform not only in religious outlook but, because church and state were intertwined, in political outlook as well. There would be religious unity and political unity, and these would be the same. In consequence not only the religious but "the *political* thought of the Middle Ages was characterized by the conviction that mankind was one and had to form one community."[27] Now politics and religion were no longer separable: "State and church, Empire and Christianity were indissolubly linked." Not without justification could Pope Boniface VIII (1294-1303) in the papal bull *Unam Sanctam* claim the Church to be "all in all."[28]

But this is not to suggest that a thousand years passed before Christianity became a powerful force in Europe. The recognition of the authority of the papacy by Charlemagne in A.D. 800 was surely indicative of the strength of the Church. Indeed, through the Middle Ages, beginning perhaps 600 years *before* the first Lateran synod and continuing until the seventeenth century, religion dominated virtually all aspects of life, both private and public, in Christendom. The basis of this domination was the Church's ability to unify and regulate actions and attitudes.[29]

For most of that period the Church was the most powerful ecclesiastical and political body in Europe, though not the only Christian one. Throughout the continent "every child of Christian parents was born into the Church almost as literally as he is now born into a state; every professed Christian was expected to conform, at least outwardly, to the doctrines and observances of the Church." One obvious result of this was that "the Church was official and public, not private and purely voluntary." Moreover, and of crucial import here, the states enforced obedience to the Church. Anyone attacking Church authority was subject to punitive action by the state.[30]

It is true that until the era of the Crusades, Christianity itself was not the force it would later become throughout Europe.[31] That power did come, however, and as it came, as the Church grew and could see to it that its demands were met, it began to regard itself *as* a state, "as a republic *to which everyone must belong."* The Church was the state, the state the Church. This is why it was possible for religion to become a "political category, even the foremost political category."[32]

The political strength of the medieval church is evident from Innocent III's view of papal power as the sun and royal power as the moon. During the papacy's apogee this was the case; Innocent virtually controlled Europe and tenaciously guarded his authority. Anyone who opposed the papacy faced execution as a criminal or blasphemer, and his works were burned along with him. When Innocent called the Fourth Lateran Council in 1215, dignitaries from all over the world attended. These men, over fifteen hundred of them, simply approved his suggestions; debate was kept to a minimum. So broad were Innocent's powers that they clearly extended past ecclesiastical consideration. With impunity he claimed that he could legally abrogate the English Magna Carta and also interfere in the election of the emperor in Germany. There was a basis for this claim: "the power of ... Pope Innocent III ... extended all over Europe, from England to Hungary (both of these countries accepted the jurisdiction of Innocent) and as far as Constantinople, which had been captured in 1204 by the Latin Crusaders."[33]

Innocent was the most powerful of the popes, and his influence was therefore somewhat atypical; but great though his power and influence were, the difference between his and those of many other popes was only one of degree. Given the *Weltanschauung* of the times this is not surprising; an English jurist living then wrote that "the Church (i.e. the Christian world) is one body," and it can have only one head, that is, the Pope.[34]

## JEWS AND NON-JEWS; SLAVERY AND HERESY

It is well to examine the position of medieval European Jewry from the perspective of the period and to recall that by comparison the situation for the vast majority of people in Europe was less than idyllic. It should not be forgotten that, bad as it was for Jews, it was not appreciably better for most non-Jews. Baron argues that it was worse, that Jews in medieval Europe fared better than most Christians, not only economically but politically. The reason for this was the Jews' unofficial status. "I may be allowed to repeat here the paradoxical statement that medieval Jewry, much as it suffered from disabilities and contempt, still was a privileged minority in every country where it was tolerated at all."[35]

Life was extremely harsh. Moreover, the acceptance of slavery as an institution could and did threaten the Christian and Pagan masses, but not Jews. Peasants in medieval Europe had good reason to fear either being enslaved or reduced to serfdom.[36] Slavery was sanctioned, in fact, by the Church. St. Thomas Aquinas asserted the moral justifiability of slavery as well as its economic necessity.

Generally the objects of slavery were heathens (the origin of the word "slave" is said to be a derivative of "Slav"), and Armenians, Bulgarians, Circassians, Serbs, and Syrians were regularly bought from the Turks by Venetian and Genoese slave traders. In 1452 Pope Nicholas V empowered the ruler of Portugal to sell all Moslems into slavery, and in 1488 Pope Innocent VIII was presented with one hundred Moorish slaves.

Slavery was not limited to the "infidel," however. In the twelfth century Christian Danes were sold as slaves, as were Italians. And during and immediately after the Children's Crusade (1212), French and Italian children were sold into slavery to Moslem businessmen. Moreover, various popes regularly threatened enemies with enslavement. For example, in 1303 Boniface VIII condemned the "companies of the Colonna," and in 1309 Clement V placed Venice under a ban of slavery.[37]

Although there may have been exceptions, in general, and unlike perhaps the majority of the inhabitants of Christendom, Jews were not enslaved or enslavable. Certainly there was no attempt to enslave them as a group. The usual state of affairs was indicated by a bull dated October 22, 1586, issued by Pope Sixtus V (1585-90) forbidding the Knights of Malta from capturing and enslaving Jews who had been traveling by ship.[38] Why was the Jew not enslaved? Clearly that possibility existed; at least one pope mentions it as a theological, if not pragmatic, reality.[39] Surely the continued freedom of Jews of medieval Europe, who were virtually helpless to defend themselves, is an enigma, since it is not true, as often claimed, that Jews were needed there. (Besides the error in the premise, the derived conclusion is fallacious: if Jews had been needed, what better way to keep them than to enslave them?) But this surely was not the case in England, France, Spain, or Portugal, where Jews were expelled en masse.

It is also of interest to examine the reaction to the growth and proliferation beginning in the early thirteenth century of the varied sects, which shocked the intensely and unswervingly religious populace. The reason for the shock was "the realization that Christendom, an indivisible unit, had suddenly become permeated and undermined by sects whose views on religion, the world, and sometimes politics differed totally from those of the church and its people."[40]

It was this change within the political and religious structure of medieval Europe that led to internal crusades, to the Inquisition, and to cries of heresy—a *crimen laesae majestatis*—and resultant horrors. Why was it that, unlike Jews, heretics were hunted with purpose and official (Church) sanction? Why were Jews not similarly hunted? The first burning of heretics at the stake occurred in 1022, and gradually the volume increased until in 1232 the Holy Roman Empire enacted a law condemning heretics to be burned to death.[41] The burning of "witches" was equally popular and equally grotesque. By 1404 over thirty thousand people had been burned, and while the exact total is unknown, the figure is undoubtedly very high.

These attacks on heretics cannot be taken to mitigate in any way the discrimination the Jews suffered; they can explain them, however, at least in the universalistic sense. After the ninth century, when it became fully established in the west, Catholicism and only Catholicism was tolerated there,[42] but if anything, the antiheretic attacks underlie the failure, indeed the lack of intent, of Christendom to destroy medieval European Jewry. It would certainly have been possible for the Church to do so, and there were historical precedents for such action. From 1208 to 1228, a twenty-year span, the Albigensian Crusades were waged, causing the total destruction of Catharism. The thoroughness and ruthlessness of this Crusade should leave no doubt about the impossibility of Jewish survival if the papacy, secular rulers, or indeed the general populace had decided to annihilate them.

And annihilation was the intent of the Crusaders. In one town close to twenty thousand people were slaughtered—heretics who had defied the authority of Innocent III. Even so gentle a man as Bernard of Clairvaux, "the uncrowned Pope of his time," who not only argued in favor of toleration of Jews but effectively protected them during the Second Crusade, denounced the heretics.[43]

The Albigensians were not the only victims of Catholic universalism; there were, in fact, other Crusades against heretics. Strayer points out that the Crusades against the heretics in Occitania—the "Albigensian Crusades—were the first large-scale use of this dangerous technique of using the Holy War to attain the objectives of the papacy in Europe." They were by no means the last. From 1185 to 1285 hardly a year passed during which a Crusade was not fought or planned. That century can rightly be called the "era of the Crusades,"[44] although in fact the period of the Crusades ran well past 1285, by which time the earlier consistency was lacking. The Lollards, for example, John Wyclif's disciples, suffered the same extinction as the Albigensians, although Wyclif himself was spared because he, like many of the Jews, was hidden by friends. He died at home in 1348. Jan Hus, another heretic, was not so fortunate; in July 1415 the heretic's hat was placed on his head and he was burned at the stake. His followers, however, did not suffer annihilation in the Hussite wars because, *unlike* the Jews of the period, they were numerous, organized, and armed. This is not to suggest that the papacy did not try to destroy them; the papacy did try but could not do it.[45]

These various crusades, so brutally effective at least in part because of their legitimization by the Church, were never directed against Jews. This cannot be taken as an indication of general beneficence; it is to suggest only that the annihilation of European Jewry was possible and that from the perspective of those in power during this period it would have been justified on the basis of existing universalistic beliefs. One must thus recognize the existence of a special and fundamental toleration of Jews during the Middle Ages, at least by the formal authorities.

The Church—both the papacy and individual members of lesser rank—specifically rejected the notion of annihilation of medieval European Jewry and offered the Jews protection, although it is true that this protection was often unenthusiastically given and lacking in efficacy. This, again, dates back to the days of Gregory I, who unrelentingly combatted Manichaeism, paganism, and heresies. Gregory had no objection at all to using force to convert heretics; yet he resolutely forbade using force to convert Jews.

Similarly, the secular rulers refused to attempt annihilation of medieval European Jewry. In fact, despite all the bloodshed during the years 1096 to 1391, there is no recorded instance of a government-instigated attack on Jews. This explains Salo W. Baron's comment that "one must admit that the prevailing legislation of practically all medieval countries tried to safeguard the legitimate interests of the Jewish minority."[46] This official acceptance of Jews and Judaism continued through and after the Reformation; secular rulers, the Catholic church, and the newly-arisen Protestant churches all refrained from seeking Jewish annihilation.[47]

## MEDIEVAL TOLERANCE, JEWISH LEGITIMACY

There were respites in medieval religious violence; even intimations of toleration. In the "Little Renaissance" of the twelfth century, for example, the idea of a plural society was given serious consideration for the first time, and some began to wonder whether people of different religions could live together without conflict. A general if not fully effective peace settled briefly over Europe during the Renaissance, but the Reformation put an end to that temporary harmony and raised the heresy issue once again. It may be true, as scholars argue, that the Renaissance and the Reformation "form the transition from the Middle Ages to modern times," and that a degree of humanism and tolerance was manifest during the Renaissance. However, as a result of the Reformation, reactionary forces dominated Europe. After the Renaissance, theology once more entered into all aspects of life.[48]

As the fifteenth century ended and the Reformation began, religion resumed its place as the basic criterion of social institutions and human actions. It is hardly surprising, then, that the religious schism between Protestants and Catholics in western Europe resulted in violent intolerance. Felix Gilbert et al. note that in the 130 years from 1559 to 1689, in the multitude of wars that plagued Europe, "the one common denominator, which constantly recurred, was Protestant-Catholic religious strife."[49] The basis of this was an incipient claim of political particularism, so that religious toleration was denied, in part, for political reasons. The political instrument was becoming increasingly dominant over the religious institution in the service of *religious* particularism; national entities would now determine what religious practices were acceptable within their boundaries. This was the case in both Catholic and Protestant countries. The followers of each faith stressed the ties between church and state, and everywhere all areas of life were regulated by the state acting under God's law. One result of this was that national rulers came to regard political unity as contingent upon religious unity. Each state, especially in western and central Europe, tried to force its citizens to follow its established form of Christianity.

Moreover, and in direct contradiction to the attitudes of religious leaders vis-à-vis Jews, anti-Protestantism and anti-Catholicism were institutionalized and legitimated. When Leo X was confronted with Luther's revolt, he not only banned Protestantism but pleaded with secular rulers to use force to crush the heresy. Succeeding popes in the sixteenth century followed a similar course. Luther, in turn, asked secular rulers to use force against Catholicism; nor did he stop there—he also asked the princes to destroy Anabaptists and various other sects. Calvin, too, was less than tolerant. Catholics and dissenting Protestants were not allowed to live in Geneva, and Michael Servetus, whose doctrines anticipated Unitarianism, was arrested, tried, and burned at the stake on Calvin's order. The St. Bartholomew massacre in August 1572, in which more than three thousand Huguenots were killed in Paris, and thousands were later killed in the provincial towns, is representative of prevailing attitudes. The Inquisition, the Index, spies, and police were used to crush religious dissent in Spain, Portugal, and Italy and to force everyone to conform to Catholicism.

In Protestant countries similar procedures were used to crush Catholicism. In Scandinavia, Finland, and Estonia the Lutheran kings either banished or executed dissenters and confiscated their property. The Catholic clergy in Scotland tried to suppress Protestantism by similar tactics, and because they had the support of the Catholic Queen, were achieving their goal. John Knox, however, urged Calvinist nobles to depose the Queen.

They did, and then seized the government and began killing Catholics. In England punitive legislation was enacted by Queen Elizabeth against Catholics, many of whom were executed because of their "treasonous" activities. She also imprisoned numerous Protestants, including Baptists, Congregationalists, and anyone else who dissented from Anglicanism.[50] These conflicts continued until Europe became de-theologized, and that occurred only when the state was fully victorious over the church, that is, over all organized religions. This process began with Henry VIII of England, reached fruition in the modern age, and brought "with it the progressive depolitization of religion" when "the secular state became the foremost political power."[51] Through this process religious universalism gradually lost its importance.

In the sixteenth century it became accepted, after these long internecine conflicts and for political rather than religious reasons, that the prince would determine the religion of his subjects. This helped to resolve difficulties between Catholics and Protestants. There was a marked paucity of Jewish princes, however; regardless of the religion of the prince, Jews remained aliens.

All of this does not in any way negate or expiate the sufferings of medieval European Jewry, any more than the bombing of Dresden could make up for Auschwitz; it does point out that Christians were no less harsh with other Christians than with Jews. Indeed, they may have been harsher with Christians. It also raises the issue of how and why Jews, without the physical power (arms or numbers or organization) of either the Catholics or the Protestants, survived amid manifest Catholic and Protestant intolerance.

Throughout the Middle Ages and until well after the beginnings of nationalism, the Jew remained a total outsider. More than this, though, "there is no denying that, in the minds of most medieval men, the Jew appeared to be a permanent stranger."[52] The operative word here is "permanent." In contrast with every other dissenting religion, Judaism continued to exist within Christendom with official sanction. Innocent IV expressed this thought in a letter to the Archbishop of Vienna (May 28, 1249): "The clemency of the Catholic religion ... allows them to dwell in the midst of its people and has decreed tolerance for their rites."[53] As in the Roman Empire, no dissenting religious group except the Jews was allowed in Europe. Jews alone among non-Catholics were not regarded as heretics in pre-Reformation Europe. Again, one must wonder why it is that they were allowed to remain there, not unmolested, it is true, but there nonetheless.

Perhaps to illustrate the oddity of this, it is best to begin with an analysis of the Jews' overall place in Christian society, that is, their legal rights and their right of residence. Simply put, Jews possessed neither; their rights and their presence were, and had to be, legitimated by special exceptional decrees and policies. Given the political ideology and the power of the Church, this cannot be surprising. Precisely because Jews in Europe had neither legal nor residential rights to protect them, their continued existence there—and indeed, after the first millennium they continued to grow in numbers—was necessarily dependent upon others. Because medieval European Jews had no legal recourse in the face of expulsions and capricious attitudes of the powers of Christendom, they had to rely on the personal support of the legitimating agencies. This support was needed, in part, because of the politicoreligious schema described above. Jews were excluded, not solely or even mainly because of prejudice and fear, but because from a political point of view the state was Christian, and Jews were not a part of it.

Besides their legal situation, their organizational vulnerability, and other factors which made existence in Europe fragile, there was an astonishing amount of hatred stirred up against Jewish people. In religious drama, the most effective mechanism for propaganda of the time, anti-Semitism was emphasized. Only in Italy was the Jew favorably portrayed.

What is astonishing, given the situation of medieval European Jewry, and what bears examination, is not that many were attacked, expelled, or forcibly converted, but that more were not. Medieval popular religion was not orthodox Catholicism but "a lively mixture of many different elements, heathen, antique, 'folk' and Christian," and thus not fully attentive to papal decrees.[54] It is not surprising, then, that the populace, given its general ignorance and the significance of religion at that time, was easily moved to violence. This, then, is another factor that explains the tenuous position of Jews in medieval Europe.

Medieval European Jewry needed protection, and the role of protector was played in the main by various popes and secular rulers. Select monks, preachers, and lesser religious figures at one time had great influence with the populace, but beginning in the twelfth century, when the danger to Jews was certainly greatest, the influence of the papacy grew. Only the popes, bishops, and secular rulers had the power and the means of providing protection. It was these authorities who tried to save Jewish lives and, intentionally or not, preserved the Jewish religion and the Jewish people. Without their assistance there can be no doubt that European Judaism, if not European Jewry, would have vanished.

One other point should be considered in conjunction with this. No ruler, however strong, however demonstrative, however secure in authority, rules alone. Secular and ecclesiastical rulers have advisors, consultants, and many other people who offer suggestions, counsel, and information. In addition to direct support from a pope or secular ruler, the Jews would receive indirect support from members of the papal court or the ruler's coterie, who would attempt to persuade the authority to grant the Jews protection or privileges. While numerous officials and intellectuals disliked Jews, numerous other officials and intellectuals were attracted to Jews, Jewish history, or the significance of Judaism for Christianity. Some were attracted to the cultural aspects of Judaism.

To support the contention that philo-Semitism was an active force in the Middle Ages, it is reasonable to take as the point of departure the notion that the continued existence of Jews in Europe depended on either (or both) papal or royal decrees and protection. Again, Jews had long since lost their citizenship and right of residence in western Europe. This fact has become so much a part of the history of European Jewry that it is hardly acknowledged, but it is of major significance. Jews had no legal right to be on the soil of Europe unless expressly granted permission by one authority or another, a fact amply demonstrated by the numerous expulsions to which they were subjected. Their continued residence within any given area was tenuous, and because medieval law was derived from either secular or ecclesiastical authority, Jews stood directly under the auspices of these rulers. The papacy and the secular rulers granted not only physical protection but legal residency. Until the institutionalization of democratic ideals and rule by common consent, every Jew in Europe, and to a lesser but nonetheless real degree, every Christian, was subject to the dictates of a secular or religious authority.

When the authority of the pope was universally recognized and accepted (after the fifteenth century, papal power was steadily reduced), Jews were subject to the dictates of the popes to a considerable extent.[55] Eventually, and especially outside the Papal States, Jews were also increasingly subject to the dictates of secular authorities. In parts of eastern Europe and throughout the west this meant that a single ruler would control the fate of all the Jews living in a vast area. In the central European states, because of fragmentation and geographical subdivisions, the authority of secular rulers was limited; that is, the area of a ruler's domain was considerably smaller than in the east or the west and the power of his office was thereby less. This meant, for one thing, that in central Europe total expulsions were virtually impossible. Jews expelled from one area could be, and usually were, accepted into another.

It is true that many acts beneficial to Jews were initiated in the rulers' self-interest and cannot simply be regarded as manifestations of philo-Semitism. Yet it is also true that Jews often gained advantages that were greater than those gained by the self-interested rulers. After all, the Jews' very lives, or at least their continued residence in the area in question, was at stake.[56] It is unlikely that the initiators of many of these beneficial acts did not recognize this. Various Christians used Jews, but various Jews also used Christians. There can be little doubt that the "beneficent greed" of several rulers helped many Jews in the Middle Ages.

However, the popes in the Middle Ages whose actions enhanced the position of Jews cannot have been motivated purely by greed. While it is true that in many instances they offered, oxymoronically, beneficent malevolence,

the popes of the Middle Ages almost unanimously condemned forced baptisms, massacres, and various lesser violations of Jewry. They also, with
varying degrees of enthusiasm, and often unsuccessfully, attempted to halt
the lesser clergy from inciting the populace to attack Jewish communities.

It seems clear, then, that the position of Jews under the shadow of
Christianity was not totally unhappy. While Jews in the Middle Ages under-
went numerous adversities because they remained Jews despite the various
pressures brought to bear on them, they still survived and sometimes prospered. This is partially explained by the fact that the penalties imposed on
them were not uniformly carried out. The ruler of one area might impose
harsh restrictions on the Jews living within his domain, while in other areas
Jews lived in relative security. Further, the disadvantages imposed on Jews in
a given area were often inconsistently applied, particularly because of actions
of individuals who arrested or repudiated the offending decrees. Although
Jews were often harassed, taxed to the extreme, and subjected to noxious
restrictions,[57] they remained a part of European life.

In speaking of medieval Jewry it is, as Baron notes, "easy to overemphasize
the Jewish disabilities and burdensome duties, as was done during the
Emancipation."[58] Throughout the terrors that comprised much of European
history, Jews survived and many prospered. This can be explained, in part,
by the allies the Jews had. Surely one cannot suggest, given the significance of
religion, the marked intolerance of the Middle Ages, and the weakness of the
Jews, that they could have survived without the assistance of philo-Semites.

## JEWISH VULNERABILITY

### Legal Restrictions and Dependencies

While there is some disagreement among scholars about when Jews lost
their rights in Europe, there is no disagreement that they did indeed lose
them.[59] Regardless of the date of this loss, by the eleventh century (which
saw, coincidentally, the beginnings of the full strength of papal power and the
start of the Crusades), Jews had no legal rights in Christendom, including no
right of residency. Even "the right to life, which Christian society granted the
merest yokel, had to be bought by the Jew at regular intervals. Otherwise,
regarded as useless, he would have been driven out or implicated in some
grim case of poisoning or ritual murder."[60] Residence, indeed existence itself,
depended on the authority of the secular ruler over a given area as well as,
less effectively, on papal decree. A French document of 1361 clearly illustrates the tenuousness of the Jews' residency in Christian Europe:

> They have neither nation nor territory of their own in all of Christendom
> where they may remain, frequent, or reside, if it be not by the strict and

pure will and permission of the lord or lords under whom they agree to remain as their subjects and who consent to receive and accept them.[61]

The residencies of Jews and their right to stay in any location were conditional; unlike Christians they had no legal basis for living anywhere in Europe. In effect they were outlaws by virtue of their very existence, and residence was permitted only by approval of an authority.

Thus it was not the threat of violence that first caused Jewish dependence on royal protection—until the era of the Crusades there was little anti-Jewish hostility—but the fact that wherever they were in Christendom, they had no legal right to be there. It is true that numerous Jewish communities in Europe predate Christianity, but this was not used as an argument for the right of residence. Jews never suggested that they had a right to remain in an area because they had lived there before their Christian neighbors.[62]

One concomitant of the lack of residential rights of medieval European Jews was their being barred from owning land.[63] This was of enormous consequence in the agricultural Middle Ages. Jews were forced into pursuits other than farming; this accounts, many scholars argue, for their reputation for economic innovation and shrewdness. It should be recalled, however, that because of further restrictions—again demonstrating the lack of rights of Jews—many were reduced to usury and the majority to the level of peddler.

Another consequence of their position in medieval Europe was various restrictions intended to keep Jews socially apart from the general population. Although enforced separateness was not always or even usually distasteful to medieval European Jewry, the methods of separation often were. Decrees specifically restricted the social intermixing of Jews and Christians, and other decrees complemented these. For example, Jews were forced to wear readily identifiable clothing or insignias to ensure that Christians would not inadvertently mistake a Jew for one of their own. The ghetto was instituted. Christians were not allowed to live in Jewish homes. Intermarriage was forbidden.

Most of these restrictions (except possibly the last) were enforced with varying degrees of enthusiasm and with varying degrees of effectiveness, as the constant renewal of these prohibitive decrees indicates. The restrictions, if fully efficacious, would have been so crushing to Jews as to destroy them. This is especially true of the social mixing of Jews and Gentiles. Consider, first, that these restrictions did not extend to business dealings in general and, second, that business associations necessarily lead to some form of social mixing. Were it not for the mixing of Jews and Christians, the Jews' place in Europe would have been untenable; their basic needs could be provided for only by non-Jews. It was necessary for Jews to deal with Christians in order to obtain clothing and food, since they were prohibited from owning land and since they required special foods. More than this, "practically every Jew was in direct contact with his non-Jewish neighbor, depending chiefly upon them for earning his living, for manual labor and for personal services."[64]

These services could have been cut off, and Christian authorities did recognize the potential here. There were instances, although brief and rare, in which Jews were denied the most fundamental needs. In Ratisbon in 1499, for example, under threat of excommunication, bakers would not sell Jews bread, nor would millers sell them flour. Jews were not permitted to enter the market place on certain days, and on others could buy what they needed only after Christians had already shopped. To ensure that these impositions were effective, severe penalties were imposed on Christians who made purchases for Jews.[65]

One might consider the possible effects of a general ban on dealing with Jews. If it happened in one area, after all, it could have happened in others and, indeed, throughout all Christendom. Granting that there existed a quid pro quo, as Katz suggests,[66] the need of Jews for Christian cooperation was considerably greater than the need of Christians for Jewish cooperation. Jews had little retaliatory power. The size of their communities was so small as to negate any attempt at economic sanction and certainly any attempt at physical sanction, that is, the use of force by Jews on Christians.

All of this is not to argue for anything other than the vulnerable position of medieval European Jewry. In addition to being legally outside society, the Jews were dependent upon Christians for their life needs. Medieval European Jewry could have been starved out. The gains to Christians in dealing with Jews were not so great as to be worth the risk of excommunication. Had sufficient secular and religious pressure been brought to bear, medieval European Jewry could not have continued to exist. It would be stretching the point to consider the tacit approval by authorities, both secular and religious, of these minimally necessary rights as philo-Semitism, but this approval does manifest a fundamental toleration of Jews.

### Expulsions

Every study of Jewish history has noted the repeated expulsions of Jews from specific countries of Europe and the refusal of numerous other countries to admit them. Jews were expelled from several countries, from numerous provinces within other countries, and from individual cities. The general expulsions, in chronological order, were from England, France, Spain and Spain's possessions, and Portugal. Schweitzer points to the "overwhelming fact" that by 1500, except for a scattering of small, hidden communities, "western Europe was devoid of professing Jews."[67] Where Jews had been admitted in central and, less frequently, in eastern Europe, expulsions occurred in many principalities. Not every European city in the Middle Ages followed a policy of periodic expulsion, but at one time or another Jews were banished from, or refused admission to, almost every major urban center.

Scholars are not altogether in accord as to which major cities did *not* expel or refuse Jews admission, although most agree that this was the case in Rome and Frankfurt.[68]

The extent of the expulsions may be illustrated by reference to a map of Europe. In the late Middle Ages, Jews were prohibited from entering Muscovy (Russia), Switzerland, and the Scandinavian countries (the kingdoms of Denmark, Norway, and Sweden). They had been effectively expelled from the west. In the remaining areas of Europe general though brief expulsions occurred in Austria in 1420, in the Low countries in 1348 and again during the Spanish Inquisition, in Lithuania in 1495, in Bohemia in 1745, and in Venice and Lower Austria in 1670. Jews were expelled from Sardinia and Sicily and several lesser areas in 1492, and from the Kingdom of Naples in 1540. Only in the north of Italy and the Papal States did Jews have a continuous, uninterrupted existence. Expulsions within the German states were extensive, occurring, for example, in Mayence, Bavaria and Cologne, Luebeck, Bremen, Saxony and Brandenberg, Hapsburg, Nuremberg, and Prussian Posen. In Germany and Italy, however, there were no general expulsions.[69] This listing by no means exhausts the full number of expulsions, major and minor, to which medieval European Jewry was subjected.

Three aspects of Jewish history become apparent here. First, these facts clearly document the precarious position of medieval European Jewry and underline the Jews' lack of a legal basis of residence in any area in Europe. Second, because the expulsions were contingent upon Jews remaining Jews—that is, if a Jew converted he was allowed to remain—it suggests that the religion, not the people, was the target of the expulsions.[70] Third, if simultaneous expulsions had occurred, Europe would have been without Jews, either because of their leaving the continent or because of their conversion to Christianity. It is not idle speculation to consider the possibility; Ben Halpern notes that "harsh conditions and harsh treatment, culminating in mass expulsions and forced conversions, had reduced the number of Jews to about 1,500,000 in the fifteenth century."[71] The continued existence of Jews in Europe was, beyond all doubt, in jeopardy during this period.[72]

In no country, however, were the expulsions totally effective. In the west a small number of Jews managed to remain hidden in a "transparent disguise of Catholicism."[73] In England, where Jews had been expelled in 1290, a number of small, hidden Jewish communities were discovered before the end of the sixteenth century. Similarly, as late as 1914, Marranos were discovered in secluded areas of Spain and Portugal, and in France, Jewish communities had existed near the borders since at least 1500. Parenthetically, one cannot doubt that the disguises of these groups were indeed "transparent" or assume the total gullibility of the Jews' Christian neighbors. Unless these neighbors were astonishingly naïve, the continued existence of these crypto-Jewish communities must have had their tacit approval if not their open sympathy. In at least one case in France, for example, when the Jews were discovered to be Jews, the authorities ignored the ban against their being there even though that ban was not revoked. Similar situations occurred in Alsace, Metz, and Lorraine.

The "total expulsions" from England, France, Spain, and Portugal were possible because of the centralization of the governments of these nations. Numerous attempts to expel Jews from the central European states were ineffective because the states themselves were fragmented and not subject to the dictates of a single ruler. For example, there was no general expulsion in the German states because of political conditions there. When Jews in one area were expelled, they were accepted into another area, so that, despite repeated but limited expulsions, there were always Jews in some part of Germany from at least A.D. 1000. The same situation obtained in Italy, which until 1848 was composed of small independent states.

## Massacres and Forced Conversions

While there is no way to estimate precisely the number of Jews systematically slaughtered during the Middle Ages, there is no doubt that the figure is extremely high. During the Rindfleisch massacre alone it is estimated that over 100,000 Jews were killed. These incidents of slaughter, those precipitated by the Crusades, and those following the Black Death were, in the west, the most destructive. In the east the most costly were the Chmielnicki massacres. There were additional, lesser massacres throughout the Middle Ages, often precipitated by specious charges of ritual murder or desecration of the Host.

Jews were often victims of forces beyond their control and also beyond the control of their Christian neighbors. The Jews often provided a ready scapegoat during times of natural disaster. During the Black Death, for example, when some 25 million people or one quarter of Europe's total population died, the Jews were deemed responsible. They were accused of poisoning wells, foods, and, incredibly, the air. In this and in other instances, attacking Jews was, as Roth notes, a "reflex action."[74]

Most scholars agree that there was no general outbreak of violence against Jews until the first Crusade. From that time until the Age of Enlightenment and the French Revolution in the west, there were regular but unofficial attacks on European Jewry. In the east, attacks continued into the twentieth century, and central Europe was, of course, the scene of Hitler's "last great pogrom."

Consider the evidence of Jewish vulnerability only in central Europe: massacres occurred in southern Germany in 1298; in Alsace, Swabia, and Franconia in 1336; in Deckendorf in 1337; and in Germany in 1336-38. Some three thousand Jews were systematically slaughtered in Prague in 1380, and in Austria the slaughter was so effective that for a time not a single Jew remained there. During the period of the Black Death, some eleven thousand Jews were massacred in Mayence, Eurfurt, and Strassburg alone. It would be impossible to list the great number of less effective attacks. Beyond any question, medieval European Jewry was extremely vulnerable.

In almost every instance the violence directed against Jews was religiously based, particularly in the western and central states. With relentless regularity, Jews were offered a choice: convert or die (or be expelled). Carl J. Friedrich is correct in noting that "the medieval Jew could . . . escape all of this horror by allowing himself to be baptized."[75] Indeed, there was often no choice. In Clermont, as early as 576, some five hundred Jews were forcibly baptized. In Mors, Jews were imprisoned and guarded—to prevent suicides—and, when the preparations were in order, baptized against their will. In Worms the bishop who tried to protect the Jews during the Crusades eventually suggested conversion when he realized that he could not prevent a massacre. Some 800 Jews died. In May 1171 nearly fifty Jews died in Blois because they refused to abandon Judaism. This was also the case in Mayence and Spires, where most of the Jews chose death. Similar alternatives were offered Jews throughout the Crusades and afterward. In Trier and Speyer and in France, some 500 Jews converted in 1236 with death as the only other option, a repetition of an earlier proposition placed before Parisian Jews in the late twelfth century. The same alternatives faced Hungarian Jews in 1348-49, Austrian Jews in 1420, Jews of Trent in 1475, Brandenburg Jews in 1510, and Jews in various other areas, including, of course, the Iberian peninsula, where in just one instance over 20,000 Jews were forcibly baptized. There were also numerous instances in which Jewish children were forcibly baptized.[76]

However, the killings and forcible conversions of medieval European Jewry did not destroy that people. Clearly the Jews were vulnerable enough, and clearly the possibility of annihilation, either through death or conversion, was a real threat. It is thus reasonable to question the means of their survival, and perhaps the first place to look is the issue of forced conversion.

One scholar notes that for a time it was decided in ecclesiastical meetings to force Jews to convert, but that the inefficiency of the program saved European Jewry.[77] This is true, but this Church attitude existed only prior to the era of the Crusades—prior, that is, to the time of the greatest dangers. Limited official sanction was then offered to those who struggled to force Jews to embrace Christianity. The fifth council of Paris in 614, for example, "the largest of all gatherings of Merovingian bishops, actually demanded that any Jew given military or civil authority over Christians should be forced to accept baptism for himself and his family."[78] As late as 937, Pope Leo VII, after trying to convert Jews, stated that "should they, however, refuse to believe you should expel them from your states with our permission."[79]

In general, however, the papacy frowned on forced conversions. This denial of forced conversion as a means of making Christians of Jews was initially stated by Gregory I and was repeated by almost every succeeding pope. The Third Lateran Council (1179) asserted, among other things, that Jews should not be disturbed, and in September 1236 Pope Gregory IX made a clear commentary on the dual issue of murder and forced conversions. The Church did not want the Jews to be annihilated nor forcibly baptized.[80] Similar positions were proclaimed in various bulls by Clement VI, Innocent IV, Martin V, and Paul III.

One reason, then, that medieval European Jewry was neither forced to convert to Christianity en masse nor wiped out was that there was no official sanction for doing so. A second reason is that the policies encouraging forced baptisms were not always enforced, and in fact, the conversions that did take place were often abrogated. King William II of England and Normandy and Emperor Henry IV of Germany, among others, after unwilling conversions had occurred, had the forced baptisms voided and permitted Jews to return to their former religion. In 1217, when Alice of Montmorency gave all Jews the alternative of conversion or death and had all the Jewish children under the age of six forcibly taken for purposes of conversion, the order was rescinded by her husband, Simon de Montfort. Similarly, after the Rindfleisch massacres in 1298, Albrecht, the newly elected emperor, halted the killings, and those Jews forcibly converted were permitted to return to Judaism, "apparently with the connivance of the Emperor and the representatives of the church."[81] The forced conversions were crippling to Jewry as a body and had catastrophic psychological consequences for individuals and possibly for all of Jewry; nevertheless, the effects did not reach their full potential. Lack of official sanction and the rescinding of forced conversions mitigated the consequences of such policies.

In the case of the massacres, a similar conclusion must be reached. During the period of the Black Death in Aragon, Jews were aided by the higher classes. Throughout the continent, the pope, kings, and members of city councils argued for reason and attempted to halt the attacks of the mobs. In Speyer, Bishop Berthold, among others, attempted to defend Jews against the usual specious and malicious charges (ritual murder, desecration of the host). Friedrich Heer, in considering the perpetrators of the massacres, notes that "large sections of the population would have no part in it, recognizing their common brotherhood with their Jewish neighbors. There were individuals, knights, townsmen and peasants, who sheltered Jews in their own houses."[82] Efforts were also made to counter the reasons for the attacks on Jews. For example, Emperor Frederick II denied the veracity of the ritual murder charge and in 1236 denied its truth publicly. Similarly, various popes decried the absurdity of the charge. Pope Innocent IV, in one particular case, not only denounced the charge, but issued a bull to the bishops of France and Germany, where the charge was most common, stating that he did not believe the accusation. Similarly, during the Black Death, Pope Clement VI once more supported the Jews. He, too, issued a bull, this one to all of Catholic Christendom, averring the Jews' innocence. Further, he produced numerous reasons to demonstrate that the charge against the Jews was ridiculous. Many other examples exist.[83]

Such actions were of enormous significance for Jewish survival. Consider the alternative: in Bavaria the dukes, the sons of the Emperor Louis, gave the people permission in writing to disregard the law in their treatment of Jews. They did; in Konigsberg all of the Jews were burned.

That medieval European Jewry survived, then, was to a considerable extent because of the assistance, support, and protection they received; it clearly could not have been because of the formidable position of the Jews themselves. "It was not possible to take revenge on the persecutors; the disproportion of strength is so obvious that the calamities that overwhelm the Jews represent to its spokesman an upheaval of nature rather than a struggle between two camps."[84] Poliakov is here speaking of the Crusades, but the same situation obtained throughout the history of European Jewry.

The issue must be restated: given the number and effectiveness of the massacres and of the forced baptisms and the possibility of their increasing in size and scope, the continued existence of Jews in medieval Europe was surely in doubt. Were it not for the refusal of the authorities to sanction such actions, the protection offered Jews by the populace and rulers, and the abrogation of the conversions, the elimination of medieval European Jewry would surely have come to pass.

### The Vulnerability of Jewish Communities

Of further significance in discussions of the vulnerability of Jews in the Middle Ages is the size of the various Jewish communities. If these communities were large, the probability that Jews would have defended themselves is increased, for they were not attacked by armies prepared to do battle with other armies, but by mobs of townspeople, often led by nobles and lesser clergy. Obviously the latter would not have attacked a large mass of individuals who, potentially at least, could have inflicted more harm than they would suffer.

It has already been noted that the Jews were a minority within each country. They were yet a smaller minority within individual localities and cities. The number of Jewish families in each community or city was, in general, quite small. For example, only ten Jewish families lived in Berlin and Frankfurt am Main in 1571. Some 150 years later, at the beginning of the eighteenth century, Berlin had only seventy Jewish families. This pattern of small numbers of Jewish families living together had existed in Germany since at least A.D. 1350, nor were small communities of Jews limited to Germany.

It is "probable" that in the Middle Ages no Jewish community contained more than two thousand people; a nucleus of "a few hundred was regarded as being of some importance."[85] Generally these groups came together only after the massacres of the First Crusade. Before that, in the eleventh century and earlier, Jewish communities consisted of small groups of perhaps ten people, and usually the number was less than that. In only a few places did the number of Jews reach the hundreds.

The defenselessness of the Jews in the Middle Ages and the vulnerability of the small groups of Jews in most localities is easily demonstrated by recalling the considerable number of communities that were wiped out; and here one must realize that many more would have similarly vanished had not an authority halted the massacres. In France and Germany alone, within the span of one hundred years, nearly nine hundred Jewish communities were destroyed.

Some understanding of the small size of medieval Jewish communities can be obtained from estimates of the total Jewish population in various countries. The expulsion of Jews from England in 1290 saw a mere sixteen thousand people leave. In Italy in the twelfth century there were ten thousand Jews out of a total population of 11 million; the numbers in Italy increased to twelve thousand out of 12 million by 1490. In the Holy Roman Empire in 1300 some one hundred thousand Jews lived amid a total population of 12 million. After the Black Death and massacres, the figures for the Holy Roman Empire in 1490 were eighty thousand for Jews and the same 12 million for the total population. In all of western Europe at the end of the eighteenth century, there were less than five hundred thousand Jews.[86] In France, for example, there were some forty thousand Jews, approximately two per thousand of the population; in Hungary one hundred thousand Jews resided in a country of 7 million; in Holland out of 2 million, only fifty thousand were Jews; and in Germany, Jews composed less than 1 percent of the population. The same proportions obtained throughout Europe.

If one considers either the small size of local Jewish communities and the extent of the violence directed toward them or the possibility of church-sanctioned forced conversion, one must conclude once more that the Jews could have been exterminated.

### The Ghetto

Perhaps the clearest indication of the position of Jews in Europe is the institutionalization of the ghettos, which existed in one form or another in every country that admitted Jews and in every city of substantial size.[87] It is not without significance that the *legal* foundation of the ghetto system was laid in 1215, for this period, as noted above, marks the high point of the Church's domination of Jews.

The ecclesiastical sanction of the ghetto might of course be viewed negatively, as a forced segregation, manifesting at best a distaste and at worst an abomination of Jews. However, it might be considered from a sociological perspective as "a way of dealing with a dissenting minority" and as "a form of toleration."[88] The suggestion that the institutionalization of the ghetto was not totally negative is supported by the reaction of the Jews of Europe, who were not at all unhappy about its official endorsement.

The ghetto served several purposes. One was the separation of Jew and Christian. This was desired by religious leaders of both groups, who feared that contact with members of the other religion would somehow "contaminate" members of their own congregations and result in a flood of conversions. It is perhaps strange that the various popes who supported the ghetto could imagine that a small number of Jews might induce many Christians to convert to Judaism. They apparently failed to consider the possibility that the Jews might be absorbed into the overwhelming mass of Christians. Thus, to prevent or at least minimize the chance of one religion "contaminating" the other, Jews were segregated (albeit not very effectively), made to wear distinctive clothing (although the repeated injunctions to this effect tend to suggest that they were disregarded), and periodically prohibited from intermarrying with Christians.

Jews were favorably disposed to some of these restrictions, especially the last; nor was the ghetto viewed with disfavor. The Spanish and Italian ghettos, for example, were requested by Jews as a physical symbol of their autonomy. In general the Jews did not resent ghettoization because "segregation ...tended to act as a powerful preserve of racial solidarity and culture."[89] In parts of Italy, for example, Jews instituted an annual feast day to commemorate the institutionalization of the ghetto. Jews had segregated themselves even before the ghetto was instituted; that is, they had voluntarily lived in separate parts of the cities.[90] One should take care, however, not to glamorize the ghetto.[91] While it benefited Jews in several ways there is no doubt that ghettoization was a stigma. Further, conditions within the ghetto were often harsh, and there were restrictions on the sizes of ghetto populations and additional restrictions on housing. In Posen, for example, the ghetto was permitted only forty-nine houses.

Nonetheless, when the abolition of the ghetto finally came, it was opposed by numerous Jews for fear that the Jewish community would be wiped out. This must be taken in two senses; the ghetto not only represented Jewish autonomy but Jewish security as well, for there can be no doubt that the ghetto was a means of protection for Jews. Even before the institutionalization of the ghetto, various secular and religious leaders placed Jews in special areas to ensure their safety.[92] Joachim Prinz minces few words: *"As a means of protection* they were assigned a certain quarter of the town which had walls to protect the Jews from the rabble."[93] In some instances the ghettos were formidable; for example, in Spain voluntary ghettos (called *castra Judaeorum*) were fortified for protection.

The Jews would not have needed the ghetto for protection if they had been able to defend themselves. The ghetto represents tangible documentation of the vulnerability of Jews within Europe and the recognition of that vulnerability by both Christians and Jews.

### Weaponry

In examining the nature of the vulnerability of medieval European Jewry, the possibility of Jewish self-defense must also be considered. There is, after all, the possibility that Jews could have defended themselves against attack, numerical differences and ghettoization notwithstanding. Such defense, however, would necessarily have required that the Jews be armed, preferably well armed.

The evidence concerning the rights of Jews to bear arms is equivocal. At least in the west that right, where it existed, vanished as the Middle Ages advanced. By the time of the Black Death (1350) it was unusual to hear of Jews forming an organized defense, so one may assume, with perhaps some exceptions, that Jews were unarmed.[94] Actually, "disarmed" is a more appropriate term; there is considerable evidence to suggest that in different places and at different times Jews could and did bear arms.[95] During the First Crusade and for some time after, at least some Jews had weapons. They fought (and lost to) Crusaders who attacked them, and they temporarily defended themselves in Cologne in 1147 and in York, England, in 1190, where they were overwhelmed by sheer weight of numbers. However, after the treaties of peace in the Holy Roman Empire, beginning with Henry IV's decree in 1103, they were systematically disarmed and eventually prohibited from carrying weapons.

This decree affected the Jews of central Europe, but there is some dispute here. Jacob Katz argues that Jews in the Franco-German areas could bear arms "well into the thirteenth century," although he adds that this cannot be taken as a sign of either Jewish self-defense or Jews' possession of weaponry in general but, rather, was an indication of an individual's political status. Katz intimates that those Jews who were permitted to carry weapons were the few who were members of the upper strata of medieval society and that their weapons were of minimal use against attacks directed towards the Jewish community as a whole.[96] This is consistent with the writings of Salo W. Baron, who, referring to the Jews of central Europe, notes the "defenselessness of Jews and their utter dependence on the government's protective arm."[97]

Jews in England were forbidden to have weapons as early as 1181 under the order of the Assize of Arms, which specified that no Jew would be allowed to keep "mail or hauberk." Spain was probably the last country in Europe to allow Jews to maintain weaponry. Eventually, in 1412, Jews in Spain were forbidden to bear arms. Forbidding Spain's Jews weaponry must have been only partially effective, however, for when they were expelled and went to Turkey they brought with them a solid knowledge of armaments, which they taught to the Turks. At a later date Jews in the east were denied the right to bear arms, although when Poland was invaded by the Tartars in the sixteenth and seventeenth centuries, both Jews and Poles were taught to handle blunderbusses and pistols to help defend the country. Apparently eastern Jews learned to use weapons with some proficiency; they received honors from the government in Prague in 1648 for fighting the Swedes.[98]

In broad perspective, European Jewry was stripped of weapons from the twelfth century. The Jews lived in small, defenseless communities and endorsed ghettoization for protection. It is apparent that the Jews of the Middle Ages were dependent upon the solicitude of the rulers for, among other things, their very physical survival. They were in no position to defend themselves even if they had wanted to challenge the numerically superior mobs that attacked them. One cannot dismiss the probability that without the protection of the various rulers of Europe, the massacres of the Middle Ages would have been worse. Again, given the essentially defenseless position of the Jews, it is not impossible that they would have been either wiped out or forced to convert to Christianity.

Parenthetically, it is of interest that in the late nineteenth century, during the pogroms in Russia, self-defense units arose in the Pale.[99] The formation of "Maccabee Clubs" eventually became a general policy of the eastern Jews when they realized that the government would not come to their aid. These clubs were not without precedent; small self-defense groups had been formed as early as 1664 in Lemberg and 1697 in Posen. It is significant that these self-defense organizations existed in eastern Europe and developed comparatively late in European history. When Jews felt that the government would not help, they began to defend themselves as best they could. One can speculate on the possibility that if Jews in the Middle Ages in the west had not been protected, they too would have formed their own self-defense units, the legality of having weapons notwithstanding—and then one can speculate on the efficacy of these defense units. In any event, it seems likely, since they did not form these units, that protection from the government was forthcoming or that the Jews felt that it was.

Two specific points are central to the sections above: the universalistic nature of medieval Christian Europe and the vulnerable position of European Jewry. Given the universalistic claims of the Church and the weak position of Jews, it is puzzling that the Church did not sanction the destruction , either physically or through compulsory conversion or exile, of the only non-Christian group within its domain. Surely that possibility existed, and surely there was "reasonable cause." A similar if not identical situation obtained during the era of heretics and the rise of Protestantism, and there was little hesitation in attempting, successfully in the case of most heretics, to crush those who defied the Church.

Similarly, one must ask why the laity—townspeople, peasants, and secular authorities—assisted Jews. Even if one wished to argue that the Church preserved Jewry because of theological considerations, that is, as proof of the "truth" of Christianity, the laity was not similarly obligated to do so. The beginnings of an answer are available in a closer look at the relationship between medieval European Jews and the three groups with whom they dealt: the Church, the secular rulers, and the general population.

## NOTES

1. It is possible, in fact, to trace the beginnings of Jewish settlements in various parts of the world from the time of the Babylonian Captivity (586-538 B.C.). See, for example, Margolis and Marx (1969), pp. 114-18, and Grayzel (1968), p. 34. Bermant (1971, p. 5) reports that in A.D. 70 more Jews lived outside of Judea than in it. Also see Schweitzer (1971), p. 35.

2. Hertzberg (1968), p. 306; Katz (1973), p. 5.

3. Roth (1970), p. 139.

4. See Cecil Roth, "The European Age in Jewish History," in Finkelstein (1974), p. 225. Also see Margolis and Marx (1969), p. 287.

5. Smallwood argues (1976, p. 5), that the Maccabean alliance was "not a formal alliance sanctioned by a law of the assembly," but only a declaration of friendship by the Roman Senate. Scholars often point out that it was in Rome's interest to sign the alliance with the Jews. Smallwood, for example, notes (1976, p. 11) that the basis for the agreement was not "philo-Judaism" but political self-interest. However, this does not in any way diminish the significance of the alliance; it was in the Jews' self-interest to sign it, too. The Jews initiated the contact with Rome, after all, and nations enter into agreements with other nations precisely because they assume that they will benefit from those agreements.

For the text of the treaty see Pearlman (1973), pp. 199-200.

6. Rome initially assumed partial control in Palestine because the Hasmonean dynasty could not control its subjects, and Augustus took complete control of Palestine because the Herodian dynasty did not have the support of the people and could not effectively rule. Smallwood (1976, p. 2), however, argues that earlier Roman international policy would have made the "ultimate annexation of Palestine . . . a foregone conclusion." She is probably correct.

7. Radin (1973), p. 215.

8. Flannery (1965), p. 15. There is considerable debate on this point, and even Flannery is somewhat skeptical (see ibid., p. 280n). Katz (1962, p. 83n) considers the alleged privileged position of Jewry in Rome as "disproved conclusively." Roth, however, states that Jews were "actually privileged." Lot (1961, p. 23) argues that Christianity and Judaism were the only religions persecuted by the Romans. The

reason he gives for Roman persecution of Judaism is "the folly and fanatical aggressiveness of its [Judaism's] followers." He fails to explain why following Judaism leads to folly and aggressiveness but following Christianity does not.

9. Poliakov (1965), pp. 11-12. He notes that the single exception to this was the anti-Jewish edicts of Hadrian, which were issued (in A.D. 135) after the Bar Kochba rebellion. However, Hadrian's successor, Antoninus, "re-established freedom of worship for the Jews" (ibid., p. 21). Millar (1966, p. 101) agrees with Poliakov, arguing that "only under Hadrian do we find an active prohibition of Jewish customs such as circumcision," and Radin (1973, p. 343) challenges even this, suggesting that the "statements connected with the persecution [are] . . . of dubious historical value."

However, 62 years earlier, after the Jewish revolt of A.D. 70-73, Vespasian had allowed only the peace-Pharisees (under Rabbi Johanan ben Zakkai) their former privileges. The Essenes and Sadducees were denied these privileges, while the Zealots, the most rebellious of the Jewish sects, were regarded by Rome as outlaws and treated accordingly. Another sect, the Jewish Christians, were subjected to sporadic persecution. Moreover, there had been still earlier instances of state anti-Semitism, although to be fair it must be noted that most of these anti-Semitic acts were politically motivated and not attacks on Jews as Jews. For example, the single ordered expulsion of Jews from Rome by Tiberius and the two by Claudius were inspired by Jewish riots, not anti-Semitism. Further, these expulsion orders were not at all effective, in part because of the large number of Jews living in Rome. It should also be considered that Tiberius was not especially anti-Jewish (he was influenced by the anti-Semitic Sejanus) and that Claudius had issued several pro-Jewish edicts. Even Vespasian, who was not a friend of the Jews, seems to have been politically motivated when he acted against them. It must be recalled that the Jews in Palestine were in almost constant rebellion against Rome, or at least some of them were, and Vespasian usually limited his attacks to the rebels. His sons, Titus and Domitian, were anti-Semites, and the Jews of the time regarded them as such. Their more odious anti-Semitic decrees were, in both cases, aborted by their deaths. Previously Caligula (Gaius) had been murdered before he could see the results of his demand that the Jews acknowledge that he was a god. He was mad, however, not anti-Semitic.

For a discussion of the position of the Jews under Roman rule see Poliakov (1965), pp. 4-16; Grant (1973), passim; Parkes (1969a), pp. 1-26; Smallwood (1976), passim; Radin (1973), passim; Brandon (1967), passim.

10. Smallwood (1976, p. 135) suggests that Julius Caesar's philo-Semitism stemmed from Antipater's help in the Alexandrian campaign as well as his "generally friendly relations with Hyrcanus II and the Jews of Palestine." She also argues (ibid., p. 41) that because of the political connection between Rome and the Jews, Caesar regarded Judea as a "client kingdom and not a province" even though it was tributary. The Jews benefited from this.

11. The Encyclopedia Judaica, vol. 8, p. 87, estimates that of the eight hundred thousand people living in Rome at the time of Christ, approximately forty thousand were Jews.

12. Poliakov (1965, p. 12) argues that the basis of Rome's "manifest philo-Semitism" was the "strong charm" of monotheistic Judaism. Flannery (1965, p. 17) concurs, suggesting that the Romans were "fascinated by the Jews' courageous

adherence to their religion, but...fear[ed] their rebellions," and Petit (1976, p. 43) states that "the Romans never knew how to handle a nation so different from others, with its love of liberty heightened by its religious separation." Grant (1973, passim) points out that many of those Romans who converted to Judaism were individuals of influence. This is true. However, it should be noted that while conversions to Judaism did occur in Rome, they were much more frequent outside of Rome, that is, among non-Roman Italians and peoples conquered by Rome. This may be one reason why Christianity, and not Judaism, became the dominant religion of Europe. Further, it should not be forgotten that though Judaism was admired, anti-Semitism, or perhaps more accurately anti-Judaism, existed in Rome too. The latter attitude was especially noticeable among the intelligentsia.

13. Another reason for Rome's toleration of Jews—not philo-Semitism—might be that the Jews and Judaism were harmless. Smallwood (1976, p. 538) argues this point:

> Judaism as a cult fulfilled the Roman criteria for permitted survival: it was morally unobjectionable and, at least among the Diaspora with whom Rome had direct contact and continuous dealings as subjects when formulating her Jewish policy in the first century B.C., politically innocuous. Rome therefore made the sensible and generous choice of a policy of toleration, and pursued it with complete consistency during the period of the pagan empire, despite the vicissitudes of her political relations with the Jews both in Palestine and elsewhere.

This is possible, but unlikely. Judaism was morally unobjectionable to Rome, but it is questionable whether the Jews, even the Diaspora Jews, were "politically innocuous" for any sustained period of time. The rebellions in Palestine were not only costly to Rome, but might have spread. Also, as Schweitzer notes (1971, p. 36), at this time Jewish religious and cultural autonomy was bound to Jewish political autonomy.

14. On Julian see, for example, Judah Goldin, "The Period of the Talmud (135 B.C.E.-1035 C.E.)," in Finkelstein (1974), p. 117.

15. Quoted in Marcus (1965), p. 113. Grayzel (1966, p. 9) has a slightly different translation of the original text.

16. See Marcus (1965), p. 111. He notes (ibid., p. 151) that "this principle of tolerance, which Gregory I had taken over from the later Roman Empire, became basic in the relations between Catholicism and Judaism."

17. Marcus (1965), p. 151. Two other theological factors, Christ's command to love one's enemies and the Pauline doctrine, influenced Christian attitudes concerning Jews. These will be discussed in Chapter 4.

18. Quoted in Baron (1965a), vol. 3, p. 28. Because it was initially otherworldly, the Church had not devised a system of secular laws. Consequently it borrowed freely from those of the Roman Empire, making modifications whenever necessary (Lot, 1961, pp. 49, 54).

19. Kohn (1967), pp. 66, 70. See also Höffding (1955), vol. 1, p. 5.

20. Kohn (1967), p. 2. This is not to suggest that Christianity in its earlier years in Rome was without travail. Sporadic persecutions of Christians began, perhaps, under Nero's rule. Initially the persecutions were not extensive, but as Christianity became

more and more powerful, they increased, reaching a peak in the mid-third century. The persecutions ended when Constantine (the Great) in 313 issued the Edict of Milan proclaiming toleration of Christianity.

The difficulties between the Roman Empire and the early Christians concerned the latter's refusal to acknowledge the absolute authority of the former in both the secular and religious areas. Obedience to the Empire's secular rulings was sanctioned by both Christ and St. Paul and did not pose problems for the Christians (except for serving in the military). Christians generally paid their taxes and were law abiding. However, obedience to the Empire's claim to religious authority was unacceptable to them, and it was because of this that conflicts existed. As the Church grew, however, and increased and secured its own authority, an apparent accommodation between the two universalistically minded institutions developed.

21. Kohn (1967), p. 73.

22. Lot (1961), p. 385.

23. Almost from its inception the Church had to contend with heretics. As early as A.D. 187 Irenacus noted over twenty forms of Christianity, and by 384 Epiphanius could cite at least eighty (Durant 1944, p. 616). The major heretical sects included Arianism, Monophysitism, and Montanism. There was "no end" to the number of minor heresies, as Durant notes (ibid., p. 605). The problem for the Church was exacerbated when, as frequently happened, pagans adopted one of the heretical forms of Christianity instead of Catholicism.

24. The Byzantine Empire lasted for one thousand turbulent years. In addition to a multitude of heresies within it, which according to McGarry (1976, p. 43) were more numerous there than in the west, it was the victim of numerous foreign invaders, such as the Huns, Goths, and Bulgars and, most powerful of all, Islam.

25. Kohn (1967), pp. 75-76.

26. Palmer and Colton (1965, p. 11) argue that "by the fifth century the entire Roman world was formally Christian." Hughes, however, suggests (1947, p. 67) that "by the end of the fifth century the whole of the west was ruled by Barbarian kings, Arians all or Pagans." The evidence seems to support Hughes' position.

27. Kohn (1967), p. 79. Emphasis added.

28. Kohn (1967), pp. 82, 88.

29. Kohn (1965), pp. 12-13. The significance of religion during the Middle Ages should not be underestimated. Kohn (1967, pp. 14-15) remarks that "religion was the great dominating force before the rise of nationalism in modern times." He later comments (ibid., p. 17), "During most of historical time, religion was regarded as the true source of cultural life."

30. Hayes (1953), p. 129.

31. Baron (1965a, vol. 3, p. 95) argues that the basis of the Crusades was that "the papacy consistently raised its sights toward world domination."

32. Kohn (1967), pp. 104-5. Emphasis added.

33. Baron (1972), p. 299. Also see ibid., p. 289, and A. L. Sachar (1965), p. 194.

34. Quoted in Baron (1972), p. 290.

35. Baron (1972), p. 259.

36. Heer (1962), p. 50. He points out that this fear explains the frequent rebellions in the countryside.

37. Heer (1962), p. 50.

38. See Graetz (1894), vol. 4, p. 656.

39. Loewenstein (1951, pp. 67-68) quotes Pope Innocent III (1198-1216): "The Jews' guilt in the Crucifixion of Jesus consigned them to perpetual servitude, and, like Cain, they are to be wanderers and fugitives. . . . The Jews will not dare to raise their necks, bowed under the yoke of perpetual slavery, against the reverence of the Christian faith."

40. Heer (1962), p. 25.

41. Heer (1962), p. 201; see also, ibid., p. 207. Heer notes the first example of a secular Heresy Law in England in 1166.

42. The alliance between the Church and the Carolingian dynasty was significant here. By the ninth century the major heretical threats to Catholicism, that is, those that were well organized, had disappeared or were in hiding. Some had dissolved after condemnation by various Ecumenical Councils; others had been persecuted out of existence; and some had been wiped out during the Islamic conquest of North Africa.

43. See A. L. Sachar (1965), p. 194, and Heer (1962), pp. 211-16. Dimont (1973, p. 275) states that one million Albigensians were killed in that Crusade.

44. Strayer (1971), pp. 44-45. The term "Crusade" applies to warlike expeditions sanctioned by the Pope to attack heretics, heathens, and in later centuries, the Turks. The Albigensian Crusade has already been cited. Consider also the following "holy wars": The First Crusade (1095-99), the Second Crusade (1147-49), the Third Crusade (1189-93), the Fourth Crusade (1202-1204), the Fifth Crusade (1217-21), the Sixth Crusade (1228-29), the Seventh Crusade (1248-54), the Eighth Crusade (1270), and the Ninth Crusade (1271-72). The Sixth Crusade is also known as the Crusade of Frederick II; the Seventh is also known as the Crusade of St. Louis. There were also the Crusades of Thibaud of Champagne (1239-41) and other, lesser Crusades such as the Crusades against the Hohenstaufen and against Aragon.

45. See Gay and Webb (1973), pp. 125-27.

46. Baron (1972), pp. 259, 265.

47. Beard comments (in Graeber and Britt, 1942, p. 384), "We must remember that while Luther, like Savonarola, assailed Christian bankers, no single great religious leader of Christendom led a serious crusade against Jews for usury or any other reason." However, she does admit Spain as an exception. Also see ibid., p. 382.

48. Kohn (1967), pp. 119, 124. See also Heer (1962), p. 147.

49. Gilbert et al. (1971), p. 179.

50. See Tawney (1954), p. 81, and Hayes (1953), pp. 176-77.

51. Kohn (1967), p. 105. Also see ibid., pp. 16, 89-90.

52. Baron (1972), p. 259. Of course, it is true that the Jews were never strong enough to pose a real threat and therefore did not need to suffer annihilation; yet beyond this, there was a fundamental right of presence granted Jews.

53. Quoted in Grayzel (1966), p. 263.

54. Heer (1962), p. 56.

55. See Gregorovius (1966), p. 56. His discussion of Rome's Jews gives a clear indication of this.

56. Besides the crucial right of residence and necessary protection, Jews were granted a substantial degree of autonomy, the right to decide legal cases involving only Jews, and the right to educate their young according to Jewish tradition.

57. Jews, for example, were taxed for crossing a bridge, for entering or leaving a town, and quite frequently for residing within a town or village.

58. Baron (1972), p. 259.

59. Parkes (1962, p. 69), for example, writes that Jews lost their citizenship from the time of Louis the Pius, Charlemagne's son (A.D. 778-840), while Schweitzer (1971, p. 165) dates the loss of citizenship of the Jews in Europe from the fourth century. Poliakov (1965, p. 117) states that in Germany the "definitive loss of ... rights of citizenship dates from 1343." Poliakov would appear to be extremely generous, however; the loss came well before that time.

60. Poliakov (1965), p. 76.

61. Quoted in Poliakov (1965), p. 114.

62. See Katz (1973), p. 16. Freud (1967, p. 115) is incorrect in arguing that Jews were not "strangers" because "in many places nowadays under the sway of anti-Semitism the Jews were the oldest constituents of the population or arrived even before the present inhabitants." Scholars generally agree with Katz (1973, p. 16), who notes not only a contractual basis of Jews' residence in many areas of Europe but that "Christian and Jewish tradition alike ... accepted Jews as strangers and exiles." That Jews may have lived in an area longer than the current population is, as Freud suggests, true. That this prevented Jews from being aliens is false.

63. There were some exceptions to this prohibition. See, for example, Margolis and Marx (1969), p. 392.

64. Irving Agus (1969) pp. 341-42.

65. See Graetz (1894), vol. 4, p. 417, and Poliakov (1965), p. 120. It is not without interest or significance that Christians *would* make purchases for Jews.

66. Katz (1962), p. 30.

67. Schweitzer (1971), p. 111.

68. See, for example, Arendt (1958, p. 26); Flannery (1965, pp. 77, 122); and Roth (1970, p. 217).

69. On Germany see Roth (1970), p. 213. Poliakov (1965, pp. 113-14) notes that Jews were recalled to Speyer and Mainz in 1352 and recalled to France by John II (the Good) in 1361; obviously, they had to have been expelled before they could be recalled. Poliakov also notes (ibid., p. 119) that the first general expulsion of Jews in Strasbourg occurred in 1394 and cites the following expulsions as well: Fribourg and Zurich (1424), Augsburg (1439), Würzburg (1453), and Breslau (1454). Poliakov comments that "the list ... could be extended indefinitely" and that some of the expulsions were permanent while others were "followed by readmission" (ibid., p. 119). On Italy see Roth (1946), passim.

70. This was *generally* the case; there were exceptions to this rule. See, for example, Prinz (1968), passim.

71. Halpern (1969), p. 6. The total population of Europe at the time was approximately 80 million.

72. The practice of expelling Jews was a Christian innovation. Moslem governments rarely used expulsion as a weapon even in their most anti-Semitic moments. Goiten (1974, p. 74) comments that expulsions were "absolutely unheard of in Arab Islam." See also ibid., pp. 80-81, 83. Nevertheless, expulsions from Arab lands did occur, however infrequently, and were directed against both Jews and Christians. In the mid-seventeenth century, for example, Omar ordered the expulsion of all Jews

and Christians from his lands. This expulsion order, however, was ineffective. In 1679 the Jews of central Yemen were expelled. They were recalled a year later.

73. Cecil Roth, "The Jews of Western Europe," in Finkelstein (1974), p. 265.

74. Cecil Roth, "The European Age in Jewish History," in Finkelstein (1974), p. 235.

75. Friedrich, in Graeber and Britt (1942), p. 2.

76. See, for example, Graetz (1894), vol. 4, pp. 202, 371. See also Schweitzer (1971), p. 108. Margolis and Marx (1969, pp. 764-66) note that massacres occurred in Fulda (Germany-Austria) in 1235; Bavaria (Germany) in 1243; Franconia, Bavaria, and the Rhine borders (Germany-Austria) in 1283-87; Troyes (France) in 1288; Würzburg and Nuremberg (Germany-Austria) in 1298; Navarre (Spain) in 1328; Alsace, Swabia, and Franconia (Germany-Austria) in 1336-38; Prague (Germany) in 1389; Toledo, Seville, Valencia, and Barcelona (Spain) in 1391; Prague (Germany) in 1394-1400; Vienna (Germany) in 1421; Franconia (Germany) in 1453; Cordova (Spain) in 1474; and Lisbon (Portugal) in 1506. They also note, among others, massacres in Limoges in 1010 and Mayence in 1012, at Würzburg in 1147, at Ham in France in 1147(?), in southern France in 1320, and at Chinon in 1321. See ibid., pp. 352, 354, 360, 399.

77. Schweitzer (1971), p. 76.

78. Baron (1965a), vol. 3, p. 51. It should be noted that the issue was not conversion as such, but conversion of Jews with authority over Christians.

79. Quoted in Baron (1965a), vol. 4, p. 6.

80. Graetz (1894), vol. 3, p. 570.

81. Graetz (1894), vol. 4, p. 36.

82. Heer (1962), p. 311.

83. For example, Graetz (1894, vol. 4, pp. 108-109) notes that the Council of Strasbourg offered protection to Jews and that in Breslau the Emperor Charles seized and punished the Jews' attackers.

84. Poliakov (1965), p. 84.

85. Roth, "The European Age in Jewish History," in Finkelstein (1974), p. 229.

86. Katz (1973), p. 9. It is obvious that these figures, and all demographic data concerning the Middle Ages, are approximations. See Baron (1972), p. 241.

87. Keller (1966, p. 296) suggests that the term "ghetto" is of uncertain origin. A. L. Sachar (1965, p. 251) agrees and offers a variety of possible bases for the term. Most scholars, however, agree with Roth, who suggests (1970, p. 273) that "ghetto," which means "foundry" in Italian, comes from the area near the ghetto neovo (new foundry) into which Venetian Jews were ordered segregated in 1516. See, for example, Schweitzer (1971), p. 123.

88. Wirth (1964), pp. 84-85.

89. Roth (1970), p. 274. Hertzler (in Graeber and Britt 1942, p. 71) argues that the ghetto was originally a Jewish innovation, designed to help maintain Jewish culture.

90. Wirth (1964), p.85. The Encyclopedia Judaica (vol. 10, p. 82) reports that Jews asked for separate quarters of residence in Constantinople, Speyer, and numerous other cities. Hertzler (in Graeber and Britt 1942, p. 72) suggests that "the ghetto was rather a privilege than a disability."

91. For example, Hertzler (in Graeber and Britt 1942, p. 72) comments that "the Jew was comfortable and happy in the ghetto." Relatively safe and secure, perhaps, but not comfortable and surely not happy.

92. To give just two examples of this: in 1084 Bishop Ruediger of Spires segregated Jews for their own protection; four hundred years later this was done again, and for the same reason, by John I of Poland.

93. Prinz (1968), p. 34. Emphasis in the original.

94. One exception was the killing of two hundred members of an attacking mob by three hundred armed Jews in Mayence in 1349. See Graetz (1894), vol. 4, p. 109.

95. It may be noted here that the ancient Jews were warriors and occasionally hired out as mercenaries and that Rome had some four thousand Jews in its army. Roth (1959b, p. 25) notes that Italian Jews were quite proficient with weapons and that some were a part of the mob that sacked Padua in 1509.

96. Katz (1962), p. 6.

97. Baron (1965a), vol. 4, p. 141. Poliakov, too (1965, p. 91), argues that in the thirteenth century Jews still had the right to bear arms. He notes, for example, (ibid., p. 93) that this was the case in Dresden in 1225; yet earlier (ibid., p. 37) he states that on the Jews' readmission to Speyer they were allowed "in defiance of traditional prohibitions . . . to carry arms." Emphasis added.

98. It might be noted that in the Arab countries Jews were not denied their weapons, with the result that, in one instance at least, the Jews of Cairo successfully defended themselves against a mob.

99. When Poland was partitioned, just before the start of the nineteenth century, Russia, which had traditionally prohibited the admission of Jews, suddenly had the largest Jewish population in the world through the annexation of Polish territory. The Pale of Settlement was created by orders (in 1790, 1791, and 1794) forbidding Jews from living in the Russian interior. Jews were confined to the Pale, "former Polish territories with the addition of certain other regions." Bernard D. Weinryb, "East European Jewry," in Finkelstein (1974), p. 359. See also Keller (1966), p. 428.

# PHILO-SEMITISM IN THE MIDDLE AGES II

## 4

## JEWS AND THE CHURCH

It is crucial to consider two aspects of European history in analyses of the Church vis-à-vis Jewry. First, Christianity was universal in outlook; that is, the Church desired and worked toward a fully Catholic Europe. Second, the Church and its official and unofficial representatives had, until comparatively recent times, great power. Because of this power the Jews could have been forcibly converted, expelled from Christendom, or exterminated en masse. The papacy had numerous agents and an effective mechanism to incite the populace if hatred of Jews in general was not already strong enough (for example, because of the image of Jews as Christ-killer and the alleged wealth of Jewry). These same forces were used during the Crusades; clearly the European Jew was more vulnerable than the faraway "infidel."

In its universalism the papacy had a motive for persecuting the Jews; toleration of Jews could be viewed as contrary to the fundamental tenet of universal Christianity. Other non-Christians were not tolerated, nor were non-Catholic Christians, until the Reformation made toleration of non-Catholic Christians a moot issue; religious forces of equal strength and the rising power of secular authority negated papal involvement. This, however, certainly did not stop the secular forces from waging wars of religion.

From its inception Christianity has been both theologically and historically bound to Judaism. So close were these ties that it was impossible for Christianity not to take the parent religion into account. However, as James Parkes notes, in doing so Christians and Christianity set Jews apart because of the charge of deicide, and the Jews' history was determined through Christian interpretation of the Scriptures.[1] Other scholars point to a second dimension of this relationship: the "historical burden of Christianity," a burden that "proved unbearable"—the burden of the "temptation of power."[2]

One reason for Christianity's inability to control its awesome power lay in the bureaucracy of the Church and the depth and breadth of its position. Christianity had inherited the organization of the Roman Empire, an effective tool for enforcing monolithic particularism, that is, a tool by which Catholicism could be made the universal religion. The Church took full advantage of this inheritance. After the reign of Innocent III (1198-1216)—the pinnacle of papal power—the social, economic, and political decline of western and central European Jewry began. More than at any other time, between 1100 and 1400 "the situation of the Jews was dominated at every level by the attitude of the church."[3]

It must also be remembered, however, that it was only within the strongholds of the papacy that Jews were never expelled or massacred.[4] Despite the general decline of Jewry in most of Europe, a degree of security existed for those Jews who lived under the direct rule of the popes. Jacob Katz suggests that the very existence of Jews was justified by papal decrees.[5] Salo W. Baron agrees, noting that "the church, despite the anti-Jewish leanings of many of its proponents, and its unceasing denunciations of Jews' 'perfidy,' insisted upon a kind of limited toleration, which alone made it possible for the Jews to survive successive waves of persecution."[6]

Insofar as the power of the Church is concerned, one must admit restraint in its use: "Fairness...permeated relations between the church and the Jews. Despite its all-embracing claims of supremacy, despite its overt attempts to penetrate all domains of public and private life, the church imposed upon itself limitations in regard to Jews which are truly remarkable."[7]

As noted earlier, the official position of the papacy vis-à-vis Jews was established during the reign of Gregory I (540-604). His attitude toward Jews became the official policy of the Catholic church in both positive and negative ways. For example, the position of St. Thomas Aquinas regarding Jews is taken almost verbatim from the letter of Gregory cited earlier: "They are not to be forced to render any service other than that which they have been accustomed to render hitherto."[8]

Although he wanted Jews to become Catholics, Gregory held to the principles of Roman law that defined the position of Jews. Jews were to be tolerated, if in a somewhat negative sense of that term, and not harassed or made to suffer physical violence.[9] This position was accepted by succeeding popes despite the fact that from a theological point of view the tenets of Christianity and Judaism could be interpreted as mutually antipathetic.[10] Thus there is the paradox of the most powerful of the medieval popes, Innocent III, who truly regarded Jews as accursed and yet prohibited forced conversions of and attacks on Jews in his *Constitutio Judaecorum*.

Earlier, on September 15, 1199, Innocent III had issued his *Edict in Favor of the Jews (Constitutio Pro Judeis)*, in which he stated a major reason for papal protection of Jews: "Thou shalt not destroy the Jews completely, so that the Christians could never by any chance be able to forget Thy Law, which, though they themselves fail to understand it, they display in their book to those who do understand." And at least part of Innocent's action was due to long Church tradition. Again quoting from the *Constitutio Pro Judeis*: "We, following in the footsteps of our predecessors of happy memory, the popes Calixtus, Eugene, Alexander, Clement and Coelestine, grant their [Jews'] petition and offer them the shield of our protection."[11]

Yet one cannot conclude that actions taken by the Church regarding Jewry have been consistent; the position of the Church, which of course means that of the papacy, vis-à-vis Jews has been correctly described as ambiguous, and this ambiguity has a long history. To illustrate, Gregory VII (Hildebrand, 1073-85) forbade Jews from holding positions of authority over Christians (a concept inherited from Gregory I), thereby severely damaging the economic position of Jews; Gregory IX (1227-41) ordered the confiscation of the Talmud; Alexander IV (1254-61) renewed the ordinance requiring the wearing of the Jews' badge in the Papal States; Clement IV (1265-71) issued a papal bull requiring the Inquisition to proceed with severity against Jews attempting to influence recent converts to Catholicism; Nicholas III (1277-80) instituted conversionist sermons; Paul V (1605-1621) deprived Jews of the protection of civil jurisdiction; and Clement XII (1730-40) drew up a new anti-Jewish code.[12]

It should be noted that these attacks were against Judaism as a religion and not Jews as people, although Jews were in fact the victims of these attacks. Indeed, Baron notes that "the very Inquisition ... was, in principle, limited to Marranos and other professing Christians and only to such Jews as were accused of attacking Christianity or of proselytizing among Christians, including backsliding converts."[13] This was the sole basis of all of the negative actions applied by the Church to Jewish people.

It is possible to argue, however, that the popes of this same era, as well as numerous others, were friendly to and protective of Jews.[14] Again, following in the tradition of Gregory I, the reasons were generally a combination of theology and humanitarianism. To illustrate, Alexander II (1061-73) cautioned Christians who were going to Spain to do battle with Islam not to harm Jews. Calixtus II (1119-24), in the bull *Constitutio pro Judaeis*, condemned all forms of persecution directed towards the Jews, which may explain why he is recalled for "his benevolent attitude toward the Jews and his solemn declaration guaranteeing their freedom in trade and worship."[15] Gregory IX ordered French priests to protect Jews and protested, in 1236, the killing of Jews by French crusaders. In 1247 Innocent IV issued the first papal bull condemning the ritual murder charge. Even Innocent III, who is generally regarded as an organizer—and possibly the architect—of medieval Church anti-Semitism, defended Jews against attacks by crusaders in France in 1199. Benedict XII (1334-42) similarly defended German Jews during a later wave of anti-Semitic violence, and Clement VI (1342-52) attempted to save Jews during the period of the Black Death in Germany; in the "friendly bull of Pope Clement VI," he prohibited Christians from forcibly baptizing Jews, from killing them without legal sanction, and from robbing them.

Boniface IX (1389-94) issued a bull of protection renewing and extending the privileges granted Jews by the Roman Republic, and Martin V (Otto Colonna, 1417-31) issued a bull whereby Jews were confirmed in their old rights and privileges and also prohibited forced baptisms. During the papal reign of Sixtus IV (1471-81) and for almost three quarters of a century thereafter, the relationship between popes and Jews was especially amicable.[16] During the papacy of Leo X (1513-21) "it was said that Roman Jews considered his pontificate a presage in messianic times."[17] Clement VI (1523-34), "a prince gracious to Israel," restored privileges to several Jewish physicians and helped numerous Marrano fugitives who had escaped from Portugal. Pope Pius IX (1846-78) had the ghetto wall razed and abolished conversionist sermons.[18] "Ambiguity" is not an inappropriate term to apply to papal actions concerning Jews.

Based on the consideration that it was not necessary to tolerate Jews and that other groups clearly were not tolerated, papal acceptance of Jews within their domain appears enigmatic. It cannot be argued that the religious leaders did not fear Jews. Their prohibitions against social intercourse between Christians and Jews, ineffective though the prohibitions were, refute this premise. Similarly, it cannot be argued that the wearers of the Shoes of the Fisherman uniformly admired or liked Jews or Judaism. The negative bulls noted above would dispute that assertion. Finally, it cannot be suggested that the popes' actions that benefited Jews were based even occasionally upon ulterior motives. Indeed, the popes had little to gain from protecting Jews.

Some scholars argue that the attitude of the papacy toward Jews was contingent upon the security felt by the Church and that when this was threatened, in fact or in imagination, the position of the papacy toward Jews changed for the worse. There is little doubt that, at least to some degree, this is correct, as the effects of the Reformation bear witness. Nevertheless, despite the inconsistencies and power of the Church, despite its attacks on all non-Catholics, and despite the vulnerability of Jews, the latter have existed within Christendom since the Church's inception largely because of the approval and occasionally even with the support of the papacy.

The two main reasons for the toleration and protection of European Jewry by the papacy, humanitarianism and theology, are often difficult to separate. A third reason, the intellectual advantages gained by having Jews in an area, was a factor in determining actions of individual popes but not of the actions of the papacy in general.

A specific theological basis of philo-Semitism dates back to the mid-fourth century. St. Jerome stated in a dictum that Jews "are divinely preserved for a purpose worthy of God." Jews were, moreover, again according to St. Jerome, to be "regarded as the virtual librarians of the Christian religion, for they had preserved the Old Testament, or rather the Law, in their Ark of the Covenent."[19] This was often repeated in papal bulls as was the letter by

Gregory I. Innocent III cited the dictum of St. Jerome as cause for the toleration and protection of the Jews. And Innocent IV, in a letter to the King of Navarre (October 7, 1246), expressed a similar opinion: "It is fitting that the Christian Faith accord the Jews the protection due them against their persecutors, and that it do so the more willingly as they have been preserved specifically to testify to the orthodox Faith."[20]

There were four basic theological reasons for the popes' protection and toleration of Jews. First, the continuing existence of the Jews in and of itself demonstrates the truth of the Bible. Second, the Jews are guardians of their scriptures, even though they do not understand them. Third, Jesus foretold their conversion, a conversion that must be patiently awaited. Fourth, some Jews will be saved.[21]

Beyond this, however, two other factors influenced the attitude of the papacy toward Jews. First, Christ's command to love your enemies, to bless, do good, and pray for them (Matthew 5:44), generally mitigated against and diminished the intensity of religious anti-Semitism. Although the term "enemies" cannot contribute to favorable Christian perspectives of Jews, it is likely that the injunction contributed to Christian tolerance of Jews. It certainly influenced the social ethics of some Christian thinkers, although the degree and depth of that influence are difficult to determine.

Less difficult to determine is the influence of Saint Paul and the Pauline doctrine.[22] Although there is more than one interpretation of Saint Paul's writings, it is certain that his doctrine helped attenuate the hatred of medieval Christians, and modern ones as well, toward Jews. Paul taught that the Jews are not lost and that God will not abandon them, regardless of their refusal to acknowledge Jesus as the Christ. The Jews are still the progeny of the patriarchs, and the covenant that God made with them has not and cannot be broken. Most important, perhaps, Paul argued that because of their original election the Jews are God's beloved. Thus they are to be forgiven and not regarded with enmity.[23] Indeed, Paul not only forgives the Jews, he justifies their position: their rejection of Christ is a part of God's plan. Further, a remnant of Jewry will eventually be saved, an event that will bring temporal history to an end.[24]

Whether or not the Pauline doctrine is so interwoven with Christian theology as to make the two inseparable, as H. J. Schoeps argues,[25] at least some of it shaped Christian attitudes toward Jews. Even if some of Paul's philo-Semitism was suppressed, his continued acceptance of the Jews quite clearly placed religious philo-Semitism on solid ground.[26]

These theological reasons for the protection and toleration of the Jews were potent. Yet along with these reasons "the pleasant fact stands out that a humanitarian note was occasionally struck."[27] Humanitarianism was a probable factor in Gregory I's position and was therefore established as a part of the Church's tradition regarding Jews. Even if papal protection of Jews was based on theology more often than on humanitarianism, the latter was nonetheless tangible and significant. Although less frequently cited in papal bulls and letters than religion as a cause for the acceptance of Jews in Christendom, humanitarianism was expressly stated as a basis of that acceptance in 1179 when the Third Lateran Council met. The council called for toleration of Jews *pro sola humanitate* ("on the grounds of humanity alone").

Thus, in addition to a theological philo-Semitism, there existed a humanistic philo-Semitism. And it is crucial to recognize that these were oriented to *Jews alone*; other non-Christians and members of other Christian sects did not enjoy that tolerance.

In the Middle Ages, indeed virtually from the beginnings of Christianity, numerous attempts were made to convert Jews. These attempts took several forms, including forced sermons (Jews had to attend lectures on Christianity),[28] religious debates (more often than not the Jews involved in these debates were under duress; their arguments and counterarguments were restricted), and not least, forced conversions (baptizing of unwilling Jews under pain of death or expulsion).

Forced attendance at sermons and participation in debates, if not totally just or reasonable, were presumably based on the power of persuasion. The instigators assumed, within protected limits, that the "truth" of Christianity and the "irrationality" of Judaism would become manifest. It is apparent that the most damaging of these techniques for conversion, as well as the most effective in pragmatic terms, was forced baptisms. The papacy did not support these; beginning with Gregory I, virtually every pope issued strong statements attacking conversion by force, although the repetitions of these statements are indicative of their ineffectiveness. The church, then, officially repudiated the practice of forced baptisms, a practice not infrequently endorsed by the lower clergy and occasionally accepted de facto by a reigning pope if a conversion had already been accomplished.[29]

The popes also, with a few exceptions, spoke out against the periodic charges of ritual murder that were directed against Jews (murders allegedly committed by Jews on Christian children to get their blood for use in Jewish rituals) and against accusations of desecration of the Host.[30] With the coming of the Reformation, of course, the charge of the desecration of the Host vanished in Protestant countries, although it still was made, if somewhat sporadically, in Catholic countries. The ritual murder charge died a slow death.[31]

In considering the position of the popes toward the Jews, one should take into account the papacy's refusal to support anti-Jewish acts of violence. Here, too, Jews were somewhat unique; the papacy was hardly nonviolent in dealing with other non-Christians, such as Moslems, and with various heretical Christian sects. But the popes did not merely refrain from directly inspiring acts of violence against the Jews; they frequently chose not to ignore the violence being done, and they acted, albeit often ineffectually, to halt it. Indeed, as Roth notes, "the popes, however much they may have desired to prevent the contamination of Christian orthodoxy through their means, always adhered to the principle of formal toleration."[32] This explains the relative tranquillity of Italian medieval Jewry.

Even the series of negative bulls did not effectively negate the general attitude of the popes. Formal toleration was a basic aspect of Jewish-Christian relations at least from the time of Pope Calixtus II (1119-24) and lasting until the Reformation. While this should not suggest that every pope was equally committed to tolerance, it does imply that within ecclesiastical boundaries, numerous popes acted to deny the more obvious of the spurious charges laid to Jews and to halt the violence directed against them; many popes did more than that. European Jewry often viewed the papacy as a protector and would turn to the pope for assistance. This was especially true when secular forces, usually nobles who were in debt and who had royal support, attacked Jews. This happened, for example, in France in 1233 and in Navarre in 1247 and 1248. In each case the Jews turned to the papacy.

It is obvious that Solomon Grayzel is correct not only in arguing that "the popes tried to protect the Jews," but in the broader view: "It is not difficult to imagine what the fate of the Jews would have been had not the popes made it a part of Church policy to guarantee the Jews life, and rights of religious observance."[33] A theological (or church) legitimation of Jews' right of presence within Christendom was absolutely vital for survival.

Any general interpretation of the Church's position vis-à-vis Jews is contingent upon how broadly the term "Church" is defined.[34] It is important to distinguish between the papacy and the lower clergy, especially during the Middle Ages. The lower clergy were closer to the population than were the popes because severe class divisions effectively separated the nobility and upper clergy from the masses. The lower clergy, especially the monks, lived and worked among, and consequently influenced, the people.[35] And the monks were often virulently anti-Semitic. It was not unusual for them to "interpret" papal bulls in a manner not at all congruent with the intent of their authors.[36] Very often monks, the lower clergy, and quite frequently Christian converts from Judaism supplied the inspiration for anti-Jewish riots and forced baptisms. More than this, it was not unusual for monks and members of the lower clergy to lead the anti-Jewish attacks.

All of the lower clergy should not be condemned out of hand, however. As some inspired, participated in, and occasionally led the violence directed against Jews, others acted to prevent such violence and to save Jews. For example, Saint Bernard of Clairvaux came to the defense of Jews who were attacked during the First Crusade and was responsible for the relative moderation of the attacks during the Second Crusade. At one point Bernard, along with Rupert of Dentz, Peter the Venerable, Abelard, and others, considered the issue of Christian toleration of Jews; they endorsed that toleration. And recall that this same Bernard encouraged the crushing of the Albigensians. The reason is clear: the Albigensians were heretics; Jews had theological (and humanistic) legitimation.

Similarly, the Third Crusade was of minimal significance for Jews because of a forthright stand by the emperor of Germany and the German bishops. It should be noted that it was in Germany that Jews were in the most precarious situation during the years of the Crusades. There are, of course, other examples of the lower clergy coming to the aid of Jews in the Middle Ages.

## JEWS AND THE PRINCES

While most if not all of the popes followed the position established by Gregory I and exerted efforts to halt the massacres and forced conversions of Jews, papal ineffectiveness here should not be ignored. Good intentions notwithstanding, papal injunctions against the absurdity of the ritual murder charge had to be constantly repeated, as did injunctions against charges of desecration of the host and charges that the Jews had caused the Black Death. This suggests that the power of the papacy in defending Jews was not nearly as efficacious as one might hope. This was not because of a lack of interest or commitment, but because of a lack of means to secure results. Medieval European society was decentralized; the bureaucracy of the Church, as powerful and influential as it may have been, was weakened because of that decentralization.

The secular authorities, more than the popes, determined the position of Jews then living within their domains, even during the years of peak papal power. While it was, of course, beneficial for Jews to be protected by the papacy and while Jews did appeal to the reigning pope for such protection, a more effective security than papal tolerance was necessary for survival. The safety of the Jews was usually in secular hands. Jews were usually granted admission to and offered security within areas in western Europe on the basis of a *privilegium*, a concession granted by local authorities, rather than through papal decree.[37]

During the peak years of papal power, secular rulers frequently made Jews within their domain *servi camerae regis*, royal serfs, following a tradition dating as far back as the reign of Charlemagne (800-14); this practice was especially prominent during the first half of the thirteenth century. It secured a legal status for Jews and offered them a form of protection the popes could not match. Lest this be misunderstood, "serfdom" was a term that was regularly used by medieval rulers to offer Jews protection; it was not used to humiliate them.[38]

Whatever physical security Jews in the Middle Ages could find was often provided by the secular authorities.[39] During the horrors of the Black Death it was the princes and magistrates who offered protection to Jews. This was most notably the case in Germany, where Emperor Charles IV tried to help the Jews, and in Austria, where the Jews cried when Duke Albert II, their protector, died. When Luther, who first appeared to embrace philo-Semitism but then adopted an anti-Semitic attitude, attempted to drive the Jews out of Saxony and Hesse, they were protected by Charles V, the ruler of the German Empire.[40]

More pointed, perhaps, was the special charter granted to Jews by Frederick the Belligerent of Austria in July 1244. This "Great Charter," which regulated Jewish affairs, was generally favorable to Jews and seems to have been based on a love of justice and humanity. This is evident from the charter itself, which contains a statement of Frederick's goals: a "desire that men of all classes dwelling in our land should share our favor and good will."[41] Frederick's charter allowed Jews to move freely, abrogated the higher tolls for Jews, and imposed penalties for desecrating Jewish cemeteries and synagogues. It prohibited the kidnapping of Jewish children and permitted conflicts between Jews to be settled in the latter's own courts. Moreover, it served as a model for similar charters for Jewish affairs in Bohemia, Moravia, Hungary, Silesia, and Poland.[42]

It is important to recall that church-state relations were rarely harmonious in medieval Europe. Although the basic points of contention appeared to have been settled as early as the sixth century by the expedient acceptance of the celebrated Theory of the Two Swords, this was not in fact the case.[43] Popes and monarchs battled over the source of kingly authority, lay investiture, and control over the Jews living within the princes' domains. All of these were struggles for power, and this was especially so in the case of the two more important issues of the time, the source of kingly authority and lay investiture. Indeed, these cannot really be separated; the first implies the right to the second.[44]

Less significant for either pope or monarch was the issue of control of those Jews living within the princes' domains, but this issue was of major significance for the Jews. The princes were a more potent force than the papacy, if for no other reason than their proximity to the area. Not only were the rulers more aware of the conditions that existed within their lands, but they could more readily command armed support to enforce the various ecclesiastical and secular decrees protecting Jews. It was this type of support—immediate and efficacious—that the Jews sought. While they wanted the popes to continue to condemn acts of violence directed against them, it was the immediate, practical aspects of protection that were first in their minds. By the time the reigning pope would have heard of the violence, the damage would already have been done. This explains why Jews wanted the secular rulers to act as their protectors; it does not explain why those rulers were willing to do so in the face of frequent popular unrest and, occasionally, papal disfavor.

The basis of the protection offered Jews by various secular rulers was generally a complex mixture of economic, intellectual, and humanistic philo-Semitism. In some instances, such as those of Henry II of the Holy Roman Empire, Casimir I of Poland, and the sultans of Turkey, another factor, loyalty (of Jews to the crown) was significant. This is not the usual interpretation. Many scholars suggest that the rulers derived specific (usually economic) benefits from having a number of Jews living within their domains, were reluctant to lose these benefits, and thus would quickly come to the aid of those Jews who provided them. Cecil Roth, for example, points out that, generally, emperors valued the economic services Jews rendered and for this reason granted Jews privileges and protection, and Frederick M. Schweitzer notes that charters were granted to Jews by individuals as well as communities for purposes of economic gain. Others agree; in fact, this seems to be the consensus of students of Jewish history.[45] A norm of reciprocity often determined the actions of the rulers.

The most important benefits the Jews supposedly offered were, first, as suggested, economic—although one must take care not to overemphasize this aspect on a priori grounds—and, second, intellectual. The economic aspect of Jewish history and the effect of Jews on European economic development have been the subject of an enormous amount of speculation, debate, and examination.[46] Scholars tend to accept the idea that Jews were invited into areas, protected, or accepted by secular rulers *solely* because of economic considerations. One student of Jewish history suggests that Christian tolerance of Jews existed *only* because of money; others imply this.[47] This is argued despite the fact that medieval Jewry generally was extremely poor. Indeed, one of the authors who argues that toleration of Jews was based on economic considerations, in pondering the question of Jewish moneylending, asks: "How... could they be expected not to devote themselves to money-making, the sole means by which they were enabled to drag out a miserable existence?"[48]

Perhaps the reason why the economic philo-Semitism of the Middle Ages has received so much attention is the benefits Jews gained upon invitation to enter various areas. Among the benefits, following a precedent established during the years of the Roman Empire, was the privilege of autonomy. Jews valued this greatly, because it ensured the continuance of the Jewish community, enabled Jews to sit in judgment of other Jews (thereby continuing the use of Mosaic Law rather than secular or, worse, Christian law to resolve disputations involving only Jews), and minimized contact with Christians, thereby reducing the possibility of mass conversion to Christianity.[49] The converse of this last, of course, was the reason the popes endorsed segregation of Jews from Christians—fear of a mass conversion to Judaism.

While there is little doubt that a good deal of the philo-Semitism that began in Rome and continued throughout the Middle Ages was tinged with economic considerations, one should proceed with extreme caution here. "Economic philo-Semitism" surely existed, as is manifest in the instances when Jews were invited into specific cities for the purpose of aiding local economic development. It is true that a number of towns welcomed Jewish settlers, especially in the early Middle Ages. There were occasions when emperors and rulers of municipalities, cities, and states offered Jews special privileges over and above that of protection to induce them to settle in their lands. This does not mean, however, that every benefit medieval European Jews received was based on presumed financial gain alone, as is often assumed.

For example, it is generally taken that the invitation to Jews to enter Spires in 1084 was based only on economic considerations;[50] yet the charter admitting Jews to that city makes no mention of economics as a cause of their admission. The charter begins: "I Rudeger, by name Huozman, humble bishop of Spires, at a time when I desire to make a city of my village of Spires, feel that it would be an honorable thing to settle some Jews there."[51] There is no mention of economic motivations here. Nor does any other part of the document imply that an economic motive lay behind the invitation. This is not to suggest that such a motive was not a cause of the Jews' entry into Spires, but it is to suggest that the causes are unknown, that the economic factor is assumed, and that other factors may have been of significance.

There were three main areas of finance in which Jews were of value to various rulers: as usurers, as tax collectors, and as financial advisors to the crown—the celebrated "court Jews." The practice of usury is prohibited in Judaism as well as in Catholicism and Mohammadanism. Jews, however, had little choice but to enter into this field. Barred from owning land since the ascendancy of Christianity, and thus from farming; driven from commerce in the western, central, and finally in the eastern European states during the sixteenth and seventeenth centuries; and long barred from entering most professions and never admitted to guilds, Jews had no alternative in terms of livelihood. As the rules against usury were increasingly ignored, Christians entered into this area of finance in greater and greater numbers, and by the middle of the thirteenth century Christian usurers were as ubiquitous as they were unpopular. Jewish prominence, not predominance, in moneylending, having begun in the middle of the twelfth century, lasted for approximately one hundred years in Europe.

It is also true—and undoubtedly this contributed to popular dislike of Jews by the peasantry—that rulers employed Jews as tax collectors. They demanded of the individual Jew or, more frequently, of the Jewish community, increasing payments to be gotten from the less fortunate of the rulers' subjects.

The economic Jew was not always the object of opprobrium, however; on one occasion Jews were recalled to France specifically because the interest rates of Christian usurers were so exorbitant as to create unrest.[52] And it was the Christian merchant princes of Hamburg whom King Frederick the Great assailed for avarice. The significance of Jews as financial advisors will be discussed below.

Yet despite the "role" of Jews as usurers and tax collectors, it must be understood that the financial world was not made up primarily of Jews; nor were most Jews a part of the financial world. Further, the majority of Jews should be distinguished from the few who were wealthy or in positions of importance. In the best of times the Jewish communities of western Europe, and the more fortunate ones in the central and eastern states, were composed of a small aristocracy at the top and a vast middle proletariat. Most Jews were hardly in a position of great wealth or, for that matter, in a position eventually to attain wealth.

Especially in the west, and extending in time to eastern and central Europe, Jews were subjected to varying degrees of economic segregation from the fourth century on. (It might be noted in passing that this was rarely the case in the Arab countries.) If Jews did at one time appear to have a monopoly on money, that appearance was shattered by the merchant republics. Even though it is true that, as merchants, Jews were of some value to economically backward countries, it is equally true that their value in those areas was soon reduced as their means of livelihood were denied them. The restrictions eventually placed on Jews forced many to become peddlers, not the most lucrative of professions or the most secure, although of value in economically underdeveloped areas.

The point, then, is not to discount either the economic usefulness of medieval European Jewry or to deny the existence of economic philo-Semitism. Rather, it is to assert the dubiousness of the idea that toleration of Jews was everywhere based solely or mainly on economic considerations. That some Jews contributed to the development of specific economic aspects of some nations in Europe is, of course, beyond dispute. But this cannot be taken to mean that all or most Jews were so involved. In fact, they were not.

The best economic historians doubt that Jews had anything special to do with the great economic upheavals of the fifteenth and sixteenth centuries. Specific Jews (those skilled in finance) may have been needed in some localities to help create, sustain, or amplify those areas' economic strength, but once that strength became manifest, the Jews in key positions were ousted, and in time only the meanest positions were available to them.

The Jews, however, were not automatically expelled after this happened.[53] It is reasonable to assume that after their "function" had been performed the Jews would always have been thrown out if, in fact, they had been tolerated or invited in only out of economic considerations. Even if one allows that the rulers supposed that financial benefits would accrue because of Jews, one cannot assume that to have been their sole motive for accepting and protect-ing Jews.[54]

If "economic philo-Semitism" was important in determining medieval Christian attitudes towards Jews, a second factor, "intellectual philo-Semitism," must be considered of greater importance. This was especially true during the peak years of medieval Jewry's contributions to science and scholarship, the period from the ninth to the thirteenth centuries. It was in the intellectual arena that the medieval Jew was outstanding, and to a much greater extent than in the economic arena.

Many scholars have noted that the connections among Jews in the various centers of the world during the Middle Ages were enhanced by the multilin-gual abilities of the Jewish traveler and tradesman. Most agree that if any single factor contributed to the success of the Jewish tradesman, it was his literacy. It is well known that literacy is fundamental to Judaism; this was of enormous benefit in an age when most of the clergy, not to speak of the peasantry, were illiterate. Through this literacy, and because only Jews were established in both the Christian and Moslem worlds and were able to travel with relative ease in both, Jews were able to bring to the west the great writings of antiquity, as well as writings within the several fields of science. This was of crucial significance; until the fifteenth century Latin Europe was primitive, the Arab world sophisticated.

In addition to introducing the west to the classics and to Arabian develop-ments in science and mathematics, the Jews made innovations in literature and science themselves. Further, Jews were involved in various technical areas such as astronomy and cartography and were sought out as translators and teachers.

It is historically true, and there are sociological reasons for this, that the natural sciences thrived on the margins of Europe and among the marginal groups of society.[55] It cannot be surprising that Jews, the most marginal of groups, contributed greatly to and played a considerable role in the scientific and intellectual development of the early Middle Ages. Jews were renowned as translators, philosophers, and theologians.[56]

If Jews were outstanding in any one area, however, it must be the field of medicine. Well *after* the peak of Jewish intellectualism, during the sixteenth, seventeenth, and eighteenth centuries, a disproportionately high number of prominent physicians in Europe were of Marrano descent. And while the Marranos were the most famous and numerically significant of the Jewish physicians, they were by no means the only ones.[57] Nor can one restrict significant Jewish involvement in the development and practice of medicine in Europe to a particular period. Jewish contributions to medicine have been similarly disproportionate since the ninth century. One proof of this is the astounding number of clergy, kings, and lesser individuals who had Jewish physicians during the Middle Ages. This was the case despite the fact that the use of Jewish physicians was specifically, although ineffectively, prohibited by papal decree in 1179 (this edict was a renewal of an older, equally ineffective decree).[58]

All of the Spanish kings, many rulers of the Franco-German states, sultans from Turkey, a host of princes, and numerous other officials made use of Jewish physicians. It was not unusual, moreover, for the Jewish physician of a secular ruler to have a substantial degree of influence with his patient. Further, the position of the Jewish court physician often remained intact in countries where Jews had been expelled. In France, for example, Marie de Medicis issued a decree expelling the Jews in 1615; nonetheless, her personal physician, Elijah de Montalto, was not only left undisturbed but because of Marie's great concern was given a Jewish burial in Amsterdam when he died.

And Jewish physicians served popes too. Canonical decrees notwithstanding, popes began to use Jewish doctors as personal physicians around 1300, although various popes had used Jewish physicians earlier than that. From the time of Alexander III in the twelfth century to Paul III in the sixteenth century, the papacy—for example, anti-Pope Benedict XIII, Pope Martin V, and Pope Leo X, among others—regularly employed Jewish physicians. Because many popes employed Jewish physicians, one must agree that despite its own earlier negative injunctions, the papacy "in general," favored the use of Jewish physicians.[59]

Despite the known and greatly-respected talent of Jewish physicians, *secular* Jewish scholarship did not continue to grow as the Middle Ages waned and as science developed to its full scope. Jewish contributions to science and secular scholarship steadily declined as the Middle Ages advanced, although Jewish scholars did appear occasionally. Part of the reason for this lies in the expulsions from the west and the concomitant growth of eastern Jewry. It is not accidental that the fourteenth century saw the beginnings of the decline of secular Jewish intellectualism. Eastern Jewry was traditional in outlook, and Talmudists make, or have made, poor scientists. A second factor was the new restrictions on university attendance by Jews. Jewish attendance at numerous universities had been prominent in earlier times, notably at Paris and Oxford in the twelfth century and, of course, throughout Spain. In Paris a Jewish school of medicine rivaled the university during the fourteenth century. As Jews moved east it became increasingly difficult for them to gain admittance to universities, and a papal bull issued in 1565 prohibited universities from granting doctoral degrees to them. For a time the only schools to which Jews were admitted were in Italy; these schools tended to disregard the papal decree, and since Renaissance intellectualism was still very much in evidence on their faculties, they were in general the finest universities in Europe. Jews were readily admitted to universities in Rome, Padua, and Ferrara. In the seventeenth century Leyden, the great Dutch school, began to accept Jewish students.

Despite this period of intellectual decline, Judaism and Jews continued to exist in Europe. Thus, despite substantial earlier Jewish contributions to medicine and other sciences, one cannot conclude that Jews received protection only because of the benefits they provided in these fields. The functionalistic approach to Jewish history (that each society regards its members from a utilitarian point of view) notwithstanding, the right of presence was granted Jews in numerous areas regardless of their functions.

## JEWS AND THE CHRISTIAN LAY POPULATION

Attention should not be limited to those Christians who were in positions of power, lest only their actions on behalf of Jews be recognized. In fact, numerous Christians were involved in securing safety for Jews in times of danger, fighting for the rights of Jews in a multitude of arenas, and in general befriending Jews in their daily lives.

It is often assumed that Jews in the Middle Ages were isolated from the Christian majority. No doubt part of this assumption stems from knowledge of the ghetto, an institution that allowed only secondary and formal contact between its inhabitants and the outside world. But one must consider the mobility of Jews in the commercial world, their involvement in cultural pursuits, and the sociological distinction between formal institutions (with their multitudinous regulations and restrictions) and the informal organization which appears within them. Despite appearances to the contrary, there was considerable contact between Jews and Christians in the Middle Ages, and despite ghettoization there was a good deal of cultural interaction between Jews and Christians, especially during the Renaissance. Even if one disregards the cultural contacts between Jews and Christians, everyday contacts were enough to ensure amiable relations between numerous members of the two religions. This was so despite rules that were designed to curtail these relations and Christian (and Jewish) religious tenets that worked to undermine them. There are indications, in fact, that social relations between Jews and Christians were more than just social; they were sexual as well. Indeed, Baron says that "illicit relations were far more frequent than is indicated in the sources," especially in the Mediterranean countries.[60] This was one reason for the "Jewish badge." Innocent IV, in a letter to the Archbishop of Besançon (October 23, 1245), justified forcing Jews to be "by their clothes . . . distinguishable from the Christians, lest Christians and Jews be able to have sinful intercourse with women of the other faith."[61]

Beyond this, numerous scholars report on the peaceful social intermixing of Jews and Christians. For example, Jews in Spain enjoyed close social relationships with various Christian patricians and nobles. Nor was the closeness between Jews and Christians limited to members of the upper class. When Philip Augustus of France expanded his territory, he discovered that Jews were living peacefully among, and on good terms with, the Christian populace. So amiable were these relations that Philip was reluctant to expel the Jews lest he anger their friends.[62]

Business dealings often brought Jew and Christian together and this facilitated social contact. This social contact involved more than pleasant courtesies. Jews and Christians, initially together for economic reasons, might become involved in one another's family celebrations. Jacob Katz points out that "for a Jew to be obliged to stay overnight in the house of a Gentile or to eat a meal there was not, perhaps, an everyday occurrence; on the other hand it was not entirely out of the ordinary."[63]

Jews also sought their clients' friendship and often won it. This could explain why numerous Gentiles helped Jews when the latter were attacked by mobs. During the First Crusade, for example, when Jews in Spires, Worms, and Mayence were in danger, a number of burghers safeguarded Jewish property and offered Jews sanctuary in their homes. Similarly, when an attack on the Jews of Cologne was imminent, no Jews could be found; they had been sheltered in the homes of Christians living in the surrounding villages. In Strasbourg, authorities tried to save Jews during attacks by a mob led by the guilds and nobles who owed money to Jews. Similar responses by Christians occurred during the Second Crusade. Jews of several cities, including among others Mayence, Worms, Spires, Strasbourg, and Wuerzburg, left their valuables with sympathetic burghers and sought and found safety in surrounding castles.

It is significant that, "on the whole, the burghers' class, not yet in official control of the cities, had no legal obligation to protect Jews. Yet having had close business relations and also some social contacts with Jews, individual citizens extended a helping hand to their friends in need."[64] Idealistic reasons—humanism, sympathy, and honor—also should be included as bases for the Christians' actions.[65]

There was also considerable social intercourse in the intellectual arena. A good deal of personal contact occurred between Jewish and Christian scholars, especially in the west. This contact was most prevalent, perhaps, in Biblical studies, although not to the exclusion of other academic interests. Indeed, Jewish and Christian scholars often exchanged ideas, and it was not at all unusual for Christian thinkers to seek out Jewish scholars for discussions of the Old Testament. Given that a disproportionate number of Jews were represented in science and that this was an era of intense religiosity, neither basis of Jewish-Christian relationships can be startling—nor can it be startling that these contacts would facilitate amiable relations between Jews and Christians.

In practice, toleration was the norm. This is why Baron will "testify to the general fairness, or at least attempted fairness, of medieval man"[66] and why in speaking of the twelfth century specifically, Heer comments that "toleration was ... a matter of practical experience; but it was also something more. Among two groups of people, liberally-minded scholars with scientific leanings, and devout laymen with a good share of common sense, toleration was a thought out principle."[67] Despite the ghetto, then, and the admonitions from both priest and rabbi, Jews in medieval Europe were a part of the larger society. Indeed,

> Ordinary people in the day to day circumstances of ordinary life, were practicing co-existence with "deadly enemies" long before, often centuries before, theologians and idealists swallowed their scruples and their pride sufficiently to provide the intellectual basis for the religious toleration which the common people had already instinctively adopted.[68]

### Summary

It is a sociological axiom that an attack by an out-group strengthens the internal solidarity of an in-group. This has been misinterpreted—almost reified—by numerous scholars as an explanation of the survival of Jewish people. Thinkers as sophisticated as Hannah Arendt and Jean-Paul Sartre have suggested that the persecutions of Jews helped them to survive as a group. Even though individual Jews died violently through the turmoil of the late Middle Ages, the Jews as a people survived because, in Arendt's words, "the Christian brand of hostility ... was indeed a powerful agent of preservation, spiritually as well as politically."[69] Sartre concurs, suggesting that "the sole tie that binds them [Jews] is the hostility and disdain of the societies which surround them."[70]

If survival is at issue, however, the axiom noted above must be qualified, just as must the comments of Arendt and Sartre. One cannot simply assert that Jewish survival was (and is) basically a function of anti-Jewish hostility.

It may be true that a threatened group is likely to manifest increased internal solidarity. But if the threatened group has neither the power nor the resources to defend itself, internal solidarity notwithstanding, that group will be wiped out, as were the Albigensians. This vulnerability has been characteristic of the Jewish community in virtually every country. The massacres and forced baptisms to which Jews in the Middle Ages were subjected may indeed have strengthened the internal solidarity of Jewry, but more importantly, they threatened the survival of the Jewish people.

That the threat was not realized cannot be attributed to Jews alone nor to the concept of Jewish solidarity. If anything is clear in the history of European Jewry, it is the Jews' astonishing vulnerability, a vulnerability that in other groups resulted in annihilation. That anti-Semitism contributed to the internal solidarity of Jewry is not disputed here; but anti-Semitism alone, while strengthening the ties among Jews, threatens the continuance of Jewry by its very nature. It is clear that philo-Semitism was practiced throughout European history, a necessary complement to anti-Semitism. While the latter contributed to Jewish internal solidarity and awareness, the former was absolutely crucial if Jews, along with their internal solidarity, were to continue to exist.

## SECURITY AND SANCTUARY

The first pogrom took place in 1096, at the same time as the First Crusade. This was not coincidence. With just cause Abraham Leon Sachar regards the beginning of the Crusades as "a turning point in Jewish history," marking "the end of settled Jewish communal life in Europe, the beginning of intense race-aversions."[71] Prior to the First Crusade, Jews were not persecuted on a large scale. From that point systematic violence was directed against them by Christians in Europe.

The Crusades were quasi-military expeditions to conquer and seize Palestine from the Moslems; there were nine Crusades in all. The First Crusade, preached by Pope Urban II in 1095, began in 1096. It was originally intended as a religious war external to Europe, but quickly degenerated into a calamitous affair in which Christians attacked Moslems, Jews, and other Christians— just about anyone who had the misfortune to be in their path.[72] This was true of succeeding Crusades as well, for the Crusaders were usually bands of malcontents, adventurers, and criminals rather than systematically organized armies. The motivation to join the Crusades was often the booty and wealth that could be gained, rather than religious conviction. Putting this motivation into practice, the Crusaders' attacks on Jews were not based on a glorification of Christ, but on an adoration of mammon.

The situation of the Jews was extremely precarious throughout Europe, although it was only in Germany that they suffered greatly. On the western side of the Rhine—in France—Jews were relatively secure, not because the bands of crusaders did not wish to attack them but because both secular and religious leaders protected them. That Jews could survive the chaos of the Crusades and settle in western lands despite the instability of the twelfth century is not unimportant. It implies that they had staunch allies even during this period. And it is of considerable importance that the burghers, their Christian neighbors, not only did not attack the Jews but, with the assistance of the bishops and counts, protected them.[73]

The most effective protection, however, came from the clergy and nobility, whose contributions to the security of the Jews were of paramount importance. This is not to suggest that all participated or that they were especially efficacious, but that attempts were made, with uneven consistency, enthusiasm, and effectiveness, to secure safety for Jews. In virtually every diocese bishops and archbishops did what they could to help the Jews; a multitude of examples demonstrates this. In Metz, Worms, and Mayence, bishops did whatever was in their power to protect Jews and their possessions. As many Jews as possible were sheltered in local churches. In Spires a young bishop used violence to control the mob. He halted the attacks with his own military force, cut off the arms of several of the leaders of the mob, and provided succor for the Jews, getting them safely into local castles.[74]

To some ecclesiastical leaders the use of forced baptism seemed the only solution. This was the case in Ratisbon, among other places. If this was less than an ideal solution, it did save lives. Moreover, the loss to Jewry was, in the main, temporary: "Whatever its canonical validity, this act at least saved the Jews from extermination and made possible the return of their majority to the Jewish faith after the storm blew over."[75]

It is indicative of the general situation that the first attempted massacre of Jews met with small success. During this first attempt, in Speyer on May 3, 1096, only eleven Jews were killed because the bishop there forced the dispersion of the mob before the toll increased. Without justifying the killing of those eleven, it is reasonable to call attention to the fact that it could have and surely would have been much worse without the assistance of various Christians: witness the tragic situation in Worms, where the bishops were ineffective and the Jews were slaughtered, and the occurrence of a similar tragedy in Prague.[76] Throughout Europe, often at great personal risk, Christians attempted to secure protection for Jews.

Many of these attempts were unsuccessful. However, this is less a commentary on the attitudes and actions of the people who tried to help Jews than on the power of the crusaders who tried to slaughter them. It is crucial to recognize that in many areas bishops and nobles risked their own lives to save Jews. This was the case in Cologne (Archbishop Hermann III), in Mainz (Archbishop Ruthard), in Worms (Adalbert), and in Prague (Bishop Cosmas). It is indicative of the situation during the First Crusade that within a relatively brief period of time after the crusade, the status of the Jews returned to normal.

The Second Crusade (1147-49) was like the first in that Jews in France suffered less than Jews in the Rhineland. Injury to the Jewish community in France was relatively mild because Saint Bernard and the king ensured that there would be no systematic slaughter of Jews there. A similar situation occurred in England, where Jews were well protected by King Stephen.

Even in Germany the consequences of the Second Crusade for Jewish communities were relatively slight. Although over twenty Jews were killed in Wuerzburg, the Jews were well protected in Cologne, Worms, and Mainz. In Cologne the bishop was so angered at the attempted slaughter of Jews that he had the leader of a mob responsible for killing Jews blinded. This cannot be taken to suggest that there was no danger to, or no violence inflicted on, medieval German Jewry during that crusade. It does mean, however, that an effective measure of protection was offered by segments of the populace, the clergy, and the nobility because of religious, economic, and humanistic philo-Semitism.

East of the Rhine, when the danger to Jews became apparent, an appeal to the princes to keep order was sent by the emperor. In addition the emperor set aside various imperial cities, including Nuremberg, as places of sanctuary for Jews. In Mayence, Archbishop Henry I, who was both chancellor and prime minister to the emperor, sheltered Jews in his own home. In Cologne the bishop not only offered Jews shelter in a castle but allowed them weapons. In Mainz, when the Diet convened, both the emperor and his son threatened severe penalties for those who harmed Jews. The bishops endorsed this position, threatening excommunication for anyone doing injury to Jews.

In part this explains why the aftermath of both the First and Second Crusades was similar. Once the crusaders had passed through the area, the status quo returned: Jews were not harmed, and those who had been baptized reconverted without incident. In fact, in at least one case and possibly many more, a priest "led those Jews who had been forcibly baptized into France and other countries where they remained till their former adhesion to the Church was forgotten. They then returned to their homes and their religion."[77]

There is little doubt that the reason the number of Jews killed in the Second Crusade was less than in the First was the effective protection given them by local secular and religious leaders. Further, in the Second Crusade the German emperor and the king of France protected Jews, preventing mobs from attacking them.

Baron, in comparing the first two crusades, notes that fewer Jewish lives were lost during the Second than the First. The reason for this was "more responsible leadership of the movement and the relative absence of unruly mobs."[78] These go hand in hand: the absence of "unruly mobs" was due to "responsible leadership." Another reason fewer Jewish lives were lost in the Second Crusade was the effective protection offered to and accepted by Jews not only from nobles and clergy, but also, and importantly, from "the masses."

Because of the decrees and protection offered by rulers and various ecclesiastics, the Third Crusade (1189-92) meant little to European Jewry on the Continent. Throughout France and Germany the situation of the Jews was relatively peaceful. Only rarely were there clashes between crusaders and the authorities about Jews, and these were minor. In Germany, the scene of the greatest danger during the earlier crusades, serious oppression of Jews was not allowed because of the influence of Frederick Barbarossa, "whose pro-Jewish sentiments had found expression in decrees issued as late as 1187."[79]

There was some movement for a new crusade in Germany, but both formal and informal protection was offered Jews. Individuals who attacked Jews or who sought to instigate violence were stopped from doing so by the government, with occasional support from some knights and priests. Moreover, German bishops threatened to excommunicate all assailants of Jews. On the Continent, then, because of the economic, religious, and humanitarian philo-Semitism manifested there, the Third Crusade meant little to European Jewry; they were effectively protected.

In England, however, where Jews had been untouched in the earlier crusades, both they and the authorities were unprepared for the riot that began in London and resulted in attacks on Jewish communities in various parts of the country. But in England's Continental possessions, no attacks on Jews took place. King Richard I was on the Continent during this period, and there is no doubt that "his measures to protect the Jews in his Continental possessions proved the more effective" than in England itself.[80] He was able, in one instance, to prevent harm from coming to Jews in Normandy and Poitou by sending messengers there warning people of the consequences should Jews be assaulted.

Because of Richard's influence, even in England the number of people who attacked Jews was reduced. In York, for example, many nobles declined to become involved in the anti-Semitic riots, even though it is probable that some owed money to Jews. The reason for their refusal to act was "fear of royal reprisals."[81] They did not help Jews as their counterparts in Germany did earlier, but their fear of Richard prevented them from injuring Jews. Nor were they incorrect in their judgment of Richard's reaction; he did deal harshly with those who harmed Jews. This is why attacks against the Jews were limited even in England.

The Fourth Crusade (1202-1204), which was especially notable for the establishment of the Latin Empire in Constantinople, did not generally affect Jews.[82] Similarly, and perhaps surprisingly, during the Albigensian crusades Jews in the towns along the Mediterranean coast were rarely disturbed. These and all of the remaining crusades were of minor significance, if any, for the Jewish communities of Europe.

The crusades, continuous during the twelfth century, were religiously motivated—at least ostensibly. Given this, it is, Baron argues, "remarkable ...how little Jews suffered directly."[83] In northern France, Italy, and Spain the Jewish communities were only peripherally affected by the crusades, and in England the royal authorities were successful in minimizing the number and intensity of attacks on the Jews. Even where Jews were attacked, they recovered with astonishing speed. For example, the Jewish communities in Worms, Speyer, Mainz, Cologne, and Treves—those in the Rhine Valley generally—were soon restored to their previous level of importance.[84] Throughout Europe, Jews forcibly converted to Christianity returned to Judaism without difficulty.

There is little evidence to suggest that Jews lost their sense of security during this period; indeed, there is some evidence to suggest that they felt quite secure. During this chaos the Jewish population in western Europe increased, several communities growing in size.[85] The basis of this security, growth, and survival was the protection offered them by numerous Christian groups and individuals and the prohibition by the secular and religious authorities against molesting Jews.

## The Need for Sanctuary

The same security, however, was not in evidence in subsequent attacks. In the later Middle Ages the protection offered Jews and the prohibitions against harming Jews were at best half-heartedly given and indifferently applied. The results of this general lack of concern are predictable: countless Jewish communities destroyed and Jews murdered. During the Rindfleisch massacres alone (1298), over one hundred thousand Jews were slaughtered. Yet the Rindfleisch and other massacres, such as those in Alsace, Swabia, and Franconia in 1336, were slight when compared with the Black Death massacres (1348-49), during which more than two hundred Jewish communities were wiped out.

Graetz has it that one cause of these massacres was the "sheer stupidity [that] made them believe that Jews had poisoned the wells and rivers."[86] Other possible causes should also be considered: "A contemporary Christian chronicler honestly confesses that the poison which killed the Jews was their wealth."[87] There is evidence to support this position. In Spires, for example, the council took over the property of the slaughtered Jews with alacrity. In other areas debts owed Jews were cancelled by fiat and Jewish homes were bought up by Christians. In general, as Margolis and Marx note, "the gain [to Christians] was enormous."[88] Whatever the causes of the Black Death massacres, the protection Jews received during the crusades was not forthcoming in later centuries.

Two factors regarding the Black Death massacres must be emphasized. First, the attacks on Jews were legitimated, that is, sanctioned and supported by an authority, usually by the city councils. Thus not only was the protection offered Jews in earlier attacks unavailable during the Black Death massacres, but those who had earlier protected Jews were now instigators of the massacres. It is true that some members of the clergy and some princes, such as Pope Clement VI (1342-52) and Emperor Charles IV of the Holy Roman Empire (1347-78), sought to put an end to the slaughter by pointing out that Jews suffered from the pestilence as much as Christians. These and similar efforts were usually fruitless.[89] Without effective protection and with their former allies turned against them, Jews could not recover from the attacks suffered during the Black Death as they had from those suffered during the crusades. In Germany, for example, where the attacks were the most devastating, Jews would never be able to attain their former numerical strength.

The second factor that must be emphasized concerning the Black Death massacres is that the massacres resulted in a mass migration of Jews to the east. The movement east had actually begun earlier, during the crusades, but it reached its peak during the mid-fourteenth century. It was made necessary during the latter period, not only because Jews were fleeing for their lives, but because most survivors were banished from their homes.

It is true, as Roth suggests, that after and even during the Black Death massacres in western and central Europe, "independent municipalities and petty nobles continued to offer a strained and far from disinterested hospitality to little groups here and there."[90] Yet sanctuary for little groups of Jews could hardly suffice; what was needed was a nation that would accept Jews en masse. A. L. Sachar sums up the tragic situation of the period: "Where indeed was a Jew to go? Half the countries of Europe had expelled their Jews, the rest were persecuting them."[91]

A parallel situation occurred some hundred and fifty years later (1492), when the Jews of Spain were expelled. The basis of their expulsion was religion, not avarice or ignorance as in central Europe; yet in terms of human cost the results were the same. The exact number of people who were dislocated by the Spanish movement is impossible to judge with any degree of certainty. An educated guess, however, has it that more than one hundred and fifty thousand Jews left Spain.[92]

In both instances, the movement from the central European states and the expulsion from Spain, the most basic of questions was where large numbers of Jews could go. With some exceptions (notably individual city-states of the Holy Roman Empire) and for a considerable length of time, the only two countries of Europe officially open to Jews were Poland/Lithuania and the Turkish Empire. Without their willingness to accept immigrants, the situation of Jews in some other parts of Europe might have sunk from intolerable to hopeless. Jews fleeing the Black Death massacres sought refuge in Poland; Turkey received and indeed welcomed the Sephardic (Spanish) Jews.

### Turkey as a Sanctuary

Perhaps the best illustration of Jews' success in discovering a sanctuary is found in the situation of those Jews who were expelled from Spain in 1492. Their situation was extremely precarious. Some went temporarily to Portugal and "a few thousand found their way to Italy. *No other accessible part of Europe being open to them*, the rest sought refuge in the Moslem world." Roth minces no words; their situation was extremely precarious:

The Jewish people must always remember the Turkish Empire with gratitude because, at one of the darkest hours in its history, *when no alternative place of refuge was open and there was no chance of succor,* Turkey flung open its doors widely and generously for the reception of the fugitives, and kept them open.[93]

Were it not for the Turks, there is every possibility that a considerable portion of the Jews of Spain would have had to convert to Catholicism or spend the rest of their days at sea. (In fact, this very nearly did happen to those Sephardic Jews who first came to the United States in 1654.) They were unwanted in France (although a few did settle there), had long been officially forbidden from entering England, and could not stay in Portugal.[94] In addition to mere sanctuary offered the exiled Sephardic Jews by Turkey, it is clear that they fared well there. The basis of this was the great freedom they were permitted.

In the Middle Ages the position of Jews under Moslem rule was considerably better than the position of Jews under Christian rule. Nowhere was this more evident than in Turkey, where they were free of the regulations demanding one third of their income in taxes and were permitted to conduct business without unwarranted restrictions. Jews in Turkey could own property and do with it as they wished. Their movements throughout the country were not limited, nor were there regulations concerning dress. They became, in a word, citizens of the country. Among the fugitive Jews the overall attitude upon taking up residence in Turkey was one of joy. One Jew living there at the time described Turkey as a country "in which nothing, absolutely nothing, is wanting."[95]

Yet the enthusiastic statements regarding Jews in the Turkish Empire should be placed in the proper perspective. Jews were elated by their treatment in Turkey, but their treatment was fair, not more than that. The joy Jews felt was an expression of relief from the exploitations, massacres, and expulsions and welcome for the pleasures of freedom; they had just come from lands where freedom was nonexistent.

The attitude of the rulers of the Turkish Empire towards the Jewish immigrants was not merely one of toleration; they welcomed them.[96] And being welcome in Turkey, Jews came to that land in droves. Constantinople witnessed a daily immigration of Jews, and within a relatively short period the Jewish community of that city grew to perhaps thirty thousand people, the largest on the Continent.

It is of some interest that the exiles from Spain were not the first Jews to seek refuge under the protective crown of the Turkish Empire. For several decades prior to the Spanish expulsion, Jews had already sought refuge there. Most of these people came from Germany and were as readily accepted in the country as the Spanish exiles.

Not surprisingly, scholars do not agree on the reasons the Turks welcomed the Jews into their Empire. One suggests that there were several causes:

trade, industry, medicine, and science were enriched by the arrival of Jewish businessmen, craftsmen, and physicians.[97] Many writers, however, argue that the primary, if not the sole, basis of the Turks' acceptance of Jews was economic. This argument is based, in part, on a correct appraisal of Turkey's heterogeneous population and the needs of the sultans to find people who were trustworthy. Heinrich Graetz, with his usual clarity, notes that "the sultans, frequently on bad terms with Christian states, could place but indifferent trust in the Greeks, Armenians, and Christians of other national creeds; they looked upon them as born spies and traitors. But they could depend on the fidelity and usefulness of the Jews."[98]

However, while it is true that the sultans were disposed to trust Jews rather than Christians because the latter were regarded as being loyal to Christendom, not Turkey,[99] other factors were also involved. The newly arrived Sephardic Jews, for example, were well known for their skills in weaponry. It was in conjunction with this, not commerce, that Sultan Bejazet II is said to have remarked, "You call Ferdinand a wise king, he who has made his country poor and enriched ours."[100] Also, as in Europe, and for the same reasons, Jews were highly regarded in Turkey as linguists and interpreters.

Above all, perhaps, just as they had been in Christendom, the Jewish immigrants to the Turkish Empire were respected for their usefulness as physicians. Jewish doctors were preferred not only to Christian physicians, but to Moslem physicians as well. As in Europe, these physicians exercised considerable influence with their patients, including the grand sultans, viziers, and pashas. This had also been true of those Jews who preceded the Spanish exiles; well before the arrival of the Marranos, Jewish physicians had worked for and enjoyed the friendship of sultans.[101] Sultan Murad II (1421-51) had begun the convention of using Jewish doctors as his personal physicians. Within a relatively short period of time other Jewish physicians were given influential positions at court.

Moreover, because the Jewish community in Spain had been by far the most intellectually advanced in Europe, the newly arrived Marranos were able to bring to Turkey a significant cultural tradition. Also, when the Jews arrived in Turkey, a large number of Moors came with them. The Marranos and the Moors had a long history of cultural symbiosis. The Turks thus benefited from admitting not only Jews but Moors as well, and from the combination of the two. Besides any economic benefit the empire derived from the Marranos, then, the Jewish and Moorish immigrants gave a rich cultural heritage to the Ottoman Empire, and did so generously. This was especially so under the reigns of Selim the Grim and Suleyman the Magnificent.[102]

All of this notwithstanding, it is possible that the foremost reason Jews were welcomed into the empire of the Turks was an inherent admiration by the Turks of Jews as people. To one scholar, for example, the tolerance of the Turks is "famed."[103] This may explain why other students of Jewish history recognize and acknowledge the Turks' generosity. Certainly the favorable attitude of the Turks toward Jews is not to be discounted. It is also possible, as some suggest, that there is "something sympathetic to the Jewish nature in Islam."[104]

Part of the reason for this appears to have been theological. Philip K. Hitti, for example, notes that in the Islamic world Jews were one of the "protected" peoples "in spite of several unfavorable references in the Koran."[105] Another reason for the Turks' acceptance of Jews may have been empathy with sufferers of persecution; as noted, Moslems had been driven from Spain along with Jews. Whatever its cause, and whether or not this sympathy was manifest throughout the Islamic world, it was in evidence in the Turkish Empire.

It is only fair to point out that a less pleasant reason for the acceptance of the Jews by the Turks and the dearth of persecution of Jews under Ottoman rule is offered by Simon Dubnov: "The role of the scapegoat, which Jews played in Russia and Rumania, had become in Turkey the lot of the unfortunate Armenians, whom the Turks assaulted periodically. Jews were regarded as loyal subjects, and the sultan Abdul-Hamid repeatedly underscored their patriotism.[106]

Without disputing the historical accuracy of this statement, exception may be taken to its interpretation, which implies that persecution of a minority (if a minority is available) is not only necessary but ubiquitous. This is questionable as a thesis; one of the purposes of this study is to demonstrate that such a universalistic proposition does not obtain.

The Turkish Empire did not last, of course, and with its collapse the situation of Turkish Jewry deteriorated. Even after the empire fell, however, the situation of the Jews in Turkey was better than the situation of Jews elsewhere, at least until the nineteenth century. It was not good in Turkey, but it still was better than under the rule of either Christians or Arabs.

### Poland as a Sanctuary

The Sephardic Jews' departure from Spain was the most outstanding example of the tragedy of expulsion because they were the most numerically significant of the exiled Jews. The greatest migratory movement of Jews, however, was to the east toward Poland. So great was this movement that eventually the majority of European Jewry lived in Poland. This eastward migration began as early as the First Crusade, increased after various demeaning papal decrees, and increased again during the period of the Black Death. Because of expulsions, restrictions, and the sporadic yet persistent violence to which they were subjected, individual Jews and occasionally whole communities from several nations moved east. These communities were mainly from Germany, France, and England, but Jews from other areas also joined in the march east. They generally settled in Poland and in nearby Slavonic areas. At least sixteen organized Jewish communities existed in

Poland by 1350. These would grow until the Polish-Jewish community was the largest in the world; by 1648 Polish Jews would number over one-half million.

Like the Marranos who entered the Turkish Empire, Jews traveling east were welcome. Their entry was supported by such Polish kings as Boleslav the Pius and Casimir the Great, among others. For the most part these Jews were not exiles (most came from Germany); yet one cannot doubt, given the physical, social, and ecclesiastical attacks they suffered, that had it not been for their welcome in the east, a great many would have been killed or forcibly converted to Christianity.

Although the great migrations eastward began in the fourteenth century, some scholars report (and legend has it) that as early as A.D. 905, well before the First Crusade, Jews were in Poland, and that, moreover, they received special privileges from Prince Leshek at that time. It was during and after the era of the crusades, however, that the large-scale movement of Jews from the Rhine and Danube provinces began in earnest. This massive migration was caused, of course, by the crusades themselves and by the intense persecution in Germany. There is, however, a paucity of sources on the early history of Jews in Poland. The absolute numbers of Jews in Poland prior to the Crusades is unknown, and it is possible, although unlikely, that the post-Crusades movement east has been exaggerated.

During the first great movement east, Jews were welcomed into and protected within Poland, at least by the kings and nobles. The probable basis of this welcome was, generally, economic; that is, it was motivated by the financial benefits Jews would provide the state. The welcome continued, for supposedly similar reasons, for some time, albeit not without vicissitudes. Well after the sixteenth century, Polish nobles, insofar as their own position was not greatly injured, defended the Jews living on their estates. Indeed, until 1648 Jews were generally well regarded and protected by Polish kings and nobles. This protection and high regard allowed the Jews there to sustain numerous prosperous and energetic communities. It also explains why, with the exception of a brief incident, Jews were never expelled from a major area in Poland/Lithuania. Similarly, because of this protection there were no large-scale massacres of Polish Jews.

It was not only the protection that the rulers of Poland offered Jews that contributed to the movement east, although that in itself was a powerful lure. Most of the rulers of Poland (not all) granted Jews privileges forbidden throughout the rest of Christendom. In thirteenth-century Polish Silesia, for example, some Jews owned lands and estates. More than this, Polish Jews were permitted to bear arms and dress as they wished, and, unheard of in the west until 1782, they could be inducted into the military.[107]

The basis of the Jews' welcome, privileges, and continued (until 1648) security in the east was to a large degree economically motivated. Jews, as Schweitzer notes, "created and built up, almost *ex nihilo*, Greater Poland's commercial, industrial, and financial structure."[108] Moreover, the Polish nobility regularly employed Jews as financial agents. Yet here too, other factors must be considered. Other forms of philo-Semitism were in evidence in Poland, besides the undeniably significant economic philo-Semitism.

It was especially during the initial stages of Poland's rise to prominence that Jews were well received and given special consideration, particularly during the "Golden Age" of Casimir the Great and Sigismund the Old. It was not during this period alone, however, nor only under these two monarchs, that Jews in Poland fared well. Nonetheless, the Golden Age was of great significance, not for the unique position of Jews in Poland, but because it was in this era that a trend, started earlier (by Boleslav), was enhanced and solidified. The favorable position of Polish Jewry lasted through the reigns of several successive kings. These kings not only offered them protection, but went to some lengths to ensure that the rights of Jews were not violated. This situation lasted well past the death in 1572 of Sigismund Augustus, the last king of the Jagellon dynasty.

It was after the middle of the seventeenth century that difficulties increased for Jews in Poland. Nonetheless, there were still those who protected them, in much the same manner as in the west. To give just one example, when Jews were forced to convert to the Greek Orthodox religion in 1649, King John Casimir allowed those who wished to do so to reconvert.

It is probably that the first great Polish leader to establish a favored position for Jews in Poland was Boleslav the Pius, although even here there were precedents. A charter issued by Boleslav in 1264 granted Jews in Great Poland both total freedom and numerous economic opportunities. The charter was not the creation of Boleslav alone; it was written in consultation with representatives from the estates as well as other influential men. Virtually all of Boleslav's successors renewed the promises he made in that charter, and they did so generally, but not always, with the consent and support of the nobles. A tradition was started and maintained, through the will of both the king and the influential members of his court, that was favorable to Polish Jewry.

Casimir the Great (1333-70), too, was beneficent to Polish Jewry, more so in fact than was Boleslav, from whom the former took his cue. Besides the specific privileges and protection granted to Jews, Casimir sought to establish harmonious relations between Jews and Christians in his domain, and to that end he encouraged close contact between them. This stands in marked contrast to the attitude of many Christian clergymen (and, in all fairness, to the attitude of many Jewish leaders), who wished for and worked toward as much separation between Jew and Christian as possible. It suggests that Casimir saw Jews not as aliens but as (potential) members of Polish society, and that he not only viewed this with favor but actively encouraged it. Under Casimir, the Jews of Poland were becoming part of the nation. Further, Jews could do so without being assimilated into the nation—Jews would remain Jews even while they became a part of Polish society. This was unheard of anywhere in Europe; moreover, it happened at a time when Jews in the west were being expelled from their homes with increasing frequency. The movement of Jewry to the east was, then, enhanced by Casimir's attitude.

There was a strong continuity between the attitudes of Boleslav and Casimir regarding Jews. This was significant in several ways, not the least of which was that Polish Jewry benefited from Casimir's efforts to unify Poland. Several decrees were issued by Casimir relating to Jews; the fourth, which is regarded by many as a restatement of Boleslav's privileges, is often termed the "Boleslav-Casimir Statute." It formed the basis of the principles by which Polish Jews were governed until Poland was partitioned in the eighteenth century. These principles had two key aims: to protect Jews and their property and to open economic opportunities to them.

In one respect, however, the reign of Casimir was unlike that of Boleslav. While Boleslav's philo-Semitic attitude was, to some degree at least, shared by his advisors, this was not the case with Casimir. Baron, in fact, notes that the philo-Semitism of Casimir was "the more remarkable as he constantly was under pressure of his anti-Jewish councilors."[109] Casimir was consistent in his philo-Semitism. A sanctuary awaited the waves of Jews entering Poland after the massacres in the west brought about by the Black Death. Increasing numbers notwithstanding, under the rule of Casimir Jews enjoyed not only security, but prosperity as well. It might be noted that there was pestilence in Poland as well as the rest of Europe, but that in the former nation Jews were rarely persecuted or massacred. This was because of Casimir's protection of them. And it must be recalled that the possibility of sustained attacks against Jews was quite real; Poland as well as Germany had heard of well poisoning.[110] All of this, his protection of and generosity to Jews as well as his high regard for the peasants of the land, earned Casimir the Great the title, King of the Serfs and the Jews.

In marked contrast to the situation of the Jews in the west, the position of the Jews in Poland and Lithuania consistently improved in the later Middle Ages. As suggested earlier, the basis for this was established in the twelfth and thirteenth centuries when Poland had not yet been united. It is only fair, however, to note that the origins of Polish Jewry's legal status came not from that nation but from decrees issued in the west. When Boleslav established the basis for the laws regarding Polish Jewry, he was following in the footsteps of the Czech and Hungarian imitators of Frederick II of Austria.[111] Unlike the successors of the Austrian, Czech, and Hungarian rulers, however, the line of Polish kings following Boleslav perpetuated his beneficence. Not only Casimir the Great, but others continued to protect and assist Jews.

For example, privileges for Jews in certain areas (Brest, Troki, and Grodno) were established in 1388-89 by Duke Vitovt. His successor, Casimir

IV, who assumed the control of Lithuania in 1440 and Poland in 1447 and reigned over both until his death in 1492, extended the privileges received by Jews to all of Poland and Lithuania and adhered to that policy all his life. During his reign Polish Jews were granted privileges unequaled in any other parts of Christian Europe.

After the expulsion of the Jews from Spain, "which had created a great sensation all over Europe," many Jews in the east were fearful that they would also be expelled. Their fears were not unfounded; there was a decree expelling Jews from Lithuania in 1495.[112] Unlike the Sephardic Jews, however, these Jews believed that the expulsion was only temporary. Consequently, instead of scattering, many simply crossed the border into the Polish city of Ratno. Their prediction was correct: when Alexander assumed the Polish crown in 1501 he renewed Polish Jewry's traditional privileges and readmitted the exiles to Lithuania and restored their confiscated property. The basis of this, again, is usually regarded as economic philo-Semitism.[113] As the years passed, the situation of the Jews did not appreciably worsen, as it did in western Europe. The reign of Stephen Bathori (1575-86) was a happy one for Polish Jewry, and Jews fared well during the reign of Sigismund III (1587-1632), a devout Catholic. It was not until 1648, during the Chmielnicki massacres, that the situation in the east took a marked turn for the worse.[114]

Some mention should be made here of Jewish autonomy in Poland. This was introduced, or more specifically legitimated, in 1551. The "Magna Carta" of Jewish self-government, issued by Sigismund Augustus, virtually gave Jews complete autonomy; Jews controlled their own courts, their own schools, and their own governing agencies. This was of profound significance for eastern Jews, who were overjoyed to receive it, but it was not in any sense a concept created solely with Jews in mind. The political ideology of the day not only permitted but encouraged the idea of a state within a state. This facilitated tax collection and was an excellent mechanism for control of minority groups. The legitimation of Jewish autonomy is not, then, a concrete indication of philo-Semitism.

In the east, as was often the case in western and central Europe, attacks on Jews were instigated by either the clergy or by the Jews' competitors. As early as 1173, well before the great migrations, Mechislav III (the Old), Prince of Great Poland, issued edicts protecting Jews from violence, most often the violence instigated by Christian "scholars" and students in religious colleges. Systematized attacks on Polish Jewry by the clergy were especially noticeable in the thirteenth century, when the Church began to exert pressure on the secular authorities to limit both the rights of the Jews and their numbers.[115]

These did not abate; quite the contrary, attacks against Jews by the clergy increased with time. In 1279 Polish ecclesiastical authorities tried unsuccessfully to force Jews to wear a special insignia, as was required in parts of western Europe. The clergy was not only a source of irritation, but agitation

as well. Similarly, those who saw Jews as competitors were less than enthusiastic in their welcome of the immigrants. This was most clearly manifest in the
attitudes of the German colonists, who worked with several Polish groups to
limit Jewish competition as much as possible and who were not very concerned with the niceties of how this might be done.[116]

To an enormous degree, the position of Jews in Poland was determined by
the reactions and effectiveness of two broad categories of people: the temporal powers would grant citizenship to Jews; the ecclesiastical forces were
intolerant and wanted the Jews out of Poland. The clergy in the east were not
especially attentive to papal decrees, and further, to a much later date than in
the west, the populace listened to and were moved by itinerant preachers.[117]
Because the power of the papacy was less efficacious here, Jews had to rely
heavily on royal protection.

Again, the protection of Jews by the nobility is taken by many writers to
have been almost solely because of the Jews' economic value. Graetz argues
that "each newly-elected king above all needed money." Moreover, ignoring
the vast number of German merchants who also migrated into Poland, he
suggests that the needed money "could be supplied only by Jews."[118] In
general, and above and beyond any individual ruler's personal needs, scholars argue that Jews were welcomed into Poland because of national economic considerations. Dubnov, for example, comments that the rulers
needed to support the Jews' economic activities for Poland's benefit.[119]
James Parkes agrees, suggesting that Jews went to Poland from medieval
Christendom because Poland profited by their being there. This same reasoning is offered to explain, at least partially, the motives of Casimir the Great
(1333-70).[120] Baron, however, suggests a dual motive: economics and loyalty
to the nation. Casimir, he suggests, "had perfectly valid political and economic reasons to try to attract to his country numerous Jews who, even if not
styled *servi camerae* as in the Holy Roman Empire, were likely to serve as the
Crown's most loyal subjects."[121] With the ascension of Alexander Yaghello to
the throne, the single motive supposedly returns. He is said to have approved
the existence of Jews in his land because of their economic importance to the
kingdom.[122]

Virtually every scholar seems to consider the Jews more necessary to
Poland than to any other country in Europe. The reason was the dichoto-
mous population of Poland; Jews filled the gap between the nobles and the
serfs. In their "role" as middlemen, Jews supplied both money and merchan-
dise. This explains why, in addition to receiving protection from the kings,
Jews received protection from the nobles; the latter benefited from them
too.[123] Further, and as intended by the aristocracy, Jews stimulated the
national economy and were subjected to heavy taxation, which went to the
nobles and the kings. This, of course, was one of the reasons for their
protection.

While it cannot be denied that Jews played an important part in the growth of Poland's economy, the evidence suggests that this point has been overemphasized, as it has been in discussions of the economic role of Jews in Europe generally. Consider, for example, the incipient stage of Polish Jewry's economic significance:

> The importance of Jewish immigration for the economic development of Poland was first realized by the feudal Polish princes of the thirteenth century. Prompted by the desire to cultivate industrial activities in their domains, these princes gladly welcomed settlers from Germany, without making a distinction between Jews and Germans.[124]

This seems a bit contradictory. There was another group that filled the "role" that, it is alleged, was reserved for Jews, and that group was Christian Germans. A multitude of Polish princes, Boleslav the Shy (1247-79) in particular, were successful in drawing Christian German immigrants to Poland. Moreover, they did so by granting them favors that some imply were reserved for Jews; that is, they gave Christian Germans numerous privileges as well as the right of self-government, the so-called "Magdeburg Law," or *ius teutonicum.*

The Germans, then, were competitors of the Jews. Further, judging from the agitation against Jews by these competitors, it is clear the Germans were numerous and powerful.[125] And in Poland as everywhere else in Europe, most Jews were poor and not at all the shrewd financial wizards of legend.

It is necessary, then, to consider the possibility of other motives for admitting and protecting Jews in Poland. One example, perhaps far-fetched though not impossible, is the rumor that Casimir had a love affair with a Jewish woman named Estherka (they supposedly had four children together). This is why, according to one scholar at least, Casimir was philo-Semitic.[126] It is, of course, impossible to know his motives and difficult to know whether or not the "affair" actually took place. Nonetheless, this particularly human suggestion of the basis of Casimir's philo-Semitism illustrates the likelihood that additional motives are necessary to explain the generally good (until 1648) situation of Polish Jewry.

A second and perhaps more substantial reason for the protection and acceptance of Jews in Poland by the kings is suggested of Casimir IV (1447-92). Casimir IV was a humanist and was influenced by the then-popular humanistic ideology; it is possible that this, not economics, was the basis of his acceptance of Jews.[127] Indeed, despite continuing pressure from anti-Semites—who eventually won out—Casimir IV consistently manifested a willingness to protect Jews.

It should also be considered that, as in western Europe, the kings of Poland enjoyed the services of Jewish physicians. These physicians included foreign as well as native Polish Jews and undoubtedly had influence with their royal patients. Other explanations of a beneficent attitude on the part of the nobility toward Jews, such as an appreciation of their cultural contributions, also attenuate, without discrediting, the importance of economic considerations. It is probable that all these factors contributed to the acceptance and protection of Jews in Poland.

From the time of Boleslav the Pius until 1648, Polish Jewry was relatively secure and prosperous. Boleslav wanted Jews and Gentiles to live together in peace and both Jews and non-Jews to be free to follow their consciences. The efforts of the kings and the nobility to secure the continuance of the harmony that Boleslav initiated goes a long way to explain why, initially at least, Jews and Christians lived together in peace, indeed on friendly terms. Finally, one cannot ignore the suggestion of Baron, which is not unlike that offered by Dubnov in his discussion of Jews within the Turkish Empire. One reason, according to Baron, that Jewry fared well in Poland was the "ethnically heterogeneous" population that existed there. This mixture of people prevented the "unruly popular massacres" or "formal decrees of expulsions." Other scholars concur.[128]

All of the factors cited above, including the philo-Semitism of specific rulers, certainly contributed to the security and prosperity of Polish Jewry. Moreover, the generosity offered Jews in the east came at a time when anti-Jewish actions in the west were especially virulent. Poland offered stability and security; to many Jews it was a haven. The situation in the east grew increasingly worse for Jews after 1648, but when it did, the west began to open its doors.

## NOTES

1. Parkes (1962), p. 64.

2. Glock and Stark (1966), p. 31.

3. Parkes (1962), p. 79. He also notes that "even where Jews were owned by secular princes the Church had the last word." See also Marcus (1965), p. 137.

4. See Roth (1970), p. 185; and Baron (1965a), pp. 6-7. There may be some dispute here, however. See Gregorovius (1966), p. 118.

5. Katz (1962), p. 4.

6. Baron (1972), p. 262.

7. Baron (1972), pp. 265-66, 284-307.

8. Quoted in Grayzel (1966), p. 10.

9. See the *Encyclopedia Judaica*, vol. 13, p. 852, for some of Gregory's negative remarks about Jews. Also see Parkes (1962), pp. 67-68.

10. Parkes (1962), p. 63.

11. Quoted in Grayzel (1966), p. 93.

12. These are documented in Gregorovius (1966), pp. 115-19, as well as in other sources.

13. Baron (1972), p. 265.

14. Thus, while Katz (1973, p. 113) argues that the Church's movement from tolerance to intolerance began in 1240, other scholars, such as Roth (1970, p. 241) and Flannery (1965, p. 101), say that the popes of the Middle Ages were the Jews' best friends.

15. Prinz (1968), p. 195.

16. *Encyclopedia Judaica*, vol. 13, p. 856.

17. *Encyclopedia Judaica*, vol. 13, p. 856. Also see Roth (1970), p. 241.

18. These are documented in the *Encyclopedia Judaica*, vol. 13, pp. 852-56, among other sources.

19. Quoted in Schweitzer (1971), p. 48, and Gregorovius (1966), p. 53. Saint Jerome derived this from the Pauline doctrine.

20. Quoted in Grayzel (1966), p. 261.

21. See Grayzel (1966), p. 12.

22. The key chapters here are Romans 9-11.

23. The nineteenth Ecumenical Council of the Roman Catholic Church (at Trent, 1545-47; 1551-52; 1562-63) cited Paul to explain why Jews should be forgiven: "according to the testimony of the same Apostle [Paul], if they had known it, they would never have crucified the Lord of Glory (1 Corinthians 2:8)." Quoted in Bishop (1974), p. 59.

24. The "saved remnant" is often cited in Christian documents as proof of Jews' worth. In light of this, Bishop Arthur Elchinger of Strasbourg asks an important, and as yet generally unanswered, question: "Don't Jews have the right to exist, not as future Christians, but as Jews?" Quoted in Bishop (1974), p. 31.

25. Schoeps (1961), p. 48.

26. On interpretations of Saint Paul's writings see Schoeps (1961); Brandon (1967); and Davies (1969). Davies does not seem to be very impressed with Saint Paul's philo-Semitism. Judaism, he insists, must be viewed on its own terms, not on Christian terms.

27. Grayzel (1966), p. 11.

28. For a discussion of compulsory sermons see Baron (1965a), vol. 9, pp. 71-75.

29. The papacy frowned on forced conversions because of a desire for only true, that is, uncoerced, Christians.

30. Among others, Innocent IV, Gregory X, and Clement XIII spoke out against the ritual murder charge, and Benedict XII repudiated the charge of the desecration of the Host. See Marcus (1965), p. 151; Margolis and Marx (1969), pp. 382, 404; Hertzberg (1968), p. 34.

31. Apparently the last accusation of ritual murder occurred in Kiev in 1911, when Mendel Beilis was charged with murdering a Christian child. He was eventually released. There are, however, cults based on the blood libel existing today, such as those of Dominguito del Val in Spain, Lorenzo Sossio in Italy, and Andreas Oxner in Austria. The Church has tried to suppress these, but it has been only moderately successful. There was also talk of ritual murders in the United States: in Massena, New York, in 1928 and in Birmingham, Alabama, as late as 1962. See Bishop (1974, pp. 105-6). She also points to the "remarkable ... fact ... that ... the ritual murder accusation was never directed against anyone but the Jews" (ibid., p. 107).

32. Roth (1970), p. 185.

33. Grayzel (1966), p. 81.

34. In fact, the Church itself did not automatically come into being when Christianity did. From 700 to 1122 Christendom was not generally controlled by the papacy, canon lawyers, or theologians from the universities, but dominated by monastic popes.

35. Heer (1962), pp. 20-24, 61-62.

36. The term "perfidious Jew," for example, was not originally pejorative: *perfidia* means unbelieving. The reinterpretation of that term by the lower clergy into a slander led Pope John XXIII (1958-63) to order it omitted from the Good Friday prayer.

37. Katz (1962), p. 48.

38. Baron (1972), pp. 307, 320. Baron notes (ibid., p. 320) that both Jews and rulers understood the true meaning of "Jewish serfdom."

39. The more powerful the ruler was, the better. Roth (1970, p. 213) writes: "So long as the central authority retained any strength, the Jews enjoyed a certain degree of protection."

40. See Poliakov (1965), p. 110; Margolis and Marx (1969), pp. 404, 406; and Marcus (1965), p. 165.

41. Quoted in Marcus (1965), p. 28. See also Margolis and Marx (1969), pp. 377-78, and Poliakov (1965), p. 61.

42. See Margolis and Marx (1969), pp. 377-78. The charter itself fell victim to the Hussite Wars (1419-36), which brought a return of religious intolerance. See the *Cambridge Medieval History*, vol. 7, p. 658.

43. The Two Sword theory divided society into two value classes, the spiritual, controlled by the Church, and the temporal, controlled by the secular powers. Pope Gelasius I (492-96) affirmed this, and the theory became an accepted tradition of the early Middle Ages, although it was ignored on more than one occasion.

44. The question of the source of the kings' authority revolved around the papacy's demand for obeisance from the secular rulers because the popes represented God on earth and, consequently, stood higher in the worldly hierarchy. The monarchs claimed that their authority came directly from God, thereby diminishing papal authority and increasing their own. For example, Henry IV, the German king, wrote to Pope Gregory VII on January 24, 1076, that he was "Henry, King ... by the holy ordination of ... God" and Frederick I (Barbarossa) told Pope Adrian IV: "The kingdom ... is ours ... from God alone." Henry II of England, Philip IV (the Fair) of France, Charles of Bohemia, and numerous other secular rulers defied papal authority and claimed that their positions came directly from God.

The lay investiture struggle concerned the right of kings and nobles to select and appoint abbots, bishops, and priests in their domains. This, too, would increase their power at the expense of that of the papacy. Although Pope Gregory VI issued a decree prohibiting lay persons from conferring ecclesiastical offices as early as 1075, the practice did not cease.

45. See Cecil Roth, "The European Age in Jewish History," in Finkelstein (1974), p. 228, and Schweitzer (1971), p. 165. Margolis and Marx (1969, p. 407) argue that soon after the massacres of the Black Death, during which Jews were "forever banished" from numerous cities, "princes and magistrates thought better of it and rescinded the drastic measures [of banishment]—not because the Jews were loved, but because taxes were high and credit conditions disorganized."

46. See, for example, Weber (1958b), p. 66, on "pariah capitalism." Weber argues that this term applies to western Jewry from later antiquity to the present. Also see Ettinger (1961), pp. 211-15, and Sombart (1951), passim.

47. H. M. Sachar (1958), p. 28. He writes (ibid., p. 28) that "hundreds of thousands of Jews have been tolerated" in Europe because "they did manage to accumulate liquid wealth; and the rulers who needed money for mercenary armies were willing to protect their Jews if only to tax that liquid wealth away." Also see Katz (1973), pp. 18-19, and Hertzberg (1968), pp. 65, 67.

Perhaps the most prevalent form of this "economic hypothesis" is found in the various "middleman" theories. See, for example, Blalock (1967), passim, and Bonacich (1973), passim. These, generally and in brief, trichotomize society into kings and nobles, peasants, and Jews as the economic connection between the first two groups. It was supposedly on the basis of their being "middlemen" that Jews were welcomed into Poland and that Cromwell worked to secure their readmission into England. But ethnic relations in general and Jewish-Christian relations in particular must be examined through more than economic prisms. Polanyi (1957, p. 46) states this succinctly and cogently:

The outstanding discovery of recent historical and anthropological research is that man's economy, as a rule, is submerged in his social relationships. He does not act so as to safeguard his individual interest in the possession of material goods; he acts so as to safeguard his social standing, his social claims, his social assets. He values material goods only in so far as they serve this end.

More than this, however, many of the assumptions that underlie middleman theories are open to question when applied to Jews. For example, Bonacich argues (1973, passim) that middleman minorities want to return home. Jews did not; on the contrary, Jews fought to remain in their "adopted" homelands. Bonacich also argues that middleman minorities are reluctant to become citizens of their "adopted" homelands. Jews struggled for and were elated by their citizenship. She also suggests that middleman minorities resist pressures to have them join unions. Jews were barred from membership in guilds and did join the only nonrestricted organization open to them, the Freemasons. Although this does not dispute Bonacich's theory—nor is it intended to— it does point out that the theory's application to Jewish middlemen is dubious.

It might also be noted that while the connection between Jews and money is often stated as a basic cause of anti-Semitism, Arendt (1958, p. 28) suggests that modern anti-Semitism is based on politics, not economics, in the west and on complex class situations in the east.

48. Graetz (1894), vol. 4, p. 128. A. L. Sachar (1965, pp. 256-57) notes not only the "money-lending by Jews," which occurred by a "queer twist of fate," but that most Jews lived at a subsistence level. He also points out that those who benefited from the moneylending of Jews were not the Jews but the kings and nobles.

49. Perhaps the most striking example of Jewish autonomy, and certainly the most important, was the Council of the Four Lands in Poland. Based on the four provinces

of Poland, the council was the most significant body of Jews that had ever been established in terms of judicial, legislative, and executive power. Lithuanian Jews, while not officially a part of the Four Lands, occasionally participated in the activities of the council and regularly coordinated their own with those of the Polish body. The apex of the Four Lands, the sixteenth and seventeenth centuries, coincided with the zenith of Polish Jewry. See Margolis and Marx (1969), pp. 538-42; D. Stanley Etzin, "Two Minorities: The Jews of Poland and the Chinese of the Philippines," in Yetman and Steele (1971); Dubnov (1916), vol. 2; Israel Halpern, "The Jews in Eastern Europe," in Finkelstein (1974); Roth, "The European Age in Jewish History," in Finkelstein (1974).

50. See, for example, Prinz (1968), p. 33, and Margolis and Marx (1969), pp. 357-60. Numerous other scholars discuss the same event and cite economics as the cause for the invitation.

51. Quoted in Snyder (1958), p. 35. It is rarely considered that Christian business-men were also asked into towns and given benefits—usually greater benefits than those given to Jewish businessmen. Moreover, the Christian businessmen suffered the same social discrimination as the Jewish businessmen. Miriam Beard, in "The Mirage of the Economic Jew" (in Graeber and Britt, 1942, p. 387) notes that Hugue-nots exercised the same function as Jews and in the same places as Jews. Berlin, for example, had a large number of Huguenots, and Berlin was by no means the only city to enjoy their services.

This, again, is not to deny the existence or efficacy of economic philo-Semitism. But one cannot take the position either that Jews and Jews alone enjoyed benefits because of their economic activity, or that they were accepted solely because of it. If others could have taken their "role," it is unlikely that their financial abilities were the only reason for their being tolerated—and others did take that role. Beard points out (ibid., p. 391) that "before the modern era of intense nationalism, there were far more 'strangers' in high places of government and industry everywhere. . . . Jews never suffered alone under popular wrath."

52. See Dubnov (1969), vol. 3, p. 55. For example, a French poet was unhappy about the expulsion of the Jews from France. The reason, as he wrote in 1306, was that "Jews were genial of heart in matters of trade—far more than Christians today." Quoted in Bishop (1974), p. 53.

53. This is not to suggest, however, that expulsions did not ever—or even often—follow. Indeed, one reason for the expulsions of Jews was usurpation of their wealth, however slight that might have been.

54. It has been suggested, for example, that the invitation to enter France that Charlemagne extended to Jews was based on economic considerations alone. It is not impossible, however, that other interests "led him to welcome Jewish immigration." Schweitzer (1971, pp. 81-82) notes, for example, that Charlemagne was interested in Biblical studies and recognized the value to those studies of Jewish translators and scholars. To judge the motives of medieval rulers from the perspective of the twen-tieth century is to do damage to both the events and the protagonists.

55. For an understanding of the sociological aspects of science see, for example, Joseph Ben-David, The Scientist's Role in Society (Englewood Cliffs, N.J.: Prentice-Hall, 1971).

56. Joseph W. Cohen, in "The Role of Jews in Western Culture" (in Graeber and Britt, 1942, p. 334) argues that "the sciences of medicine, optics, mathematics, astronomy, and geography were brought to life by . . . Jews and Arabs." Heer agrees, pointing out (1962, p. 309) that "there can be no denying the unifying and unique contribution made by Jewish learning and piety to the intellectual and religious culture of earlier medieval Europe." Quite naturally, there was social interaction between Jews and Christians based on this.

57. See Charles Singer, "Science and Judaism," in Finkelstein (1960), p. 1402; and Poliakov (1965), pp. 149-53.

58. See Margolis and Marx (1969), pp. 419, 424, 437, 453, 460, 483, 487, 513, 516, and 562. Also see Poliakov (1965), p. 150; Schweitzer (1971), p. 104; and Hertzberg (1968), p. 12. Graetz comments, in referring to the prohibitions against using Jewish physicians (1894, vol. 4, p. 275):

> The practice of medicine was still entirely in the hands of Jews, and opened to them the cabinets and the hearts of kings and nobles. It was in vain that papal bulls proclaimed that Christians should not employ Jewish physicians. There were few or no Christians who understood the healing art, and the sick had no recourse save the skill of the Jews. Even the higher clergy had but little regard for the [prohibitive papal] bulls. They had too much care for the health of the flesh to refuse the medical aid of the Jews on account of a canonical decree.

This should not be taken to imply that there were no Christian physicians; there were. Graetz (1894, vol. 4, p. 131) notes that in the 1360s Christian physicians complained about the number of their Jewish counterparts' patients.

One reason for the success of Jewish physicians in the Middle Ages is noted by Roth (1959b, p. ix): They were "wrongly" imagined to have "access to stores of recondite information not available to other men." Thus Roth (ibid., p. 214) argues that "when a ruler or prelate took a Jewish physician into his service, it was not simply out of belief in his competence, but because he was thought to have at his command vast stores of secret medical doctrine which was unknown to or even kept from Christians." Yet the Jewish physicians must have been effective, or else they would not have been constantly used, "secret medical doctrine" notwithstanding.

59. Arturo Castiglione, "The Contributions of the Jews to Medicine," in Finkelstein (1960), vol. 2, p. 1363. Roth (1959b, pp. 214-15) states that "from the thirteenth century at least, pontiff after pontiff had a Jew in his employ as his personal medical attendant, and almost every ruler in Italy followed this example."

It might be noted that Jews also served as military physicians in Italy. They performed a similar role in several other countries as well.

60. Baron (1972), p. 245; see also ibid., p. 250.

61. Quoted in Grayzel (1966), p. 259.

62. See Baron (1965a), vol. 4, p. 38, and the *Encyclopedia Judaica*, vol. 7, p. 14.

63. Katz (1962), p. 38. See also Agus (1969), p. 348, and Prinz (1968), p. 33.

64. Baron (1965a), vol. 4, p. 100.

65. Poliakov (1965), p. 45.

66. Baron (1972), p. 264. See also ibid., pp. 246-53.

67. Heer (1962), p. 150. See also Agus (1969), p. 341.

68. Heer (1962), p. 150.

69. Arendt (1958), p. 7.

70. Sartre (1962), p. 91.

71. A. L. Sachar (1965), p. 192. See also Poliakov (1965), pp. 15, 100, 105.

72. Graetz (1894), vol. 3, p. 298. Dimont, with justification, terms the crusades "ecclesiastical imperialism" and argues (1973, p. 272) that "although they suffered grievously, the devastation which befell the Jews does not compare in total horror to what befell Christians." He suggests (ibid., p. 273), for instance, that over two hundred thousand crusaders were killed in Hungary.

73. See Baron (1965a), vol. 4, p. 90; Graetz (1894), vol. 3, p. 299; and Parkes (1962), p. 75. Parkes notes that the burghers were not successful in protecting Jews. Usually "the mob prevailed."

74. Baron (1965a), vol. 4, pp. 198-99; Margolis and Marx (1969), pp. 360, 368.

75. Baron (1965a), vol. 4, p. 100.

76. Poliakov (1965), p. 45, states that "a final massacre occurred in Prague despite the efforts of Bishop Cosmas."

77. Graetz (1894), vol. 3, p. 356.

78. Baron (1965a), vol. 4, p. 119.

79. Baron (1965a), vol. 4, p. 129.

80. Baron (1965a), vol. 4, p. 128.

81. Baron (1965a), vol. 4, p. 127.

82. Baron (1965a), vol. 4, pp. 119-26.

83. Baron (1965a), vol. 4, p. 131.

84. Encyclopedia Judaica, vol. 5, p. 1143.

85. Encyclopedia Judaica, vol. 5, p. 1143.

86. Graetz (1894), vol. 4, p. 106.

87. Margolis and Marx (1969), p. 405.

88. Margolis and Marx (1969), p. 406.

89. Schweitzer comments (1971, p. 90) that Jews "suffered noticeably less from it owing to the specification in their law of an elaborate code of cleanliness and hygiene." See also Roth (1970), p. 214, and Margolis and Marx (1969), p. 404. Graetz (1894, vol. 4, p. 103) suggests that Clement VI was effective in helping the Jews in Southern France.

90. Roth, "The European Age in Jewish History," in Finkelstein (1974), p. 242.

91. A. L. Sachar (1965), p. 203.

92. Roth (1970), p. 227.

93. Roth, "The European Age in Jewish History," in Finkelstein (1974), p. 253. Roth 1970), p. 256. Emphasis added. See also Ben-Zvi (1961), p. 339.

94. Curiously enough, the Jews of Spain had once sought refuge within Christendom. In 1110, when the Almoravides tried to convert Jews to Islam, the Jews fled to the Christian kingdoms to the north "where they were welcomed and accepted" (Schweitzer, 1971, p. 63). It was, as Roth notes (1970, p. 164), "fortunate that the Christian kingdoms had by now [1172] begun to make headway in the north, providing a haven of refuge in which Jewish life could take root and flourish again."

95. Quoted in Graetz (1894), vol. 4, p. 271.
96. Especially important here were the Sultans Bajazet, Selim I, and Solyman I.
97. A. L. Sachar (1965), p. 221.
98. Graetz (1894), vol. 4, pp. 400-401.
99. Gibb and Bowen (1957), vol. 1, p. 219.
100. Quoted in A. L. Sachar (1965), p. 221.
101. Gibb and Bowen (1957), vol. 1, p. 217. Roth (1959b, p. 213) notes that in the pre-Renaissance Moslem world "Jewish physicians were highly esteemed for their ability."
102. Gibb and Bowen (1957), vol. 1, p. 218.
103. Goiten (1974), p. 86.
104. Gibb and Bowen (1957), vol. 1, p. 218.
105. Hitti (1947), p. 138.
106. Dubnov (1969), vol. 1, pp. 638-39. He is speaking here of the late 1890s, but the situation he describes was apparently not limited to that period.
107. See Baron (1965a), vol. 10, pp. 31-36; A. L. Sachar (1965) pp. 224-27; and Dubnov (1916), vol. 1, pp. 40-42.
108. Schweitzer (1971), p. 147.
109. Baron (1965a), vol. 10, p. 44.
110. Graetz (1894), vol. 4, p. 111. Some ten thousand Jews were killed throughout Poland.
111. Baron (1965a), vol. 10, pp. 41-43.
112. Baron (1965a), vol. 10, p. 39.
113. Baron (1965a), vol. 10, p. 39. Margolis and Marx (1969, p. 531), however, have a much less favorable interpretation of the event. They view Alexander as anti-Semitic.
114. It might be noted that Poles were killed, too.
115. Baron (1965a), vol. 10, p. 33.
116. Baron (1965a), vol. 10, pp. 34-35. See also Rivkin (1971), p. 135.
117. One of the most forceful and effective preachers was the Franciscan monk, John Capistrano, who was responsible for a multitude of Jewish deaths and forced baptisms. See Margolis and Marx (1969), pp. 414-15, 430, and A. L. Sachar (1965), pp. 202-3.
118. Graetz (1894), vol. 4, p. 642.
119. Dubnov (1916), vol. 1, p. 50. See also ibid., p. 45.
120. Parkes (1962), p. 150.
121. Baron (1965a), vol. 10, pp. 44-45.
122. Dubnov (1916), vol. 1, p. 71.
123. See, for example, Graetz (1894), vol. 4, p. 263. Poliakov (1965, p. 225) calls the nobles the Jews' "natural protectors." In 1519 Sigismund I stated that because he did not derive benefits from Jews whereas the nobles did, the nobles must try the Jews' cases. Because Jews gave the king no advantage, Sigismund felt that he was "not obliged to secure justice for them" (Dubnov, 1916, vol. 1, p. 84).
124. Dubnov (1916), vol. 1, p. 43.
125. See Baron (1965a), vol. 10, p. 37, for an example of their effectiveness. It should be considered, however, that the Poles were fearful of becoming too dependent upon Germany. Jews could not draw upon the political and military support of a state and therefore would be more loyal to Poland.

126. Dubnov (1916), vol. 1, pp. 43-44.

127. Dubnov (1916), vol. 1, p. 61.

128. Baron (1965a), vol. 10, p. 43. It should be noted that this interpretation is in opposition to that of this author. See also Graetz (1894), vol. 4, p. 112. Graetz, too, disagrees with this author's interpretation.

# JEWISH EMANCIPATION I

5

## THE ISSUE OF JEWISH EMANCIPATION

### The Return to the West

At the beginning of the seventeenth century there were comparatively few Jews in the central European states and, officially, no practicing Jews in western Europe. Expulsions and massacres had forced the overwhelming majority of European Jews to seek sanctuary in the Turkish Empire and, to a greater degree, in Poland. In time, however, the Turkish Empire crumbled, and by 1574 the golden age of Turkish Jewry had ended.

There was no radical change in the situation of Jews in Turkey; for example, there were no massacres, expulsions, or charges of sacrilege; there was, however, a shift in the status of Jews. The distinction between Jew and "true believer" (Moslem) became increasingly apparent through laws and restrictions.[1] There was also sporadic persecution of Jews by various Pashas. By the beginning of the seventeenth century, then, one of the two havens no longer offered Jews the sanctuary it once had.

The second haven, the vast Polish Empire, was still a land of relative beneficence and would remain so for another fifty years. In 1648, however, and for ten years thereafter, a continuous series of massacres occurred that would, in terms of lives lost and human misery, exceed the earlier devastation of the Black Death massacres. The cause of these seventeenth-century massacres were the Chmielnicki attacks.

Chmielnicki and his followers were Cossacks, Greek-Orthodox peasants. Their quarrel, at least ostensibly, was not with Jews but with the Catholic Polish nobility, who they regarded as both heretics and economic and political oppressors. Jews, to some degree, were simply caught in between the two warring groups. Yet the Jews were not merely innocent bystanders. They had done well in Poland for several hundred years and, therefore, were loyal to the kingdom. Moreover, Jews were frequently employed as financial agents and tax collectors for the Polish nobility. Chmielnicki and his followers could reason that by attacking Jews, they were attacking allies of the Polish nobility. For these reasons, in addition to the anti-Semitism which was prevalent among the Cossacks, Chmielnicki and his followers made no distinction between Polish Catholic and Jew (except that Jews who converted to the Greek-Orthodox religion were not harmed). In fact, Chmielnicki and his followers attacked Jews with greater ferocity than they attacked Poles. The Jews were unorganized, less numerous, without an army, and extremely vulnerable.

Within the period 1648-58, well over one hundred thousand Jews in Poland were killed. As a result of these massacres, the movement of Jews and the areas of sanctuary shifted toward the west.

It has already been noted that there were groups of Jews who remained in central Europe even after the Black Death massacres. Generally for economic reasons, Jews were readmitted to various cities within a few years after the Black Death by German citizens and magistrates, who conveniently forgot their vow that for one hundred years or more no Jew would be admitted within their walls. Similar invitations to take up residence were extended by Nice, through the Duke of Savoy; by Reggio, through the Duke of Modena; and by Naples and Ferrara, as well as by other small nation-states. In 1622 Christian IV of Denmark asked a small number of Jewish families to settle in various Danish cities, promising them numerous privileges for doing so.

These small city-states and nation-states could not themselves offer sanctuary to the large numbers of Jews migrating west. This movement of Jews to the west coincided with new policies of readmission and acceptance into western Europe generally and into England and France in particular. Further, France and England would set the tone of European history for the next three hundred years. They would be instrumental in the struggle for emancipation of Jewry throughout Europe.

### The Stages of Emancipation

The full emancipation of European Jewry was a long, difficult struggle that entailed reform not only of the perspectives of Christians and Jews but of European social and political ideology as well. The term "Jewish emancipation" itself is understood to mean "the legislative equalization of Jewish rights."[2] This meant that the usual meaning of justice, equal application of the law, would henceforth include Jews, a radical, tradition shattering concept. It also meant that Jews would be "of" as well as "in" society, with all the attendant obligations and privileges that membership entailed.

The ideology of reform for Jews began in Germany, but the pragmatic basis of that reform originated in France. The Enlightenment and liberalism were manifest in France both earlier and in greater depth than anywhere else in Europe.[3] It is no surprise, then, that it was in France that Jewish emancipation first occurred (in 1791). The immediate social catalyst was the Revolution, which facilitated the change from subject to citizen. However, in France and throughout Europe the idea of Jewish emancipation had been in the air for several decades.

Jacob Katz argues that Jewish emancipation occurred "more or less simultaneously" in western Europe, that is, in France, Germany, Austria, Hungary, Holland, and England.[4] This is true only if emancipation is viewed within a very broad perspective. Adopting an equally broad overview, Simon Dubnov notes that "'emancipation' [became] a political fact only after the emergence of a new order—government based on human rights instead of the class system and police repression. In Europe, this occurred in 1789 in France and 1848 in other western countries; in Russia it began only in the 20th century." He adds that in England Jewish emancipation was a result of "evolution," which was unlike the situation in other western countries.[5] With the exception of the statement concerning England, neither position is absolutely correct. France and Holland emancipated their Jews almost at the same time, although the Dutch had a strong stimulus from France's conquest of Holland. It is true, however, that the Dutch had been seriously discussing Jewish emancipation prior to their being conquered and that after the withdrawal of French troops they did not rescind the emancipation edict. Fifty years after the emancipation of French and Dutch Jewry, similar emancipation was still being debated in most European countries, including Austria, Hungary, and Germany.

A more reasonable analysis is offered by Dubnov when he divides Jewish emancipation into two stages and two negative reactions, spanning the years between 1789 and 1914. The first emancipation (1789-1815) took place in France, Holland, and parts of Germany, Italy, and Russia. The first reaction (1815-48) negated all gains except those in France and Holland. The second phase (1848-80) completed western European Jewish emancipation, although it aroused the second reaction (1881-1914), which entailed increasing anti-Semitism.[6]

Only a very small number of Jews benefited from the emancipation decrees issued between 1789 and 1874 (that is, from the French Revolution until the beginning of the massive migrations from the east in the late nineteenth century) because comparatively few Jews lived in the west at that time. It could be inferred that the small number of Jews in the west (nowhere were they more than 2 percent of the population[7]) facilitated emancipation in that Jews constituted such a negligible threat to the majority. This follows a more or less standardized sociological perspective, but the argument is flawed. Europe was still conceived of as a Christian society by the vast majority, and this worked against Jewish emancipation. Further, the idea that the smallness of the group facilitates its emancipation is premised upon the assumption of the relative invisibility of the group. This was not the case with

European Jews, who were distinctive in matters of dress, language, and customs—differences that raised, to many, the question of their ability to be assimilated into the larger society. Moreover, individual Jews in prominent positions were often brought to the attention of the public by anti-Semites for the specific purpose of retarding emancipation (they would point to the "takeover" of the nation by Jews). Thus their limited numbers did not further emancipation. Quite the contrary, their very modest numbers made it necessary for the Jews to receive consistent and considerable assistance in securing their emancipation.

## Christians and Jewish Emancipation

Because this book is not concerned with Jewish history as such, but with a specific interpretation of that history, it will not examine Jewish emancipation in every European country. Instead, indications of the struggle in various countries will be noted and the situations in France and England will be examined in detail in the following chapters. The intent here is to demonstrate that throughout Europe Jewish emancipation was, in the main, the direct result of the efforts of Christians rather than of Jews. This was not because of a lack of concern or involvement on the part of Jews, but because they simply did not have the power to effect the changes necessary for their emancipation.

This, however, does not seem to be recognized by a good many students of Jewish history. Abraham Leon Sachar, for example, notes that "by the third quarter of the nineteenth century Jewish political equality had been won in nearly every western European country." He argues further that this emancipation was brought about by numerous influential Jews and that during the second phase of their emancipation, after 1815, "the Jews themselves labored for their freedom."[8] This implies a substantial degree of efficacy on the part of Jews in securing their own emancipation.

Almost every historian of European Jewry agrees with this position. Each considers the significance and influence of specific Jews who contributed to the emancipation of their coreligionists. But while one must acknowledge the emancipation efforts of such Jews as Moses Mendelssohn, Gabriel Riesser, Isaac Cerf-Berr, and a multitude of others, it should be realized that only Christians could emancipate Jews and that the decisions of these Christians regarding emancipation would be most effectively influenced by other Christians. Until they were emancipated, Jews individually or as a group had no official power to effect any change. Jews were tentative members of society until political equality was attained; until that was achieved, the possibility of expulsion was as real in the nineteenth century as it had been in the Middle Ages.

Even influential Jews could accomplish very little without the help of an astonishing number of Christians. In fact, such Jews were considered influential precisely because of their success in influencing key Christians to support

Jewish emancipation. The efforts of those Christians were highlighted by the presence of intense countervailing pressures, in particular the anti-Semitism that was so virulent during the nineteenth century. Jews struggling for emancipation not only welcomed Christian assistance, but could not have achieved their goals without it. In western Europe, Jews were increasingly accepted due to efforts of various Gentiles, and full emancipation there was a real possibility. The Jews of the time knew this. That is why Zionism rose not in the west, where support was manifest, but in the east, where Jews had no support for and thus no hope of emancipation.[9]

### Social Factors

In addition to arguing that Jewish emancipation was brought about in a large degree by the efforts of Jews, scholars turn to certain social changes to explain that emancipation. For example, Howard Morley Sachar argues that Jewish emancipation was a consequence of both the rationalistic ideology and the spirit of fraternalism that permeated the Continent during and immediately following the Age of Enlightenment and the French Revolution.[10]. Other scholars agree.

> The origins of Emancipation . . . are to be found in the secular and mercantilistic conception of the state and society as well as in the ideology of the enlightenment, while the actual instrument for cutting through the Gordian knot of ancient prejudice and antipathy was the French Revolution of 1789.[11]

To Joseph W. Cohen the combination of economics and politics, manifested in and by liberal democracy, provided the basis of Jewish emancipation.[12] Ellis Rivkin takes a more forceful stand, arguing that "capitalism and capitalism alone emancipated the Jews."[13] However, he also suggests that capitalism had other effects in the world, specifically a reinterpretation of the concept of freedom: "The emancipation of the Jews was an inevitable result, then, not only of the development of capitalism, but of the new order of freedom that capitalism generated and sustained."[14] Finally, Jacob Katz argues that the Jews were not granted citizenship because of an "appreciation of [their] quality," but because of a "general principle" including them in "the category of man." That principle suggested that the Jews would eventually acquire the "necessary attributes of the enlightened man and citizen.[15]"

While correct in tone, each of these is too broad in scope. The length and intensity of the struggle for Jewish emancipation suggest that initially only a limited number of people regarded as viable the inclusion of Jews in European society. These difficulties also make it unlikely that a change in the economic structure could in itself have provided the impetus for Jewish emancipation. It was crucial that philo-Semites argued that the Jews belonged in the "category of man" and would acquire the "necessary attributes of enlightened man and citizen." At the same time, others argued that the Jews could not and would not become enlightened citizens. And changes occurring in the marketplace did not alter the opinions of either group.

James Parkes, then, is partially right when he says that Jewish emancipation came about because of "a change in temper among the intellectuals" and because of "a vague belief in the rights of man." Yet one must view with skepticism his claim that the efforts of politicians, Christian religious leaders, Christian charity, or philo-Semitism had little to do with that emancipation.[16] It is true that there were positive changing social conditions vis-à-vis Jews and that these facilitated emancipation,[17] but anti-Semitism, which would increase in intensity during the nineteenth century, proved to be a powerful obstacle to Jewish emancipation in many countries. Thus, while a "change in temper" did occur, it was both positive and negative, both philo-Semitic and anti-Semitic. This change, incidentally, did not occur among the intellectuals alone, but among a large portion of the people, especially the political leaders. Nor should it be forgotten that while many intellectuals supported Jewish emancipation, not all did so by any means.

It is also true that a "vague belief in the rights of man" helped Jews, although to many people there were questions about the definition of the term "man." In most countries "man" was equated with "countryman," or Christian. Coupled with this was the potent concept of the nation itself, which raised the question of whether Jews belonged to the state or were a separate entity, a nation apart living within the host country's borders.

It is probable that the most important factor in bringing about Jewish emancipation was a change in the attitudes of both Jews and Christians. A majority of the former were willing to give up their autonomous status and did so with alacrity; many of the latter were willing to accept this as evidence of Jews' willingness to become members of the state. To a large degree, philo-Semites were the catalysts for these changing attitudes.

This, however, was a gradual process. It is optimistic to argue that emancipation "not only explicitly abolished the legal discriminations and disqualifications of the Jew but actually implied an invitation to him to participate in political, artistic, intellectual, economic and social life of the respective peoples as an equal."[18] This participation, where it did occur, was hard won.

One clear indication of this is the scope of the change that was needed. Katz notes that it was not merely a political change that was required; more importantly, and prior to political change, a psychological change was necessary.[19] The idea that Jews could be accepted in society had to precede their actual acceptance. It was specifically philo-Semites who contributed to and argued for changing attitudes towards Jews.

Finally—again—the economic issue must be considered. Numerous scholars have noted the connection between the influence of a rising economy on western European society in general and on the status of Jews in particular. For example, Dubnov suggests that, in general, "the economic factor played a great role in the liberal and the reactionary movements,"[20] and A. L. Sachar, in speaking specifically of Jews, notes that "in a period of expanding capitalism inherited prejudices were not permitted to interfere with profits, and they were conveniently pushed into the background. Economic changes were therefore more crucial in winning political equality for Jews than all the glittering generalities about the rights of man and the sanctity of human personalities."[21]

This would seem to be a one-sided interpretation, however. If economics could be taken as a major cause of Jewish emancipation, it could also be taken as a major obstacle to that same emancipation. For example, in almost every instance when the issue of naturalization of English Jewry was considered, it was the merchants who opposed it—opposed it so vociferously that the issue either failed to reach the floor of the House of Commons for consideration or was defeated there. It was the merchants who, with the support of some conservatives, caused the approval of Jewish emancipation of 1753 to be rescinded in that same year. The issue was unwanted competition, not blatant anti-Semitism; the same merchants protested with equal fervor against all "aliens." Moreover, it was not the demands of finance, but the philo-Semites' support of the rights of man and the "sanctity of human personalities" that had facilitated the entry of Jews into broader areas of economic activity.

## The Difficulties

Without the tenacity, integrity, ability, and persuasiveness of philo-Semites, Jewish emancipation would have been much longer in arriving, "rights of man" and spirit of the Enlightenment notwithstanding.

This is not to deny the significance of the social changes occurring in Europe at that time or the fact that philo-Semites used the concept of the rights of man as well as political change to secure Jewish emancipation. These appeals to humanity, tolerance, and reason were the substance of their arguments. Nonetheless, the catalysts for Jewish emancipation were the philo-Semites, whose actions and attitudes were partially a result and partially a cause of all of these changes (that is, the Enlightenment, growing capitalism, and nationalism). Sociopolitical changes alone could not and would not have brought about the emancipation of western Jewry. Katz is incorrect in suggesting that the Jews' political fate was not contingent on Christians supporting their cause but on the "general way in which the modern state was developing."[22]

Not only the social integration/acceptance of Jews, but their political emancipation depended upon Christian support. This is true from two perspectives. First, social integration or acceptance implies political emancipation, especially within an increasingly modern, industrial state. One cannot be fully *in*, as opposed to *of*, society without being part of it politically as well as socially. Second, given the numerical paucity of Jews in western Europe, the support of Christians was not merely an additional contribution to their cause, but the sole political means of achieving the desired goal. That the modern state was developing in a way that *could* benefit Jews cannot be taken to mean that it was developing in a way that *would* benefit Jews. Were it not for the assistance of various philo-Semites in all countries of Europe, it is possible that the modern European states would have excluded European Jewry.

The objections to and activities opposing Jewish emancipation suggest that attributing emancipation to "the times," economics, or any other single factor is historically unwarranted.[23] The reasons for the rejection of the idea of Jewish emancipation, although many and varied, were all based on one of two different ideologies. The first viewed Europe as Christian, secularization notwithstanding; thus Jews were, and would remain, an alien people in a Christian society. The second ideology set Jews apart not only religiously, but racially. Supporters of this position regarded Jews as not only fundamentally unassimilable, but genetically different as well.[24] A common denominator underlies these ideologies: not only do Jews not belong *within* Christian society, they cannot be *of* Christian society. It was over this that the philo/anti-Semitic battle raged.

In a large measure Rashi's dictum, "once a Jew always a Jew," and Joachim Prinz's theory of "Jewish inescapability"[25] were supported by the situation in post-French Revolutionary Europe. It is equally true, however, that the situation of Jews in Europe had changed; that a shift in the perception of Jews had become increasingly manifest; that Jews were able to enter into the arts and sciences; and more important in terms of their social acceptability, that Jews were accepted into the military and into national politics. In a word, much of European Jewry was emancipated in the nineteenth century, both in theory and to a considerable degree in fact. This was the result of a multitude of forces, but a primary one was the involvement of those Christians who presented, supported, and fought for the idea of Jew as human being.

## SOCIETAL CHANGES

Toleration has a negative quality built into its meaning. To "tolerate" is to endure, to overlook the unpleasant aspects of what is tolerated. It is, as Allport notes, "merely a negative act of decency."[26] Nevertheless, toleration was hard won for European Jewry because toleration also has built into its meaning an acceptance, if an unhappy one, of others' differences and the recognition, however reluctantly given, of their right to be different. In Europe religious toleration first began to reach fruition in the seventeenth century, after a long history. A full two centuries earlier, during the Renaissance, the idea of a "natural religion" was becoming acceptable, as was an increasingly manifest willingness to accept individual differences. This was part of the growing intellectualism of the period, an intellectualism nurtured by the increasing number of writers, statesmen, and philosophers who endorsed these views. Works written earlier than the seventeenth century, then, contained indications of the coming era of toleration even though the major intellectual defense of religious tolerance in general and of Jews in particular was a seventeenth-century phenomenon. The political emancipation of European Jewry would have been impossible without this religious toleration.

But religious toleration depended upon two interrelated factors. The first was the dissolution of the concept of religious unity; the second was the separation of religion from everyday life. The forces that would bring these about were the Reformation, the growth of the nation-state, and the liberal/ democratic ideology of the Enlightenment.

## Toleration

As suggested, earlier indications notwithstanding, scholars tend to agree that the seventeenth century was the time when social and political issues took a decisive turn. Theological and traditionalistic universalisms gradually began to evolve into secular nationalism.[27] Beginning with the Edict of Nantes (1598), which granted French Protestants an enormous degree of religious freedom (by the standards of the time), there grew throughout Europe an increasing willingness to grant religious liberties to Christian minorities. A similar, though not so thorough or efficacious, tolerance of Jews by Christians was beginning to take hold. This in part explains the marked decrease of expulsions of Jews.

The beginning of religious toleration throughout Europe was based on pragmatic politics, not morality. The very concept was a part of the emerging idea of the *raison d'état*. If there were several religions within a given area and these religions battled, the state itself could not survive. This point was suggested by the territorial principle of the Peace of Augsburg (1555): *cujus regio ejus religio*, ("whose the region, his the religion"). This principle "assigned a religion to a political framework though based upon the principle of the rule of intolerance within the one state in which all must belong to the religion of its ruler, nonetheless recognized the fact that within another political unit another religion may be practiced."[28]

The initial phase of this toleration grew out of the growth of and disputes among Christian sects. In time, and after prolonged internecine religious warfare, people began to realize that no one side would be able to eradicate the others forcibly. In consequence there developed an increased understanding that religious toleration was a pragmatic, though not a theological, necessity. The main breaking point here was the Reformation, which led to the separation of church and state.

The significance of the Reformation is that the unity of Christianity was now obviously at an end (although in fact it had never actually existed[29]). The old notion of the one true faith had lost its meaning, undermined in part by the numerical strength of the Protestants, whose membership soon approached that of the Catholic Church. The significance for Jews of the shattering of monolithic Catholicism was that, paradoxically, in their isolation they were now no longer alone. Protestants now had Catholics and Jews living in their countries, while people in Catholic countries had to adjust to Protestants as well as Jews living among them. And the fact that there were numerous Protestant sects added to this religious heterogeneity.[30]

However, Jews did not immediately benefit from the Reformation. To begin with, a fierce reactionary movement swept Europe as a result of the new divisions within Christianity. Moreover, most of the Protestant denominations did not initially preach tolerance, and most were not conspicuously more accepting of Jews than the Catholic Church, at least in an immediate theological sense.

The Reformation was more than a "theological movement," however; it was a political and economic movement as well, and in time it brought changes to numerous institutions of European society.[31] Because of these changes the Reformation eventually helped European Jewry, not only by increasing the religious diversity within Europe, but also by evoking social change. More than this, Protestantism in itself, apart from the new dichotomy of Christendom, contributed to the *idea* of tolerance, if only indirectly, in that it saw every man as a priest unto himself. Further, although this did not immediately have the positive effect for Jews that it eventually would, Protestantism retained the Catholic tradition, and resulting tolerance, of the Jew as history's witness to Christianity.

Indeed, the Reformation enhanced that tradition, and this became a major factor in changing Christian (specifically Protestant) attitudes regarding Jews. Protestantism enthusiastically revived interest in the Old Testament, Hebrew, and Biblical studies. One important result of this was that more and more theologians and scholars began to regard Jews with sympathy. The Jew was beginning to be seen not as a deicide, but as a descendant of the patriarchs. This was especially true in England, where several groups of Puritans began to identify with the Old Testament Israelites. In consequence, they "evolved a kind of philo-Semitism whereby they created a favorable atmosphere for contemporary Jews."[32]

The Reformation thus offered Jews two specific advantages. First, monolithic Catholicism was shattered and a multitude of sects, of which Judaism was only one, existed throughout Europe. Second, a new attitude toward and definition of Jews was discernible. The new attitude and definition were religiously oriented, it is true, but they presented Jews in a positive light. The first necessary condition for Jewish emancipation, then, an incipient and growing toleration of different religions, obtained in parts of Europe.

### Liberalism and Nationalism

At least two other changes were also necessary before Jewish emancipation could be achieved. One was the growth of liberal philosophy. The second was the acceptance of the state as a morally self-sufficient entity. Those who supported the secular state also endorsed the admission of Jews into society, and they did so without hoping for or expecting their eventual conversion to Christianity. Thus, for example, John Locke's classic argument for a secular state includes a recommendation for Jewish participation in it.[33] With the growth of the state, coupled with a liberal ideology and its accompanying idea of tolerance, European Jewry and its Christian allies began to envision the possibility of sociopolitical acceptance.

The ideology of liberalism was in symbiosis with the growing sense of nationalism. Eventually, during the nineteenth century, the century of Jewish emancipation, the two would become intertwined; overwhelmingly nationalists were liberals and liberals were nationalists. Each not only supported the other but needed the other. One reason for this was that liberalism and nationalism initially had an identical goal, a goal of crucial and beneficial significance for Jews: the establishment of a nation-state that guaranteed the safety and legal rights of its citizens in exchange for legally specified obligations. Thus it was not liberalism alone, but liberalism in conjunction with the rise of nationalism, that saw secular ideology win over religious ideology.[34] In France, for example, "it was under the influence of liberal English nationalism, that the . . . *philosophes* fought in the eighteenth century against the authoritarianism, the intolerance, and the censorship of their church and state."[35]

At the core of the liberal position was a rational philosophy that stemmed from the Enlightenment, the ideal of which was to free all peoples. The mechanism for freedom would be the truths established by science and man's innate intelligence. The theological basis of truth was to be superseded. One consequence was that the new standards of scientific truth were pragmatically oriented; a second consequence was the primacy of these same pragmatic considerations in social values and institutions. This meant that talent, not religion, would become the criterion by which European society lived. Not surprisingly the groups on the fringes of society, the minorities who had previously been prohibited from being a part of society because of iniquitous discrimination, enthusiastically endorsed this turn of events. No group was more a minority than the Jews.

Another result of the Enlightenment was the growth of humanitarianism. This quite naturally fed the post-Reformation idea of toleration, although an important distinction must be made. The toleration growing out of the Reformation was based on political expediency; the toleration growing out of the Enlightenment was based on an idea of freedom—political, intellectual, religious, economic, and national freedom.[36] The Reformation brought a reluctant acceptance of toleration; the growing liberal philosophy that developed from the Enlightenment enhanced that acceptance and reshaped it into a form beneficial to all minorities, not least to Jews.

## Nationalism

The growth of nationalism was neither smooth nor uniform in Europe. In the west it was predominantly political; in the central and eastern states, nationalism rose later and at a time when those states were less advanced both economically and politically. Outside the west, nationalism found its first expression in the cultural field; that is, the central and eastern states' main expression of nationalism was in the form of national culture. In Germany, for example, the concept of citizenship was of less significance than that of *volk* ("the folk") a more vague and emotional term. From the point of view of European Jewry, the positive aspects of nationalism were most manifest in the west, that is, in England and France. Nationalism in these countries tended to be expressed politically, in an attempt to increase and secure civil rights and to curtail the power of government. A part of the Age of Enlightenment, the movement toward nationalism in western Europe was a movement toward a rational and a liberal society.[37]

The intertwining of nationalism with the ideology of individual liberty not only began in the west, it remained there. This conception of nationalism, if it ever did penetrate the central and eastern states, failed to take a firm grip. Beginning in the 1820s and culminating in the years following the revolutions of 1848, nationalism in these states evolved into an ideology that stressed collective power and unity at the sacrifice of individual liberty.

This helps to explain the general difficulties that hampered the fight for Jewish emancipation in those states. Eventually, and most regularly in the eastern and central states, nationalism became something of an obsession and ancient hatreds and fears were aroused. As one result, these nations, especially the newly emerging ones, looked with disfavor upon minority groups within their borders as a threat to homogeneity. Under these conditions it was difficult for Jews to be accepted. They were regarded as aliens, as an unassimilable people, as a state within a state.[38]

Even in France, after the first flush of victory, problems arose. The political-ideological view there moved toward a type of nationalism that embraced Christian romanticism, and the social distance between Jew and Gentile increased. Nor was this the case only in France. The Napoleonic wars were followed by a reactionary period and a return to Christian exclusiveness in most, if not all, of Europe.[39] Extreme patriotism and a drive toward demographic homogeneity were two of the reasons why it became necessary for Jews to be willing to change, to accept citizenship in a political society, if they were to be emancipated.

Given the growth of nationalism, and given the state as the unit of measure, it was obvious to all that the Jews had to become "new men." That is, they had to renounce the self-segregated Jewish community. In France they had to stop being Jews living in France and instead become Jewish Frenchmen.[40] This was true, in fact, everywhere. Each parliament that debated Jewish emancipation raised the issue of renunciation by Jews of their special privileges. Jews could retain their religion, but they would have to give up their autonomy, their Jewish nationalism, and the institutions that nationalism bred. This view was endorsed by supporters of Jewish emancipation in Holland, for instance. Civil rights for Jews in Germany were contingent upon several conditions, among which were assumption of surnames, wearing of German clothing, shaving of beards, and use of the German language in account books and commercial documents.[41] Similarly, in Hungary Jews were told that they must abandon the idea of a Jewish nationality and become assimilated. The granting of Jewish civil rights was contingent on the Jews becoming Magyarized.

But this was not simply a matter of volition on the part of Jews. The most fundamental issue to be decided concerning Jewish emancipation was whether Jews could become members of the societies in which they lived. Supporters of emancipation argued that Jews could and would become citizens of the various European countries, while their opponents argued the contrary position.

To cite just two examples of the rhetoric which was heard in every parliament in every nation in Europe: When the issue of emancipation was first being debated, Abbé Jean Sieflein Maury, speaking in the French National Assembly in 1789, stated: "The word *Jew* is not a name of a sect; it is the name of a nation." This sentiment was echoed by opponents of Jewish emancipation throughout Europe. Supporters of Jewish emancipation answered in the manner of Stanislas de Clermont-Tonnerre, who in the same assembly argued: "Jews, as a nation, are to be denied everything; but Jews, as a people, are to be granted everything." In 1847, during debates concerning the emancipation of Jews in Germany, Prussian Cabinet Minister Tiel asserted that "Zionism constitutes the fatherland of Jews; their religion teaches them that essentially a Jew can have no other fatherland."[42]

### The Jews

The Jews—particularly the better educated ones—were overwhelmingly in favor of emancipation, especially in the west. European Jews generally denied their separate nationality and awaited emancipation with great anticipation.[43] But by no means was there unanimity within the Jewish communities; conservative Jews regarded emancipation with varying degrees of trepidation. They regarded it as a major step toward the eradication of Judaism.[44] And while their fears did *not* come to pass, there were undeniably some problems of adjustment as Jews began to enter European society.

It might be said, however, that greater problems preceded their emancipation. There was, as Katz notes, a growing tendency among Jews to convert to

Christianity.[45] This tendency ebbed markedly after the emancipation edicts became law and most Jews adjusted to their new status. In Germany, for example, there was serious discussion of the possibility of intermarriage, a topic that had been anathema to Jewish leaders for over two millennia. In England a new synagogue opened in 1842, the West London Synagogue of British Jews, that would not differentiate between Spanish and Germanic Jewry but would be a *British* synagogue.[46] In short, virtually all of the acts favoring Jewish emancipation had the support of most of European Jewry.

## PRECURSORS: INDICATIONS OF THE COMING EMANCIPATION

The Enlightenment itself did not affect the masses to any great degree. Political leaders and intellectuals notwithstanding, religion was still the popular basis of nationality: "The Spaniard was defined by being Catholic, the Russian by being Orthodox."[47] Moreover, even during this time of great sociopolitical change, the European world remained parochial, with illiteracy the norm and communications slow. Yet there were some indications that the general citizenry was beginning to see Jews in a new light, and the humanism of the Enlightenment as propagated by Europe's ideological leaders may have been the catalyst for this.

When viewed in broad perspective, the changing status of European Jewry, the transition from what was at best second-class citizenship to full membership in the European polity, was almost covert. Arnold A. Rogow notes that "gradually, almost imperceptibly, the situation of European Jewry began to improve. By the end of the eighteenth century, a variety of influences—political, economic, intellectual—had combined to create a movement for Jewish emancipation."[48] Nevertheless, a close examination of the situation reveals that, beginning even earlier than the eighteenth century, a barely discernible reshaping of the "Jewish question" was taking place. There were indications that the "Jewish question" was evolving into a political matter concerning both Jewish contributions to the state and the state's contribution to the Jews.[49] There were, that is, indications of a reinterpretation of the centuries-old Christian problem.

It is not suggested here that Jews and their allies had merely to bide their time until this trend reached fruition. The emancipation of European Jewry was not an easy or readily accomplished task: "General legislation," as Katz points out, had little to do with the Jews' political emancipation, and "mutual adaptation" on the part of Jews and Christians had little to do with their social emancipation. The possible consequences of Jewish emancipation, both political and social, were discussed with considerable passion in the legislative arenas of Europe as well as the "arena of public opinion."[50]

Again, because Jews themselves could not participate in the discussions, in all of these various arenas philo-Semites were their representatives and staunch supporters. And the difficulties these philo-Semites faced were substantial. They had to overcome not only reactionary political ideologies, but perhaps more importantly, ancient stereotypes and prejudices. It can hardly be surprising, then, that Jewish emancipation was a slow, painstaking process.

Emancipation could only be accomplished by eradicating images of both real and imagined differences between Jews and Christians, images that prevented many from even conceiving of a Christian society that included Jews. It fell to the philo-Semites to eradicate the stereotypes and prejudices and to break down innumerable anti-Semitic barriers. Indicators of emancipation for European Jewry facilitated these tasks and intimated that such emancipation was a viable possibility.

## Social and Political Trends

It was not accidental that France and England were the first to embrace the eighteenth-century trends of humanism, liberalism, and rationalism that would later influence the rest of the world; nor was it accidental or insignificant that the changes in the status of European Jewry were first considered seriously in France and in England. The influence of these two countries cannot be denied. The world in this period (1789-1814), as Hobsbawm notes, "—or at least a large part of it—was transformed from a European, or rather a Franco-British base." This transformation came in three key areas, the economic, political, and ideological.[51] The sociopolitical emancipation of French Jewry and the continuing social emancipation of English Jewry was of monumental importance for Jews throughout the rest of Europe. It was to a large degree because the leaders of France and England were receptive to that emancipation that the concept spread and was accepted throughout the Continent.

In both countries there were discernible indications of readiness for emancipation well before the fact. In France, for example, an edict of expulsion was reissued in 1615 and never repealed.[52] During the reign of Louis XIV, however, individual Jews as well as entire communities were granted letters patent, and these documents specifically mentioned Jews. In effect, the Edict of Expulsion was ignored rather than repealed.[53] This evasion was based, in the main, on the economic contribution of the Jews. Yet suggestions of a general and humanistically based tolerance were also being heard, and this, too, was significant.

In England a general acceptance of tolerance increasingly became the norm. As early as 1693 Sir Joshua Child, the president of the East India Company, demanded naturalization for English Jewry. One reason for this was that Jews living in the American colonies had been naturalized and it seemed inconsistent, even foolish, to grant colonial Jews rights that were denied Jews in England. To correct this anomaly, Pelham, the new prime minister, proposed a naturalization measure to Parliament in 1753. The measure passed both houses and was signed by King George II.[54] Prior to both the French and the Industrial Revolutions, then, a movement toward Jewish emancipation existed in France and England. Similar movements existed elsewhere.

Yet one must exercise caution. As noted earlier, the naturalization measure in England was rescinded. And, disregard of the Edict of Expulsion notwithstanding, the problem of what to do with French Jewry was not automatically or immediately solved. When discussion of this topic began, only two equally radical possibilities existed: expel the Jews or grant them citizenship. Thus, for the first time, the issue of the right of presence was joined with a new issue, the right of membership. If Jews were allowed to remain in France, the French would no longer be tolerating a "state within a state," but accepting Jews as members of the larger state. This, clearly, was crucial for France, crucial for Jews, and crucial for the whole of Europe; for the first time in the history of Christendom, Jews would be members, not "guests," of a Christian nation.

The final decision favoring membership was not lightly taken nor easily decided. It was agreed to, but only after the National Assembly engaged in a lengthy debate concerning the ability of Jews to be assimilated and the desirability of that assimilation, if it were possible. It may be that "Latin logic," as Cecil Roth suggests, "forced upon the National Assembly of France . . . the conclusion that even Jews must enjoy benefit of the Rights of Man."[55] But these benefits were not won by reason alone; nor did they flow automatically because the "rights of man" implied the "rights of Jews," too, for at least initially they did not. In France, and in England and throughout the Continent, Jewish emancipation had to be fought for, intimations of emancipation notwithstanding. In no nation was it granted automatically.

One especially significant indication of the coming emancipation of European Jewry was discernible in the Edict of Toleration issued by Joseph II of Austria in 1782.[56] The edict was important for two reasons. First, it represented the first pragmatic effort to emancipate Jews. Second, it was "a significant act of friendship, the first in centuries which Jews had enjoyed from any great European state."[57]

The edict, through separate rulings enacted between October 1781 and March 1782, dealt with Jews in lower Austria, including Hungary, Silesia, Moravia, Bohemia, and Vienna.[58] It included, among other things, the right (or obligation) to be recruited into the military, the first time a European Christian state expressed a willingness to induct Jews into its army. This, above all, was a clear indication to Jews that their status paralleled that of their Christian fellow countrymen.[59] A major step toward the emancipation of European Jewry had been taken. Although many of Joseph II's policies were reversed upon his death, the Edict of Toleration was not revoked. Even after legislation was enacted that "set him back practically," the Austrian Jew emerged as not just a permanent resident but a citizen, and officially recognized as such.[60] Moreover, the edict influenced the attitude of Louis XVI's government toward Jews. In several ways, then, Joseph II's action was immensely beneficial to Jewish emancipation and pointed to the future.

Scholars have disagreed about the reasons for Joseph's actions, some suggesting that the cause was the "spirit of the time."[61] This, however, ignores the forces of political pragmatism. Earlier, in 1781, when an outline of the future reforms was presented to the Austrian council, Joseph II stated part of his reason for issuing the edict: "In order to render the members of the Jewish nation more useful for the state, it is necessary to grant them education and to extend the circle of their occupations."[62] In keeping with this intention, Joseph II supported a condition of Jewish emancipation that was repeated wherever that topic was discussed: Jews would be granted freedom if they denied Jewish nationalism, that is, Jewish national identity.

This suggests that Joseph was less concerned with human rights than with state efficiency; yet other factors must be considered. As in France, Jews in Austria had secured the right to exist within the nation. The issue now was what to do with them. Again as in France, the decision was to make Jews members of the state for the benefit of the state, but also for the benefit of the Jews. This is why in Austria, as elsewhere, Jews were generally happy to comply with enculturation (renunciation of national identity).

Beyond state concerns, however, Joseph's issuance of the edict was prompted at least in part by humanitarianism. The edict itself reflects both aspects of Joseph's position. It begins: "Convinced on the one hand of the perniciousness of all religious intolerance, and on the other hand of the great advantage of a true Christian tolerance to religion and the state...."[63] It would seem, then, that Peter G. J. Pulzer is correct in suggesting that Joseph II was willing to grant Jews—and Protestants, too, it should be noted—restricted toleration for two reasons, a genuine humanism and a recognition of the stupidity and inefficiency of discrimination.[64]

However, at least one scholar finds little comfort in the actions of the Austrian emperor and indeed considers his policies no better than "the stagnant, Prussian, anti-Semitism."[65] But this was not the attitude of Austrian Jewry; nor would it be that of European Jewry in general. Most Jews cheered Joseph II, even though they recognized that one feature of the edict, perhaps even one of its intentions, was the abolition of Jewish national identity. They understood that the emperor had tried to benefit them as well as the state. For example, Joseph II demanded that Christians befriend Jews or at least act amicably toward them. He also forbade the circulation of a vicious work that attacked Jews. This was necessary; Jews were elated by the edict, but not all Christians were, especially those who saw Jews as competitors.

Another indication of the future emancipation of European Jewry was the attitude of the Freemasons toward Jews. The Freemasons are important for two reasons. First, they may be taken as representative of the middle classes. Although they were a secret organization and atypical in certain respects, they were not intellectual, political, or religious leaders. Second, Freemasonry was not limited to a single nation; its ideas penetrated most of Europe. Beginning in England in the early eighteenth century, Freemasonry quickly spread to Holland, France, and Germany, as well as numerous other countries.[66] As early as 1732 in England, the constitution of the Freemasons approved admission of Jews, and by 1756 a significant number of Jews belonged to the lodges. Similar situations existed in Holland, France, and Germany, although in the latter two countries church pressure eventually prohibited Jewish membership. Until the Revolution in France and the 1830s in Germany, when it became superfluous, many intellectual Freemasons supported toleration of Jews for humanitarian and liberal reasons. The revolutions of 1848 swept away the old restrictive laws in all of the German states save Prussia.

This is not to argue that the position of Jews in the lodges was always satisfactory to them. Even in England discrimination existed, but this became less and less the norm. That the Freemasons were antitraditionalistic in numerous ways had an influence on their policies; nonetheless, their acceptance of Jews as members cannot be attributed only to this nonconformist aspect of their orientation. The increasing degree of toleration in the eighteenth century must have facilitated the Jews' acceptance into the lodges and eased the work of the Jews' champions who brought their admission to the fore.[67]

It seems too negative to assert, as Katz does, that because the Freemasons tried to avoid the public eye, the acceptance of Jews into their organization did little, if anything, to enhance toleration.[68] This acceptance was an indication of things to come. Moreover, it indicated that what was to come would come through the efforts of Christians and that the "common man" was beginning to accept Jews.

## Intellectuals

Aside from specific political acts such as the Edict of Toleration, the clearest portent of the coming emancipation of European Jewry was probably the increasing intellectual support it received. Growing numbers of writers, philosophers, and social critics voiced their support for Jews and Jewish emancipation. This support was not only potent but manifest in virtually every country in Europe.

During the eighteenth century toleration of Jews came to be recognized throughout western and central Europe as an issue to be debated. This idea had, as noted, a precedent in the seventeenth century and, to some degree, before that.[69] Writers, scholars, philosophers, theologians, political figures, and virtually every individual who was in any way cosmopolitan had discussed the topic of European Jewry. Even prior to the Reformation, the idea of tolerance of Jews had been endorsed by men like Saint Thomas More and

Desiderius Erasmus. As religion diminished as a force on the Continent, and as nationalism grew to take its place, it followed logically that the issue of toleration of Jews would grow and, in time, evolve into the issue of Jewish emancipation. Not unreasonably, if toleration became the norm in various European countries, and if these countries were no longer to be defined as Catholic, Protestant, or simply Christian in the broadest sense, Jews might have a say in affairs of state. This possibility was raised by various writers, statesmen, and philosophers, possibly because it is often the intelligentsia who set society's trends or are the first to understand and express those trends while they are in a formative or embryonic state.

In Gentile discussions of Jews, a period of neglect had followed the hostility of the earliest Christian writers. The Reformation aroused a new interest in Jews. Eventually there appeared "a modern note of sympathy, first for the aspirations of the Jews for the rights of citizenship and then for the establishment of a Jewish homeland."[70] This was discernible in virtually every European country. After the Reformation the idea began to take firmer root, especially among religiously oriented intellectuals. Hugo Grotius, the eminent Dutch thinker, pointed out that there existed "the desire of some to raise the Old Testament to the position of natural law."[71] This view did much to transform the negative image of Jews into a positive one, especially in some intellectual circles. Moreover, Grotius's tolerant views, if hardly universal, were not eccentric; in Holland, Germany, and other countries, there were other authors who championed the Jews as a people during the sixteenth century.

The basis of this change was a newly awakened religious philo-Semitism, one that went beyond the older papal version. The new religious philo-Semitism was, in one sense at least, based on a universalistic perception of Christianity in concert with Judaism. Consider the words of William Surenhuysius (d. 1698), a Dutch Protestant:

He who desires to be a good and worthy disciple of Christ must first become a Jew, or he must learn thoroughly the language and culture of the Jews, and become Moses's disciple before he joins the Apostles, in order that he may be able through Moses and the prophets to convince men that Jesus is the Messiah.[72]

Judaism was ceasing to be regarded as the mistaken, and occasionally malevolent, but necessary precursor of Christianity. Instead it was now regarded by some as the necessary condition for the existence of Christianity and therefore a religion that should be understood, respected, and admired.

This conception gained force as the sixteenth century gave way to the seventeenth and eighteenth centuries. To illustrate: The Mishnan was translated into Latin by Surenhuysius, and Jacob Basnage wrote a history of the

Jews and of Judaism. This study was unique in that it was an unbiased account of both the people and the religion, and it documented the struggles of the Jews. Basnage's study, the first of its kind, was widely read. It was a factor in Christians' changing attitudes towards Jews; their hostility was evolving into understanding and respect.[73] However, it was in France and England that the strongest arguments for religious toleration were heard.

Before Grotius wrote, Michel Eyquem de Montaigne, whose mother was Marrano, endorsed a tolerant philosophy. The basis of this philosophy was simple humanism. Consider the force of his words:

> You Christians complain that the Emperor of China roasts all Christians in his dominions over a slow fire. You behave much worse towards Jews, because they do not believe as you do. If any of our descendants should ever venture to say that the nations of Europe were cultured, your example will be adduced to prove that they were barbarians. The picture that they will draw of you will certainly stain your age, and spread abroad hatred of all your contemporaries.[74]

Another Frenchman, Richard Simon, wrote works praising Jews before the end of the century, and for similar, that is, humanistic reasons.

However, it is probable that the most significant pre-Enlightenment writer in France was Jean Bodin, whose philo-Semitism was well known. Bodin, a political thinker of considerable significance, regarded Mosaic Law as the embodiment, the "supreme authority," of natural law. This, quite logically, contributed to a newer, greater regard for Judaism.[75] Once again, the new religious philo-Semitism stressed a religious universalism that encompassed both Jew and Christian. More than this, however, it was the Old Testament that was the "supreme authority," and not only Jews but Christians ought to recognize and respect it.

The most significant thinkers of the time, however, were the Philosophes of the Enlightenment, men who admired the sophistication and humanism of the Renaissance and brought these views to contemporary Europe. They were the greatest single influence for toleration of Jews throughout Europe, and especially in France. The reason for their tolerance and the actions they took to spread that tolerance to others is suggested by Arthur Hertzberg: "The majority of the Philosophes sincerely believed that it was their moral duty to extend equality to all men and that even the Jews would be regenerated by the new order."[76] A new perception of the Jew, then, was beginning to take shape: the Jew as man, as human being. This concept would be of great significance in the struggle for Jewish membership in European society.

Among the more philo-Semitic works of the Philosophes were those of Montesquieu and Abbé Charles Irenée Castel de Saint Pierre, fierce opponents of religious prejudice, as well as the writings of Claude Adrien Helvétius and Pierre Bayle. It was in England, however, that the most potent philo-Semitic writings existed. There, and especially because of humanistic and religious philo-Semitism, John Selden, Samuel Pepys, and Samuel Butler, among others, wrote in praise of Jewry.

The most significant writers in England to advocate religious toleration during the seventeenth century were John Locke and, somewhat later, John Toland. Both argued in favor of admitting Jews into England and granting religious toleration to them, although both opposed extending this toleration to Catholics. Locke's main concern, as noted in his *Letter Concerning Toleration* (1689), was the way in which various Christian sects dealt with and regarded one another. Consistency of argument demanded an extension of this principle, and he concluded that "neither Pagan, nor Mahometan nor Jew ought to be excluded from the civil rights of the commonwealth because of his religion!"[77] The essence of Locke's position, most clearly seen in his political philosophy and in his epistemology, is that individual liberty and conscience are inviolate. Therefore, conditional to acceptance of and obedience to the "social contract" that constitutes civil government, no individual ought to be excluded from membership because of religious conviction.[78]

In the light of this it is possible to understand, if not justify, Locke's exclusion of Catholics from membership because their loyalty would not be directed toward England but toward the pope. Jews, on the other hand, would be loyal to England. Locke, then, anticipated and discounted a problem that would become a focal point in subsequent discussions of Jewish emancipation.

The key issue of Jewish emancipation, however, was expressed some twenty-five years after Locke wrote, when John Toland came on the scene. Toland was more interested in practical politics than in theoretical concerns. Specifically, he directed his attention to the topic of general naturalization, a subject that had been a major political issue since the Restoration. The law favoring general naturalization granted English citizenship to any professing Protestant. Toland suggested that Jews be granted citizenship as well (although he—like Locke, and for similar reasons—would not grant English citizenship to Catholics). The significance of this position is that, first, Toland endorsed an unqualified acceptance of Jews during a time when the readmission of Jews to England was in full debate. Second, as Katz notes, the reasoning of his argument is unique: religious doctrine should not influence political decisions. Thus the Jews' denial of the "truth" of Christianity cannot be a barrier to their emancipation.[79]

Toland, like Locke, endorsed a universal citizenship of all men who would be loyal to the state, regardless of religion. The only exception would be Catholics. (Toland, incidentally, had been raised a Catholic.) Religious differences were of no consequence. Part of the basis of this position was Toland's religiosity. A deist, Toland doubted the absolute truth of religion: "I acknowledge no Orthodoxy but the Truth."[80] Religion, therefore, did not belong within the dictates of the state, but within those of one's individual conscience. And if church and state are separate, there is no reasonable cause for the exclusion of Jews from membership in the state.

The views of Locke and Toland were not accepted throughout England; they were, in fact, quite clearly minority opinions. Nonetheless, they indicated a trend that was to gain increasing strength.

As noted, a new perspective, most clearly voiced by the Philosophes, was developing that would alter Christian perceptions of Jews. Beginning slowly in the eighteenth century and increasing thereafter, the image of the Jew changed from villain, to Biblical witness, and finally to full human being. In England in 1794, Richard Cumberland's *The Jew* had, for the first time in English literature, a Jew as the hero. Other works portraying Jews in a favorable light soon followed by such authors as Thomas Dibdin, George Walker, and Maria Edgeworth.[81] The works of William Hazlitt and Thomas Babington Macaulay, among numerous others, were specific in their support of Jews and Jewish emancipation. Two particularly influential writers were Sir Walter Scott and George Eliot (Mary Ann Evans). The former, in *Ivanhoe*, analyzed Jewish history in an altogether new light: Jews were the victims, not the villains. Scott portrayed the Jews as unjustly persecuted and exiled, as forced into the avaricious trade of moneylending. It is possible to argue that "throughout the book . . . Jews reveal more of the Christian virtues than the Christians. And when at the end Rebecca and her father prepare to exile themselves abroad, the meaning of their departure is that England still cannot behave with Christianity to its Jews."[82] One Jewish scholar writes that George Eliot used Jewish history to create "artistic images" and "immortalized the Jewish national and Messianic dream in the novel *Daniel Deronda*".[83] The humanistic aspect of Eliot's position, the view of the Jew as a human being, is clear in her work. Eliot, a Christian scholar writes, "would have her readers understand that Jews are precious to the human family, that the world would be poorer without those qualities."[84] This clearly points to the changed image of the Jew.

In France the idea of toleration took on a political overtone, suggesting the beginnings, or at least the first overt signs, of what might be termed political philo-Semitism. Logically, this basis of toleration of Jews was seen as the first step towards full emancipation of Jews. Anne Robert Jacques Turgot argued this position in his "Letters to a Grand Vicar on Toleration."[85] Pierre Bayle took a similar stance. Perhaps the best example of this position was offered by Abbé Henri Grégoire, whose *Essay on the Physical, Moral, and Political Reformation of the Jews* had great influence on the Continent and was soon published in an English translation. These men were not alone in voicing opinions supporting toleration and membership in French society; Montesquieu and a host of other political writers supported Jewish freedom. Jewish emancipation could hardly have been accepted by the Assembly in the absence of such intellectual support.

As Cumberland introduced the Jew as hero and human being into English literature, Gotthold Ephraim Lessing, "perhaps the most notable of the German philo-Semites," presented a similar image of Jews in eighteenth-century Germany. Rejecting the image of the Jew as usurer and villain, Lessing presented the Jew as an honorable individual, as, for the first time, a noble figure.[86] His *Die Juden* was one of the first favorable portrayals of Jews; the same author's classic statement on Jews and his plea for religious tolerance, *Nathan der Weise*, came a full generation later.

Lessing's philo-Semitism was motivated to a great degree by his genuine belief in brotherly love and toleration. And it is crucial to consider that during the Enlightenment many, if not most Christians, felt that brotherhood and toleration were the crux of Christianity. Beyond this, Lessing was undoubtedly moved by his friendship with, and admiration and respect for, Moses Mendelssohn. *Nathan der Weise* is a portrait of Mendelssohn.

As indicated earlier, many literary works supportive of toleration were published well before and continued to appear throughout the period of public debate over the specific issue of Jewish emancipation. This was the case in most European countries. Prior to the Age of Enlightenment and continuing through the nineteenth century, there was an increasing number of works endorsing toleration of Jews, although not every thinker supported the idea.[87] Nonetheless, throughout this period in Europe there was a substantial increase in the number of writers who held favorable perceptions of Jews. Sympathy for and support of Jews is clearly manifest in, if not the intended reason for, numerous works.

Part of this sympathy and support was undoubtedly brought about by the growing acceptance of a new social outlook. Many of the intelligentsia considered liberal, rationalistic tolerance the only acceptable social philosophy. Coupled with this was an acceptance of the arguments in, and sympathy with, earlier writings that supported tolerance. The works of Cumberland and Lessing, among others, permitted, even encouraged, a reexamination of Jews and Jewish history. Jews could now be seen as an unjustly persecuted minority, and many writers did see them that way; they viewed the plight of the Jews with compassion and were outraged at the persecutions Jews had suffered and did suffer. Underlying this was a religious, humanistic, and liberalistic philo-Semitism coupled with belief in brotherhood, in Christian and humanistic tolerance, and in a world based on reason and freedom.

Whatever the cause of any individual writer's sympathy with European Jewry, there was an outpouring of philo-Semitic literature throughout Europe. For example, in Czechoslovakia, Karal Klostermann's *Surl* was sympathetic to Jews, as were, in Holland, the writings of Anthony C. W. Staring. Also in Holland, journals such as *De Denker* (1764), *De Opmerker* (1778), and *De Koopman* (1768-76) suggested the positive side of economic and cultural Jewish emancipation. This, in turn, contributed to the enculturation of Dutch Jewry. In Hungary, Mihaly Vitez Csonkonai (1773-1805) viewed hatred of different nationalities as "uncouth Magyarism," and said so; and Jozef Katona (1791-1830), Hungary's greatest tragic dramatist, regarded Jews with sympathy in his *The Destruction of Jerusalem*. Even in Poland, where the situation of the Jews was steadily worsening, writers showed an increasing sympathy for the situation of Jews. Notable here was the Polish authoress Eliza Orzeszkowa.

In Scandinavian countries Jews were increasingly portrayed in a favorable light. Denmark's Jens Baggeesen, in his book *Labyrinthen* (1792), was supportive of Jewish emancipation, and Hans Christian Andersen included favorable portrayals of Jewish characters in several stories. The same situation obtained, albeit to a lesser degree, fewer Jews lived there, in Sweden and Norway, where Jewish emancipation began to be viewed sympathetically. In Sweden Pastor Karl Herman Lewin wrote a long poem in 1847 supporting equality for Jews, and in Norway, to which Jews were not admitted until 1851, Henrik Arnold Wergeland, in his struggle to win equality for Jews, wrote about their plight often and with sympathy. The later works of the Russian, Ivan Sergeevich Turgenev, show a degree of sympathy toward Jews, and Tolstoy came out against anti-Semitism in his ethical writings. The pre-Revolutionary era in Russia saw some increase in pro-Jewish literature with the works of Anton Pavlovich Chekhov, Vladimir Galaktionovich Korolenko, Maxim Gorky, and others.

And in Germany, Christian Fuerchtegott Gellert's play "The Swedish Countess" viewed the Jew as a hero; Friedrich Gottlieb Klopstock wrote praising Joseph II of Austria for emancipating the Jews.[88] Notable also are the works of Christian Wilhelm von Dohm, whose *Über die bürgerliche Verbesserung der Juden* supported and contributed to Jewish emancipation in the years surrounding the French Revolution.[89]

Thus, beginning during the Enlightenment and continuing through the nineteenth and indeed into the twentieth century, a literary movement in virtually every European country portrayed Jews in a comparatively favorable light. Again, this is not to argue that all literature that dealt with Jews during this period was favorable. But, the fact that a large and increasing amount was favorable is indicative of a change in the perception of Jews by numerous Christians. That many of these individuals were among the intelligentsia adds to the significance of those changed perspectives and perceptions.

### The Court Jew

A final point must be considered here: the alleged influence of the court Jew. Although some scholars suggest that the court Jew was a crucial factor—perhaps *the* crucial factor— in securing emancipation for European Jewry, his influence has been greatly exaggerated.[90]

Relatively little is known about the court Jews in England and France, although they probably existed in these countries.[91] They were, as Katz notes, ubiquitous. History offers countless examples of Jews (and Christians) who served the powerful. For some Jews this was a way of achieving power and influence in a Christian world and, not to be discounted, a way of securing protection.[92] William the Conqueror and Charlemagne both had Jewish financial advisors, and in Spain the court Jew was an important figure down to the time of the expulsion. Nor was he unknown in the east. Despite these precedents, however, the fame of the court Jew peaked in the seventeenth and eighteenth centuries, when his power was at its height.[93]

Probably the most famous of the court Jews, and certainly among the most influential, was Joseph Oppenheimer—*Jüd Süss* (1698-1737)—who worked for and was admired by Duke Karl Alexander of Wuerttenberg. Oppenheimer and other "agents" handled the finances of the state, supplied armies, raised money, manufactured textiles, leased tobacco and salt taxes, and engaged in a host of other enterprises that provided their rulers with arms, food, and money. For these purposes Moyses Isaac was employed in Bamburg, Samuel Oppenheimer (Joseph's uncle) in Vienna, Bernd Lehmann in Saxony, and so on in all the German courts. Though a few court Jews ended their lives peacefully, most lasted only as long as their rulers; Joseph Oppenheimer, for example, was hanged soon after Duke Alexander died.

For the most part the court Jew reached his greatest influence in the years preceding Jewish emancipation, especially in the central European states. Virtually every king and prince there had a court Jew to handle his business affairs. After the middle of the seventeenth century, he was found in the principalities and courts of Germany. Regardless of the general status of Jews within the rulers' domains, court Jews were often able to exert considerable influence. Indeed, as Joachim Prinz notes of the more important court Jews, "even in the day of medieval anti-Semitism, when church and state had succeeded in restricting Jewish commercial activities, the important minters were elevated to the position of court Jews. They had easier access to the ruler than most noblemen; . . . the doors of the palace were readily opened for them."[94]

All of this notwithstanding, the privileges received by court Jews were earned. There was never any question concerning the relationship between the court Jew and the ruler. The social distance was well understood and well maintained. Further, each acknowledged the clear and overt connection between benefits received and services offered.[95] Nevertheless, the court Jew, the *Hofjude*, and the ruler had at times a "genuinely friendly" relationship. In numerous instances an affection between court Jew and ruler so developed that although the former gained his reputation through financial expertise, he was occasionally given great responsibilities in other areas of importance, such as military affairs or diplomatic concerns.[96]

Because of their intimate relationship to and influence with various rulers, court Jews were able to intercede on behalf of their coreligionists, securing for Jews rights and privileges that would normally have been denied them. This, of course, is the basis of various claims that the court Jew was instrumental in securing emancipation for European Jewry. Frederick M. Schweitzer notes that "sometimes royal confidence in and dependence upon a Jewish minister was such that he could intercede with his master to relieve some of the disabilities of his ghetto bound coreligionists, to prevent their expulsion by this princeling or that town, and to gain for them greater security and prosperity."[97] Prinz suggests that court Jews were "their fellow Jews' most convincing spokesmen."[98] Even assuming this alleged degree of influence of the court Jews, however, it would still be incorrect to assert, as Heinrich Schnee does, that *"the emancipation of the Jews was the work of the Hoffactoren."*[99]

It must be recalled that the points of departure for the emancipation of European Jewry were in France and England, where the court Jews were, at best, of minimal influence.[100] In France, in marked contradistinction to Germany, the court Jews, and indeed Jews in general insofar as financial affairs were concerned, were numerically insignificant and relatively inconsequential.[101] In England the court Jew played an even smaller role; indeed, the court Jew was not needed there. The Resettlement gave Jews de facto social emancipation, and in the open economic system in England there was no need or place for the court Jew. Moreover, and of enormous import, the two most significant acts in support of Jewish emancipation in Europe, the Edict of Toleration of the Emperor Joseph II and the granting of Jewish citizenship in France by the National Assembly, were proposed, discussed, and effected without the assistance of court Jews or, in fact, any Jews at all.

This is not to deny the court Jew some degree of influence on or significance for Jewish emancipation, especially in the central European states and most particularly within the Germanic states. But even here one must be cautious. David Friedlander's efforts to improve the status of Prussian Jewry had limited success at best, and the Arnsteins accomplished almost nothing at the Congress of Vienna.[102] Katz is attuned to the overemphasis on the significance of the court Jews; he points out that the status of the court Jew was determined in part by the various social changes occurring at the time and that these changes were not unrelated to the efforts of the court Jews to help their coreligionists. If this had not been the case, Katz wonders why the court Jews could not have brought about improved conditions within the Jewish community before these social changes occurred, when the court Jews were at the height of their power.[103]

Although many scholars consider the court Jew to have been a potent force in Jewish history—especially after the Reformation—geographical limitations preclude any unqualified assertion that he had great influence or general effectiveness. Court Jews were of some significance in the German states, but not throughout Europe. One scholar warns that in the financial field the contributions of the court Jews "should not be overestimated."[104] Surely the warning applies a fortiori in the political arena; if his influence can be questioned in the area of finance, where his power was alleged to be great, then his political influence must be questioned still more closely.

## NOTES

1. Roth (1970, p. 255) notes that during this period "we begin to read, at increasingly frequent intervals, of lapses from the old standards; of sumptuary laws, intended to mark out the Jews for contumely from true believers; of persecutions at the hands of various pashas; of terrorization by the Janissaries."

2. Dubnov (1973), vol. 5, p. 493. The word "emancipation" comes from the Latin *emancipacio*, "enfranchisement of a slave."

3. To Becker (1970, p. 33), the Enlightenment was "not . . . particularly French but [an] . . . international climate of opinion." His partial listing of Enlightenment names reflects this: Leibniz, Lessing, Herder, Goethe, Locke, Hume, Bolingbroke, Ferguson, Adam Smith, Price, Priestly.

4. Katz (1973), p. 3.

5. Dubnov (1971), vol. 4, pp. 493-94.

6. Dubnov (1971), vol. 4, pp. 495-96.

7. See Parkes (1962), p. 142, and Katz (1973), pp. 9-10. Of course, all demographic information is based on estimates.

8. A. L. Sachar (1965), pp. 297, 295, and 112.

9. Although Theodore Herzl is generally viewed as the Father of Zionism, that conception was adumbrated as early as 1862 when a German Jew, Moses Hess, wrote *Rome and Jerusalem*. The conception was elaborated on in 1882 when a physician in Odessa, Leo Pinsker, wrote *Auto-Emancipation*.

10. H. M. Sachar (1958), p. 70.

11. Schweitzer (1971), p. 157.

12. Joseph W. Cohen, in Graeber and Britt (1942), p. 342.

13. Rivkin (1971), p. 159.

14. Rivkin (1971), p. 164.

15. Katz (1973), pp. 74-75.

16. Parkes (1962), p. 129.

17. All of these social changes were not aimed at or specifically caused by the situation of the Jews; rather, they focused on the general notions of man, the state, religion, and human rights. Acceptance of their general arguments led to acceptance of Jews in numerous cases. In these instances lay the border between philo-Semitism and a-Semitism, that is, the outer limits of philo-Semitism. To some these changes and the situation of the Jews were not separable. Jews were almost always and everywhere regarded as a special group. To a number of Christians the specific application of these changes for the emancipation of Jews was of as much significance as their general application.

18. Hertzler, in Graeber and Britt (1942), p. 63.

19. Katz (1973), p. 83.

20. Dubnov (1971), vol. 4, p. 495. See also ibid., pp. 270-72.

21. A. L. Sachar (1965), p. 295. Also see Katz (1973), p. 22, and Hobsbawm (1962), p. 238.

22. Katz (1973), p. 83.

23. See Katz (1973), pp. 80-103, for an insightful discussion of these objections. Very few scholars assert that the emancipation of Jews was monocausal; none, however, acknowledge philo-Semitism as a factor in bringing it about.

24. Katz (1973), p. 87.

25. Prinz (1968), p. 14.

26. Allport (1958), p. 398.

27. See, for example, Kohn (1967), p. 187; A. L. Sachar (1965), p. 253; and Katz (1973), p. 15.

28. Ettinger (1961), p. 196. Also see ibid., p. 197.

29. Gay and Webb (1973, p. 124) note: "To speak of the Reformation as a shattering of Christian unity is in an important sense misleading.... Christendom had been deeply, often furiously, divided for centuries, long before Martin Luther made that division final."

30. Not only were there splinter groups, but splinter groups that broke off from other splinter groups, such as the Arminians in Holland and the Deists in first England and then throughout Europe.

31. Pulzer (1969), p. 29. Of course, as Katz notes (1973, p. 14), these changes did not automatically benefit Jews, nor did they automatically imply future benefits for Jews. Changes that could and would contribute to the emancipation of Jews did not, merely by their occurrence, have to be contributory.

32. Katz (1973), p. 15. Kohn (1967, p. 187) writes:

Though the State emancipated itself from the Church, it remained in Europe inseparably connected with religion. But in the British Empire a daring example was set. Roger Williams founded in Providence the first society which completely separated the state and religion, and this new principle was acknowledged in the charter which Charles II granted in 1663 to Rhode Island and Providence Plantation.

33. Katz (1973), p. 38.

34. See Hobsbawm (1962), pp. 260-63. Baron (1972, p. 326) suggests that this was the case in most countries, although there were exceptions such as in Germany, where Protestantism "stimulated" nationalism. Also see Pulzer (1969), p. 34.

35. Kohn (1965), p. 18.

36. Artz (1968), p. 40.

37. Kohn (1965), pp. 29-30.

38. A. L. Sachar (1965), p. 338.

39. Katz (1973), pp. 201-2. Although Katz is speaking here of Germany, this was the case throughout Europe.

40. Hertzberg (1968), pp. 364, 350.

41. Dubnov (1971), vol. 4, p. 498, and vol. 5, p. 609. Pulzer (1969, p. 226) notes Heinrich von Treitschke's demand: *Sie sollen Deutsche werden* ("They should become German").

42. Quoted in Dubnov (1971), vol. 4, p. 497, and vol. 5, p. 53. Emphasis in the original.

43. Janowsky (1966), p. 384. Hertzberg (1968, pp. 188-89) comments that Mendelssohn defined Judaism as a religion and rejected the existence of a separate Jewish community.

44. A. L. Sachar (1965), p. 281. See also Hertzberg (1968), p. 8. So extreme was some Jewish leaders' desire to retain Jewish autonomy that they would reject freedom to sustain it. Margolis and Marx (1969, p. 630) note that Shneor Zalman, the leader of the White Russian Hasidim, was opposed to Napoleon's efforts to free Russian Jewry because it meant the disintegration of Judaism. It was, in Zalman's opinion, better to live without civil rights under the Czar if that "preserved the inviolability of Judaism."

45. Katz (1973), p. 121. See ibid., pp. 104-23, for a discussion on converts in pre-Emancipation Europe. While there are no exact data available, there can be no doubt that there was a substantial loss to the Jewish community.

46. See Katz (1973), p. 207, and Roth (1964), p. 257.

47. Hobsbawm (1962), p. 168. See also Artz (1968), p. 32.

48. Rogow (1961), p. 112.

49. Hertzberg (1968), p. 71. Katz (1973, p. 58) suggests that by the end of the eighteenth century the Jewish issue was not only one of being admitted, but also one of being "accepted as citizens."

50. Katz (1973), p. 7.

51. Hobsbawm (1962), p. xv. He also points out (ibid., p. 74) that "if the economy of the nineteenth-century world was formed mainly under the influence of the British Industrial Revolution, its politics and ideology were formed mainly by the French."

52. Poliakov (1965, pp. 176-77) notes that expulsion edicts did not apply to the Marranos of Bordeaux or Bayonne because they were too profitable. Moreover, these Marranos superficially satisfied the requirements of being Christian.

53. Katz (1973), pp. 10-11.

54. A. L. Sachar (1965), p. 275.

55. Roth (1964), p. 246.

56. There is some dispute among scholars whether or not the Edict of Toleration was concerned exclusively with Jews. Dubnov (1971, vol. 4, p. 339) argues that it was; Katz (1973, p. 164) that it was not. It might be noted that an earlier toleration edict applied to Protestants.

57. A. L. Sachar (1965), p. 274. See also Hertzberg (1968), p. 315.

58. The contents of these rulings varied slightly for each country, but the meaning of each was the same. See Katz (1973), p. 162.

59. Katz (1973), pp. 164-65. Accepting Jews into the army suggests recognition that Jews of one nation will fight Jews of another nation.

60. Katz (1973), p. 164.

61. See, for example, Dubnov (1971), vol. 4, p. 336.

62. Dubnov (1971), vol. 4, p. 337. Jews were now permitted to engage in science and the arts and to become craftsmen and farmers, although certain conditions

affected their entry into the latter occupation. They were also admitted to the universities. Joseph II decreed that Jewish adults "learn the language of the country" and removed all attempts at religious compulsion. An ordinance of November 2, 1781, stated that Jews were to be considered "fellow-men" (Graetz, 1894, vol. 4, p. 357).

63. Quoted in Pulzer (1969), p. 129.

64. Pulzer (1969), p. 129.

65. Dubnov (1971), vol. 4, p. 459. Margolis and Marx (1969, p. 597) suggest that the purpose of Joseph II's edict was "to break down from above Jewish separatism."

66. Katz (1973), p. 44. He notes (ibid., p. 45) that Freemasonry approached the ideal of religious toleration.

67. See Katz (1973), p. 46. Also see Katz (1967), passim, and Hobsbawm (1962), pp. 37-38, 259.

68. Katz (1973), p. 47.

69. It is probable that the first practical instances of toleration in medieval Christendom occurred in Italy in the second half of the fourteenth century. Humanism was a popularly accepted concept in Italy at that time, and toleration is fundamental to humanism.

70. *Universal Jewish Encyclopedia*, vol. 3, p. 175. Rosenberg (1960, p. 39) notes that "the good Jew is of relatively recent origin" in literature.

71. Quoted in Ettinger (1961), p. 198.

72. Quoted in Graetz (1895), vol. 5, p. 194.

73. *Universal Jewish Encyclopedia*, vol. 3, p. 176.

74. Quoted in Graetz (1895), vol. 5, p. 336. Also see Katz (1973), p. 78.

75. Ettinger (1961), p. 197. See also Poliakov (1965), p. 197; Kohn (1967), p. 133; and the *Universal Jewish Encyclopedia*, vol. 3, p. 175.

76. Hertzberg (1968), p. 338. Hertzberg also points out (1968, passim) that some of the Philosophes were agents of modern anti-Semitism.

77. Quoted in Roth (1964), p. 246.

78. Locke's most important works, *An Essay Concerning Human Understanding* and *Two Treatises of Government*, are available in numerous editions.

79. Katz (1973), p. 39.

80. Quoted in the *Encyclopedia of Philosophy*, vol. 8, p. 142.

81. Roth (1964), p. 244. See also the *Universal Jewish Encyclopedia*, vol. 3, p. 106. There is a major debate on the attitude of Charles Dickens toward Jews. In *Oliver Twist* Dickens portrays a Jew as an avaricious, evil character; in *Our Good Friend* Dickens portrays a Jew as humane and generous. See Rosenberg (1960), pp. 15-16; Calish (1969), p. 108.

82. Johnson (1970), p. 745. Rosenberg (1960, pp. 73-115) is unhappy with Scott's representation of Jews in *Ivanhoe*. To Rosenberg, idealizing Jews is as damaging to Jews as continually portraying them negatively.

83. Dubnov (1973), vol. 5, p. 378.

84. Schweitzer (1971), p. 254.

85. Turgot wrote this in 1753-54. He argues that intolerance is unworthy of a gentle and charitable Christian.

86. H. M. Sachar (1958), p. 46. See also Schweitzer (1971), pp. 162-63.

87. For example, Jonathan Swift, Daniel Defoe, and Alexander Pope all wrote works that may be regarded as anti-Semitic, or at least anti-Jewish.

88. See the *Universal Jewish Encyclopedia*, vol. 3, pp. 100-125. See also Kohn (1967), pp. 347, 420.

89. *Universal Jewish Encyclopedia*, vol. 3, p.176. See also ibid., vol. 3, p. 111 for a further discussion of German writings on Jews in the nineteenth century.

90. On the court Jew generally, see Stern (1950), passim. See also Coser (1972) for an excellent sociological analysis of the relationship between the court Jew and the ruler.

91. Schweitzer (1971), pp. 176-77. Scholars are not totally without information however; see, for example, Prinz (1968), p. 29.

92. Katz (1973), p. 29. Miriam Beard in "The Mirage of the Economic Jew" (in Graeber and Britt, 1942, p. 385) points out that both Christian and Jewish business-men were in unhappy situations: they all had to grovel before the mighty and beg for favors.

93. See Margolis and Marx (1969), pp. 349-50; Roth (1970), p. 165; and Katz (1973), pp. 28-29. Schweitzer (1971, pp. 176-77) dates the preeminence of the court Jews from the fifteenth to the nineteenth centuries.

94. Prinz (1968), pp. 31-32.

95. See Poliakov (1965), p. 232; Arendt (1958), p. 17; and Katz (1973), p. 43. This was the case despite a "natural attachment" that may have grown between the two.

96. Poliakov (1965), pp. 228-32. Also see Cecil Roth, "The Jews of Western Europe," in Finkelstein (1974), p. 261. This was especially the case in Arab lands and most particularly in Turkey.

97. Schweitzer (1971), p. 177.

98. Prinz (1968), p. 32. Roth (1962, pp. 293-94) attacks this position. Although speaking specifically of England and Anglo-Jewish aristocracy, by implication Roth condemns all court Jews. Roth suggests that these men did their coreligionists "more harm than good," because the Christian populace began to associate Jews with wealth and poor Jews paid the price.

99. Quoted in Katz (1973), p. 30. Emphasis in the original. It should be noted that Schnee wrote during the Hitler era and was anti-Semitic.

100. This is not to dispute the significance of the Rothschilds, the Goldsmids, or other influential English Jews. It only argues that they were not the catalysts for Jewish emancipation in England. See Roth (1962), pp. 283-84.

101. See Katz (1973), pp. 15, 30, and Roth (1962), p. 282.

102. Katz (1973), pp. 30-31. Carsten (1958, p. 140) comments that it was "only in Germany and Austria that the court Jews achieved . . . pre-eminence" and that the Hapsburg emperors relied on Jews.

103. Katz (1973), p. 31.

104. Carsten (1958), p. 156.

# JEWISH EMANCIPATION II

## 6

## FRANCE AND ENGLAND

This book does not attempt to detail the process of the emancipation of Jews in every European nation. Two nations, however, are of special significance: France and England.

The domination of Europe by France and England in the eighteenth and nineteenth centuries, respectively, makes the emancipation of Jews in those countries important events. The emancipation of French Jewry marked the first time since the rise of Christianity that Jews were accepted as full citizens of a European nation. This event was not only prophetic, but was a force behind future emancipations. The emancipation of English Jewry illustrates the difficulties involved in accomplishing that task; further, it was of momentous significance in that Jewish emancipation in England paralleled the industrialization and increasing powers of that island nation. Moreover, it was from a British base that the internationalization of philo-Semitism began and was nourished.

It is necessary, then, to examine in some detail the mechanisms and causes of the emancipation of Jews in these two countries. In addition, because of their significance for this analysis, the effects of Napoleon and of the Dreyfus Affair in France and of the process by which Jews were readmitted to England will provide postscripts for, and an introduction to, discussions of the emancipation of Jews in these countries.

The purpose here is to give some idea of the significance of philo-Semitism for Jewish emancipation and to illustrate the changing social structures and perceptions of Jews that facilitated emancipation. Although the process of the emancipation of Jews in each country was to some degree idiosyncratic, in that it was contingent upon specific national conditions, a general idea of the factors that brought it about can be gleaned from an examination of the processes in England and France.

### Emancipation: France

Christians who struggled for Jewish emancipation had themselves little to gain by so doing. This was certainly true in France and England, the two most important countries in Europe in the eighteenth and nineteenth centuries, the period of Jewish emancipation. The emancipation of French and English Jewries was not simple. In each case another religious group (in France the Protestants, and in England the Catholics) had been emancipated prior to the Jews. But in neither country did this mean that Jewish emancipation would automatically follow; even after other minorities had been unfettered socially and politically, the issue of Jewish emancipation brought debates, denunciations, progress, and regression. The eventual emancipation of French and English Jewry was, to a great extent, the achievement of those men who had fought in the Jews' behalf.

The crucial issue in France was whether or not Jews could be citizens of the nation, whether or not they would relinquish their special status and privileges, such as internal autonomy and self-government. This was less an issue in England, where Jews had already demonstrated their ties to that land to the satisfaction of most people. In England the antiemancipation forces were organized on the basis of religion and were so conservative that they viewed virtually any social change as anathema.

Four years before the French Revolution, when Jews were not official residents of France, the Royal Society of Arts and Sciences in Metz offered a prize for a discussion of the subject: "Are There Means of Making the Jews Happy and More Useful in France?" In 1788 three prize winners were announced; one was a Polish Jew named Zalkind Hourwitz and the other two were Catholic, Aldophe Thiéry and Henri Grégoire, a lawyer and an abbot, respectively. The unanimous conclusion of the winners was, as Grégoire said, that Jews "were men like ourselves before they were Jews."[1] They could become Frenchmen, and they should become Frenchmen.

There is much speculation over Grégoire's motives. Many people suggest that he was, above all, a conversionist, that he saw the emancipation of French Jews as the first step toward their becoming Catholics. The reaction of others to his ideas must be considered, however. Many accepted the more rational points of his position and ignored their theological implications. More than this, Grégoire's "appeal struck the proper chord among influential philosemites,"[2] and it was on the advice of these "influential philosemites" that the Assembly took the first step toward emancipation of French Jews. On September 28, 1789, Jews were freed from local jurisdiction and their security was placed in the hands of royal officials.

Even Grégoire's critics acknowledged that at least in part his motives were based on the humanistic sentiments of the time. Indeed, Arthur Hertzberg suggests that Grégoire was sympathetic to the Jews' plight, that his writings were often "generous, humane, and deeply felt," and that he did work for Jewish emancipation in France.[3] At minimum, then, he spoke for Jews not only because he wanted to convert them, but because of a fundamental humanism as well. Further, if Grégoire, a cleric, supported toleration for Jews, laymen would be hard pressed to reject that toleration on religious grounds, although of course many did. Grégoire's arguments not only stimulated the move toward Jewish emancipation in France but offered a substantial degree of legitimation for it.

The situation of French Jews was unlike that of Jews in any other European nation. In the first place, French Jews were divided into two groups, the Sephardic, who had lived near the Spanish borders for centuries as transparently disguised Catholics, and the Ashkenazim, who lived in the eastern part of the country. The former were westernized and could easily become acculturated, or at least many leaders supposed that they could. The latter were less westernized.

In the second place, French Jews had very little influence, either political, economic, or social, as contrasted with, for example, some English Jews. It is true that some Jews were well thought of, if only by reputation,[4] but by and large no French Jews were so influential as to be able to help direct the course of the events that would so greatly affect their lives and the lives of their French coreligionists. In fact, when the Estates General convened in the spring of 1789, Jews were not permitted to attend the meeting because they were not considered subjects of the king.[5] Virtually all of the struggles for their emancipation were waged by their allies; indeed, the emancipation of French Jewry came about through the political efforts of Gentiles and through these efforts alone.

Necessarily, then, and throughout the relatively brief struggle for sociopolitical emancipation, French Jewry had numerous influential spokesmen: Honoré Gabriel Riqueti de Mirabeau, the Abbé Grégoire, Bishop Talleyrand, Clermont-Tonnerre, Maximilien Robespierre, Adrien Duport, and the Protestant pastor Rabaud-Saint-Etienne. The Jews had to have such allies; without them the struggle could not have occurred. In addition to being excluded from the meeting of the Estates General, even though that body had invited all segments of the population to voice their discontents, Jews were barred from attending the National Assembly. At that assembly, where decisions of great importance to Jews would be made, it is apparent that, initially at least, most representatives did not feel very strongly for or against Jewish emancipation; they were concerned with other, more pressing issues. Only representatives from the northeast and some conservative Catholic deputies were interested in the status of French Jewry, and they, if anything, were anti-Semitic.[6]

In fact, the Estates General had considered the plight of French Jews as early as 1789, and in April of that year had submitted a single petition to the attorney general, who in turn presented it to the king. The petition did not speak at all about emancipation; it only asked for "the alleviation of the harsh treatment of the Jews,"[7] and there was no suggestion of granting Jews equal status with Catholics. The revolution changed all that, and the "Jewish Question" began to receive more and more attention. At a meeting of the National Assembly (during, not incidentally, a discussion of the Declaration of the Rights of Man), the status "of freedom of religion" was being considered. One deputy, Castellan, expressed the issue succinctly: "No one should be persecuted for his religious convictions."[8] Defenders of Jewish equality were enthusiastically in support of Castellan. Mirabeau argued that "unrestricted freedom of belief is... 'sacred'," while Rabaud-Saint-Etienne demanded "liberty for the nation of the Jews" and continued: "Banish forever the aristocracy of thought, the feudal system of opinion, which desires to rule others and impose compulsion upon them." Castellan's statute was passed, although there was substantial opposition to it. The law, which forms the basis of the French constitution, states: "No one shall be molested on account of his religious opinions, in so far as their outward expression does not disturb public order as established by law."[9] It would seem, then, that there was to be no problem in securing full social and political rights for Jews, but this was not the case. The battle for Jewish emancipation lasted for two more years, during which time the Jews' Christian allies would prove to be unswerving in their devotion and friendship.

One reason for the delay in securing Jewish emancipation is that the law and the lawmakers were concerned not with Jews but with religious freedom, and the "Jewish Question" per se was not very important to most members of the assembly. Moreover, many pro-Jewish deputies, especially the more moderate ones, were far more concerned with the rights of Protestants than with Jewish emancipation.[10] It should not be surprising that the French were principally concerned with the religious minority that, outside of France, encompassed a good portion of Europe. This is why, when Grégoire spoke in support of Jews, he was silenced not only by northeastern and conservative anti-Semites but also by philo-Semites.[11]

Not until December 21 of the same year (1789) did the National Assembly meet to take up the "Jewish Question." The topic of discussion was ostensibly the voting franchise. The questions to be settled concerned eligibility for full and active citizenship and the right "to elect and to be elected to administrative and municipal posts."[12] None of this hid the fact that the key issue was the political rights of French Jewry, a subject that warranted and received the full attention of the assembly. This time the situation of French Jews was at the heart of both the liberal and conservative positions. It was during a speech given that day that Clermont-Tonnerre uttered his famous remark: "Jews, as a nation, deserve nothing, but Jews, as people, deserve everything."

The debate was preceded by arguments about the meaning of the Declaration of the Rights of Man and apologies for the circumstances of French Jewry.[13] Robespierre, for example, more than once argued that the Jewish question should be based on the principles embodied in the declaration. Duport, an eminent author of the liberal constitutional parts, who would perhaps be the most important figure in securing Jewish emancipation in France, argued the same point. All of this, however, was to no avail; French Jews were denied emancipation.

Jewish emancipation in France, when it finally did come, arrived piecemeal. First, Sephardic Jews were declared free Frenchmen; then, after a twenty-month hiatus, the Ashkenazim. There was, in fact, an aborted attempt by Talleyrand to subdivide Sephardic Jewry and grant emancipation to only one part of that group. Talleyrand, a fierce defender of toleration, both religious and racial, suggested that the assembly should enfranchise the Bordeaux Jews. Those Jews were Sephardic, but were not all of the Sephardic Jews in France. It was Grégoire who protested, arguing that such a policy would divide the Jews, and it was Grégoire who secured from the assembly the enfranchisement of all the Sephardic Jews. On January 28, 1790, with the vote 373 for and 225 against, the assembly adopted the following resolution:

All Jews living in France known under the names of Portuguese, Spanish and Avignonian will continue to enjoy the rights that were accorded them until now by the royal patents. Therefore they also enjoy active civil rights if they will meet the requirements that were established by the National Assembly in this instance.[14]

There was still the issue of the Jews in the German districts, the Ashkenazim. Initially at least, the Ashkenazim had fewer supporters, but they were able to secure the services and support of Jaques Godard, an articulate and forceful ally, who pleaded their case cogently and effectively. At their behest he drew up a petition to the National Assembly arguing that the emancipation of French Jewry—all of French Jewry—was consistent with the principles of the Constituent Assembly. To deny such emancipation, Godard argued, was "cruelty."

Perhaps because of Godard's plea, the president of the General Assembly, the Abbé Mulot, was won over to the side of the French Jews. His support apparently was based on the principles of the Enlightenment: "The chasm between their religious conceptions and the truth which we as Christians profess, cannot hinder us as men from approaching each other, and even if we reproach each other with errors and complain of each other, at least we can love each other."[15] Others, too, offered their support for total emancipation of French Jewry. Abbé Bertolio, Mayor Bailly of Paris, and Cahier de Gerville, for example, argued strongly for full emancipation. These were intimations of equality, perhaps, but in fact the situation did not change. When the constitution was ratified by the king in September 1791, the Ashkenazim still had not been enfranchised.

The only benefit the constitution offered was the paragraph in the Rights of Man that protected everyone from molestation because of religion. This did not satisfy the advocates of Jewish emancipation, nor did it quiet them. As the National Assembly was about to disband, Duport had his say.

I believe that freedom does not permit any distinction in political rights on account of a man's creed. The recognition of this equality is always being postponed. Meanwhile the Turks, Moslems, and men of all sects, are permitted to enjoy political rights in France. I demand that the motion for adjournment be withdrawn, and a decree passed that the Jews in France enjoy the privileges of citizenship.[16]

The motion for adjournment was withdrawn, and Jews in France became citizens. On September 27, 1791, the National Assembly adopted Duport's proposal. On the next day, a new law was formulated that prohibited regulations specifically directed against Jews and allowed German Jews to take the oath of citizenship. For the first time since Europe became a Christian continent, the Jews within a Christian nation were fully accepted as members of that nation. And, as it turned out, that nation would, to a great degree, shape European history for the next hundred years, if only indirectly, and it would shape the development of Europe for the next twenty-five years, through its emperor, very directly indeed.

It should not be assumed that Duport's proposal was automatically passed. There were dissenters, but they were quieted by, for one, Deputy Regnault, who compared rejection of the proposal to abrogation of the constitution. Louis XVI, on November 13, 1791, signed into law the decree granting all Jews full equality in France. "They were not required to swerve one iota from their religion as the price of emancipation; all demanded of them being that they forego certain ancient privileges."[17] French Jews had officially become Jewish Frenchmen.

It is abundantly clear that it was Christians who emancipated French Jewry; the latter had little to do with it indirectly and nothing to do with it directly. The time it took for emancipation to come about, the tenacity of its opponents, and its revolutionary implementation indicate the dedication of the philo-Semitism of the Jews' Christian friends.

The emancipation of the Jews of France was important in two respects. First, France was the first nation to emancipate its Jews, establishing a precedent that was to be carried throughout western Europe (with the exception of Spain and Portugal). Second, it was the French armies that did the carrying. As the French military advanced under Napoleon, Jews in Holland, Belgium, Prussia, and Italy became free men and women. It is true that there was a reactionary response to this when France was defeated, but the reactionary backlash did not affect Jews in all of these countries. Moreover, even where there was a backlash, it was not so forceful that it could fully turn the clock back.

The struggle for Jewish emancipation must be distinguished from the increasingly accepted ideas of freedom of religion, human rights, and citizenship. These concepts quite naturally played a part in the willingness of some to accept Jews as members of the state, but the concepts did not automatically include Jews. Jews were regularly singled out for consideration, both positively and negatively, regardless of the prevalent ideologies of the time. The struggles for Jewish emancipation and citizenship revolved around the application of these concepts of freedom of religion, human rights, and citizenship specifically to Jews.

## Napoleon and European Jewry

It is probable that no historical figure is more controversial than Napoleon Bonaparte; this controversy also involves scholars of Jewish history. Thirteen years after French Jewry was emancipated, Napoleon became emperor of France. Three years later he had conquered virtually all of Europe save England. For a period of time, then, the fate of European Jewry was directly in his hands. Even after his defeat the force of Napoleon was felt throughout the Continent, a force that influenced the Jewish communities and also affected Christian attitudes towards those communities.

The position of Napoleon in relation to the Jews was complex and contradictory. Numerous scholars attack Napoleon for his actions toward Jews. These attacks in the main are based on his "infamous decrees," which dealt with the commercial activities of French Jewry and were, in many cases, not only capricious but paralyzing. One especially distasteful decree regulated the movement of Jews within France. This was particularly pernicious in that "it struck at Jewish equality before the law—in short at emancipation."[18]

At the same time, Napoleon has apologists for his policy toward Jews. Hertzberg states that French Jewry remained equal under Napoleon's rule "as a matter of course," and Cecil Roth argues that Polish Jewry was helped by Napoleon. Other scholars point out that European Jewry in general and French Jewry in particular liked, admired, and respected Napoleon,[19] and Louis R. Gottschalk remarks that Napoleon wanted to win "the support of the Jews of Europe."[20]

Even in considering the "infamous decrees," caution is advised, at least by Leo Gershoy. While granting that some have considered them "oppressive in character," he suggests that "most students of the question are of the opinion that Napoleon's solution benefited both the Jews and the state."[21] Some who attack the decrees do not deny their importance for Jews. Howard Morley Sachar notes that the decrees "probably hastened the decline of moneylending, peddling, and old-clothes dealing as major fields of Jewish enterprise; by 1810 and 1811 Jews were moving rapidly into retailing, crafts, the mechanical arts, and the professions." He adds that the "readjustment undoubtedly would have taken place without Napoleon's gratuitous and insulting discrimination."[22]

But this, surely, is conjecture. While an occupational shift might have occurred, it is impossible to state when that would have come about and how many Jews would have "readjusted." Then again, a readjustment might not have come at all; it did not happen in Russia. Another historian, Abraham Leon Sachar, in considering the effects of the decrees, suggests that the ledger is balanced: Napoleon was almost as injurious to Jews as he was beneficial to them. However, after the decrees were issued the climate became much more positive, and for the remainder of Napoleon's reign "he proved to be a magnificent Jewish benefactor."[23]

Napoleon's attitude toward French Jews can be summed up in two words: Become Frenchmen.[24] This was the reason for calling together the Paris Sanhedrin, a body of representative Jews that had last met more than two thousand years before. The group was convened in order to determine the attitude of Jews toward the new concept of the nation-state. It is probably true that, as Glazer notes, "if his [Napoleon's] assembly of Jewish leaders had been from east of the Elbe, the story would have been quite different."[25]

But the representatives were not from the east. They were western, recently emancipated Jews, and they would not jeopardize their new freedom. The members of the Sanhedrin agreed to become Frenchmen, to abandon their Jewish nationality, and to renounce independent Jewish statehood. The magnitude of this event is obvious; it was a major turning point in Jewish history. This is why, to A. L. Sachar and probably to other scholars as well, the Revolution in France and Napoleon were both responsible for allowing the Jews to become part of Europe.[26]

Those who attack Napoleon and the Sanhedrin note that Napoleon's motive was, as the Emperor tactfully phrased it, to "correct" French Jewry.[27] Nevertheless, French Jewry accepted his conditions with alacrity; moreover, there is some evidence that this famous and controversial meeting was at least in part instigated by Jews. If Napoleon's actions were in his own interests, these interests coincided with those of the Jews affected by his actions.

It is undoubtedly true that Napoleon's actions did not arise from a love of Jews, but by the same token it is not easy to decide exactly what his attitude toward Jews was. Interpretations tend to depend upon an author's personal like or dislike of the Emperor. Arguments suggesting that Napoleon was an anti-Semite as well as a philo-Semite can be cogently offered. There were instances in which he clearly showed antagonism toward Jews. Moreover, several of his edicts can be regarded as anti-Semitic. Yet there were times when he was friendly toward Jews, and he was regarded by Jews in both France and Germany with admiration, even affection. Indeed, Jewish life improved throughout Europe because of Napoleon. As his armies marched through the Continent, the ghettoes were torn down and the Jews freed and protected. German Jews still regard him as the father of their emancipation.

The major issue was not the situation of Jews in Germany, however, but the continued nationalization of Jews in France. Like Charles II of England 150 years earlier, Napoleon accepted and even strengthened the position of his nation's Jews. This was not trivial. Moreover, as judged by the responses of French Jewry, it was welcome.

It seems incautious to label Napoleon a philo-Semite; yet there can be no denying that his presence was beneficial to Jews. Even if one disregards the theory that Napoleon wished to reestablish a Jewish homeland in Palestine—which would certainly have violated his supposed goal of assimilating Jews into European, or more specifically French, society—his continuance of the emancipation of French Jewry, his spreading of the idea of Jewish emancipation, and his effecting of Jewish emancipation wherever he went must be viewed today as philo-Semitic in consequence, as it was by the Jews of the period. The "infamous decrees" were (in tone if not in effect, for there were many exceptions to their application) clearly not specifically philo-Semitic, but they cannot by this token be defined, as they have been by many, as anti-Semitic. They were basically pro-French, or more accurately pro-Napoleon. In the final analysis, nonetheless, Napoleon's acts benefited Jewry and Jews, and Napoleon knew this.

## The Dreyfus Affair

The Dreyfus case (1894-1906) ostensibly revolved around the guilt or innocence of Captain Alfred Dreyfus, a Jew, a member of the French general staff, brilliant, and falsely accused of selling military secrets to Germany. But the ostensible meaning did not hide, nor was there any attempt to hide, the other aspects of the case: the integrity of the French judicial system, national loyalty and loyalty to the army,[28] social reform and social reaction, anti-Semitism, and, to a lesser degree, philo-Semitism. The intensity of the affair within and outside of France was enormous. Families and friendships were shattered; duels were fought; and the nation was almost torn asunder by the case. *L'Affaire* was omnipresent.

The Dreyfus case broke at a peculiar time insofar as French Jewry was concerned. Among Jews a sense of security was curiously juxtaposed with increasing incidences of anti-Semitism. That period has been described as "a glorious and golden age for French Jewry," no less in the military than anywhere else; yet anti-Semitism, already becoming a "national pastime,"[29] was exacerbated by a multitude of Jewish refugees pouring into France at that time because of the Russian pogroms (over two thousand Jews were murdered in Russia from 1881 to 1914). In France at the time, anti-Semitism was tinged with xenophobia.

It was also tinged with an anticapitalistic bent. Most of the anti-Semitism in France of the 1880s was directed from the political left. More than this, Robert F. Byrnes correctly points out that "the French Socialists, who claimed to be working for a new society free from all exploitation and discrimination, contributed most to the strengthening and deepening of the anti-Semitic prejudice in France."[30] Strong public anti-Semitic statements also came from

Edouard Drumont, author of *La France Juive*, a noxious anti-Semitic work, and publisher of *La Libre Parole*, a newspaper preaching expulsion of Jews from France.[31]

French Jewry simply ignored the anti-Semitic campaign throughout the country, and as far as Dreyfus and the Affair itself, French Jewry wanted it to go away. Dreyfus's family, serving as the catalyst that brought about the inquiries that eventually resulted in Dreyfus's release, evidenced familial concern, not Jewishness. French Jews tended to ignore anti-Semitism, as they had in the past. Specifically referring to Drumont, "French Jews before the Dreyfus Affair generally showed little alarm at Drumont's campaign and were careful not to increase its fury by offering resistance."[32] The reason for this attitude was that French Jews, particularly the intellectuals, believed that anti-Semitism was alien to France. They regarded it as German and thought that the answer to the problem was assimilation.

French Jewry believed that Dreyfus was guilty. The Jews saw the affair that grew out of his case as at best a source of embarrassment and at worst a real danger to themselves.[33] An exception to this was Bernard Lazare, who was persuaded, however, to protest Dreyfus's innocence by Mathieu Dreyfus, Alfred's brother, and further was only of Jewish origin; at the time of the affair Lazare was Christian.

The obvious conclusion is that French Jews did not take part in actions designed to save Dreyfus, to see that honest judicial practice was carried out, or to negate the catastrophic effects of the affair. All of this was left entirely to Christians. Even before such actions could be taken, the issue of anti-Semitism had to be dealt with and eradicated, or at least blunted. This, too, had to be done by Christians. Nor was it an easy task. Many in France, not least the anti-Dreyfusards, were obsessed with the "Jewish Question." There can be no doubt of the connection between the cries of the anti-Semites and the Dreyfus case.

Those who supported Dreyfus, then, had to attack an increasingly virulent and vociferous anti-Semitism before that support could be effective. It was necessary for those who believed in Dreyfus's innocence to defend the integrity of French Jewry. In this sense Byrnes suggests that the Dreyfus Affair can be interpreted as "one of the glories of France."

> One only has to recall the desertion by the Liberals in Germany to Bismarck, the anti-semitic outrages in Russia in the 1880's and 1890's, which called forth significant protest only outside of Russia.... The Dreyfus Affair is a glory of France because the French made it their *affaire*. In France, from 1897 through 1900, hundreds and thousands of Frenchmen of every religion, profession, and class rose to denounce iniquity, to demand the rule of law, to defy the powerful corporate bodies, and to put their positions and even their personal safety in peril

before enraged mobs. Not only did these thousands stand up and fight, but they won.[34]

In time more and more leftists, though never all of them, and a limited number of the military joined the Dreyfusards and demanded justice.[35] There was a growing distaste for and distrust of anti-Semitism by an increasing number of people, especially, but not only, the intellectuals. Of special significance here is Émile Zola, "France's leading novelist, even then a writer of world renown, [who was] shocked by the filthy spew of anti-Semitism that accompanied Dreyfus's conviction."[36] There is no need to detail here the involvement of Zola in the affair or his magnificent essay "*J'Accuse.*"[37]

Without the efforts of Christians, Dreyfus undoubtedly would have remained imprisoned on Devil's Island. And without the help of Christians, the anti-Semitic epidemic that swept through much of France as a result of the affair, or at least in a large part because of it, would have worsened. Hannah Arendt, as usual, puts her finger on the matter: "the Jews failed to see that what was involved was an organized fight against them on a political front." One consequence of this was that they "resisted the cooperation of men who were prepared to meet the challenge on this basis."[38] It follows that those Christians who did "meet the challenge" and fought for Dreyfus and against anti-Semitism, did so alone. If philo-Semitism was not manifested there in full force, intimations of it were clearly exhibited.

### England: The Readmission

The reentry of Jews into England was unofficial yet legitimated, obvious as well as covert, and above all unique. The mechanics were simple. In 1655 Rabbi Manasseh Ben Israel, the leader of Dutch Jewry, came to England to petition Oliver Cromwell, the Lord Protector, for readmission of Jews into that country.[39] Cromwell himself endorsed the idea and proposed that "the Jews deserving it may be admitted into this nation to trade and traffic and dwell amongst us as providence shall give occasion."[40] If there is one point on which students of Jewish history are in unanimous agreement, it is that Cromwell was very sympathetic to the petition of reentry.

Despite his own enthusiasm for the readmission of Jews to England, Cromwell could not persuade the Council of State in Whitehall to support it. He was not a man to be denied, however, and subsequently arranged for a conference to be held at Whitehall on December 4, 1655, to consider the issue. When Cromwell addressed the assembly, he reduced the question of the Jews' return to England to two fundamental issues: Was the reentry of the Jews legal, and if it was, what should the conditions of reentry be?[41] Sir John Glenn, Chief Justice of the Upper Bench, and William Steele, Chief Baron of the Exchequer, represented the conference's legal opinion. One succinct sentence issued by these men was to have a profound effect on Jewish, British, indeed world history: "There was no law which forbade the Jews' return into England."[42]

It is true, as Roth notes, that from one point of view all future discussions on the readmission of Jews to England, and there were many, would be anticlimatic, since the declaration of Glenn and Steele had decided the "essential point" on that first day.[43] But this is true only within a long-term historical perspective; officially it was not the case: Jews had not been formally admitted into the country. Moreover, strong opposition to readmission was heard, most especially from merchants who did not want additional competitors. In addition, there was little applause from some members of the church. Cromwell, in fact, never defeated those who were opposed to the Jews' returning to England. Instead he ignored them and acted as though Jews had been admitted. There were no general outcries; both the populace and the government gave tacit approval to the existence of Jews on the soil of England. The people just accepted the fact that some foreigners had "formed a religious commune" in London, "although in principle the monopoly of the government church prevailed."[44]

The breaching of the fortress by Jews did not at all imply permanence, however, particularly since they had not been legitimately received. Legitimation was established, again unofficially, soon after Cromwell's death in 1658. The possibility existed then that the restored monarchy would prevent Jews from living in England. This did not happen. Quite the contrary, when Charles II, who assumed the crown in 1660, was still in Holland, he had offered his assurances to the Jews of Amsterdam that if he became king he would not only protect the Jews in England but "ameliorate the harshness" of the anti-Jewish laws then in existence.[45] It is probable that economic factors coupled with irreligiousness prompted Charles's promise, but whatever the cause, he was as good as his word, and more. During the difficult period that followed his ascension to the Crown, his position became official. He rebuked the merchants who feared competition from the Jews and wanted them barred from England: Jews in England would have royal protection as long as they obeyed the law, behaved peacefully, and did not jeopardize the government or put it in an awkward position. From that point on, the position of English Jewry was increasingly strengthened.

Despite their unofficial existence from the time of their reentry, and in England alone in western Europe, Jews "had unrestricted (or rather unchallenged) rights of settlement."[46] In 1673 Charles II granted the Jews partial naturalization or citizenship. A similar policy was followed by James II, Charles's successor. James, incidentally, was also a supporter of Catholic rights when these were challenged by the ruling Anglican church, a challenge neither he nor any English king would be forced to take up in behalf of Jews. Each succeeding king either maintained the status quo or advanced Jewish integration into England. Despite some early protests from merchants—

never from government officials or, for that matter, from the Anglican church as a body—the position of English Jews remained secure and their status on a par with that of Anglican Englishmen.

Roth argues that this "new state" of the history of Jews in England was without precedent anywhere. English Jews were given a degree of "general social equality, such as [was] then known in no other country of Europe, or indeed of the world, not excepting even Holland. For by and large, it is true to say that from the period of the Resettlement native-born Jews enjoyed the same rights, protection, and privileges as other non-Protestant Englishmen."[47] This is not to suggest that the position of English Jews was initially on a par with that of Anglican Englishmen. England was, after all, a country with an official church. Yet Jews were singled out for tolerance; the situation of other non-Anglicans, such as Catholics, was substantially worse than that of the Jews. Moreover, the social situation of English Jews was one of total emancipation from the beginning, and so was the economic situation; only minor occupational restrictions were placed on them. This shattered a thirteen-century tradition that was still in force elsewhere in Europe.

The "why" of this readmission of Jews to England is of more importance here than the mechanics of that readmission. Indeed, "readmission" may be the wrong word. The Jews, in fact, had never completely left England. From at least the time of William the Conqueror in 1066, despite the general expulsion in 1290, there was no period during which Jews were complete strangers in England.[48] Notwithstanding this, Jews were tacitly readmitted to England, and their readmission, if not officially legitimated, was surely officially sanctioned.

Roth argues that the basis of this readmission was a fundamental philo-Semitism that had three causes:

a sympathy for Hebraic idealism as expressed in the Bible, the fundamental religious document both of Christian and Jew; an intense sympathy and even shame for Jewish sufferings, both past and present; and a fervid hope for the fulfilment of the prophecy in the restoration of the Jews to Palestine, and of Palestine to the Jews.[49]

Roth's analysis of the causes of readmission is unusual in that he does not cite the usually accepted motive: economics. Other scholars, however, do not eschew economic explanations. Even those who sympathize with Roth to some degree suggest a connection between the two. Most scholars, in fact, suggest both religious philo-Semitism and economic considerations as the basis of Jews' reentry into England. H. M. Sachar succinctly states that readmission was brought about by a combination of "hard headed mercantilist reasoning and the typically Puritan brand of Old Testament sentimentality."[50]

Emphasis on the economic advantages of having Jews in England is supported by noting that the English affection and respect for Jews continued after the Glorious Revolution of 1688. At that time William of Orange "brought a number of wealthy Jews in his train, and he encouraged the arrival of more."[51] Too much should not be made of the fact that William allowed rich Jews to enter England; it is hardly surprising that he did not encourage the arrival of paupers into his realm, whether they be Jew or Christian.

Cromwell, too, was concerned, at least partially, with the economic advantages of welcoming Jews. A. L. Sachar comments that Cromwell "required no persuasion to convince him of the commercial usefulness of the Jews." This suggests that economic considerations might have been, if not the sole basis, then at least a factor in Cromwell's fight for the readmission of Jews. Even Roth accepts, somewhat reluctantly, this possibility.[52]

Yet Roth argues elsewhere that it was the fundamental philo-Semitism of Cromwell that encouraged him to support the reentry of Jews. Indeed, this "unaffected pro-Semitism" was more important for reestablishing Jews in England than mercantilism. Nor was this attitude confined to Cromwell; it was manifest throughout English society and in fact had preceded the Jews to England.[53]

English philo-Semitism was based in part on religion and in part on a growing nationalistic liberalism. Indeed, these were intertwined. There was a sympathy for Jews based on Puritanism, in conjunction with which the newly conceived concept of nationalism was becoming manifest in England. In fact, England regarded itself as the new Israel—which helps to explain why England's American colonies felt the same way. The new nationalism, influenced undoubtedly by the innovative thinkers of the time, tended to be both liberal and universal in outlook. Thus England, even if it did not immediately grant a substantial degree of liberty to everyone, gave support to the idea of liberty as well as to the idea of equality of all individuals. The catalyst for this was the civil war in the seventeenth century. During that war nationalism first came to the fore, and not only was religion freed from the restrictions of national boundaries, but it was separated from politics as well.[54]

In addition to the liberal nationalism that ripened in the seventeenth century, Judaism became increasingly important to numerous people, Cromwell among them. They were deeply moved and inspired by the Old Testament. More than this, "the whole thought and style of the period was deeply colored with Hebraism." In England this religious philo-Semitism dates from the Reformation, when there developed an intense interest in studying the Bible. The religion of the Jews became fundamental to Puritanism. Hebrew phrases increasingly appeared in English speech, Hebrew ideals in English thought, and, amazingly perhaps, Hebrew history in English politics. The Puritans regarded themselves as Israelites.[55] So potent was this Hebraism that a number of Christians at the start of the seventeenth century, prior to the reentry of Jews, carried matters to an extreme. Several converted to

Judaism and went so far as to have themselves circumcised. Others vociferously demanded that the Jews be readmitted.

To a large degree, then, English Puritanism saw itself as an extension of the parent religion. There was, as Max Weber notes, a strong relationship between Puritan morality and Talmudic Judaism.[56] Not surprisingly, then, Puritans agreed to the validity of Mosaic Law. It is likely that this is why philo-Semitism was so prominent in England, more so, for example, than in other Protestant countries, for much more than Lutheranism, "Calvinistic doctrine was characterized by a marked benevolence toward [Jews]."[57]

The Puritans also endorsed the arrival of Jews in England for another religious reason: Biblical prophecy. According to the New Testament the second coming of Christ could occur if, and only if, Jews were scattered throughout the world. They were not yet officially resident in England. A good deal of the support for readmission of the Jews came from those who anticipated the second coming of Christ. A. L. Sachar suggests that Cromwell, too, was influenced by this.[58]

But it must be clearly understood that support for the return of Jews to England came from other than social deviants (the eccentric fringe) or even from the religiously inspired masses. Sanction for the return originated within "the palladium of English common sense and balance—the judicial bench." This, while "more restrained" than the religiously based support, was more effective.[59]

Roth suggests that the English, and the English alone, felt some degree of contrition for the persecution of the Jews during the Middle Ages. As a consequence, some people perceived the readmission of Jews to England as both a justifiable "act of repentance" and as "moral compensation" for the sins of the past.[60] This is probable, but it should also be recognized that the growth of a multitude of religious sects in England facilitated the reentry of Jews. Each sect in its struggle for recognition contributed to the acceptance of numerous and sometimes disparate religions. In fact, this concept was put to a pragmatic test "in the winter of 1648-9 in a remarkable attempt to establish in England a 'universal' religious toleration for all—'not excepting Turkes, nor Papists, nor Jewes.'"[61] The "Jewes," in fact, had their own special supporters. A small group, mostly Baptists, argued specifically for them.

The reasons for readmission of Jews to England are intricate, interwoven, and complex. Explanation by a monocausal theory, such as economic considerations, must be suspect. Beneath all possible causes for the readmission of Jews to England lay barely concealed philo-Semitism in a number of forms.

## The Political Emancipation of English Jewry

The emancipation of English Jewry was unique in several ways. Its most irregular feature was the absence of the lengthy struggle that occurred in most other European nations; yet this is not to suggest that there was not a fierce battle for Jewish political freedom in England or for their right to be admitted into Parliament. It is true that, virtually from the moment of their readmission, Jews in England were granted full, unswerving social emancipation,[62] but it is also true, as Roth suggests, and as events in Anglo-Jewish history demonstrated, that social emancipation is not political emancipation. The latter had to be fought for.

A second aspect of the emancipation of English Jewry was that the barriers were exclusively religious, rather than racial, ethnic, or based on a misguided sense of nationalism, as they tended to be on the Continent. The prohibitions against Jews entering Parliament as members did not apply to Jews as a race. A Jewish M.P., however, would have to take an oath to be seated, and the oath stated that the Member of Parliament swears to uphold the laws "upon the true faith of a Christian."[63] The struggle for admission of Jews to Parliament involved changing the wording of that oath.

This was not easily accomplished. Most conservatives, almost all of them Tories, saw themselves as protectors of the Church of England. They felt duty bound to deny admission to Members of Parliament who would reject Christ's divinity since they would be empowered to legislate on the organization and, worse, the doctrine of that church.[64] The supporters of admission of Jews to Parliament felt no such obligation. This, in broad terms, was the situation when, in 1828, the "Jewish Question" was initially considered by the British parliament. The first of a long series of debates on the question began when Lord Golland argued that the oath was unacceptable to Jews and that they should be allowed to take another one. He was told that the Chamber of Parliament would not alter the status of the Jews. Thirty years later it would.

In retrospect, given the generally happy situation of English Jews, it seems odd that they should have suffered political exclusion. One explanation offered by Roth is that acceptance of Jews in virtually every other area of English life made the final step seem relatively trivial. This is especially true when the situation of the Jews in England is compared with the situation of Jews throughout most of the rest of Europe, where Jewish equality—where there was Jewish equality—was usually a constitutional issue. Precisely because Jews in England suffered few disabilities, their political disadvantages were regarded as almost inconsequential.[65]

There is considerable reason to endorse this view. Despite the refusal of Parliament to seat a Jew, several Jews advanced politically during the nineteenth century. In fact, throughout the difficulties that ensued, Jews were elected to Parliament with some consistency (but were not seated).

Consider the political progress of English Jewry during the time Parliament was closed to them. In 1837 Queen Victoria knighted Moses Montefiore, the first Jew since Solomon de Medina to be so honored. In that same year Jews were admitted to the University of London.[66] In 1841 E. Emanuel was elected City Councillor in Portsmouth; as early as 1838 Abraham Abrahams was elected to the same position in Southampton. In 1839 David Barnett was elected to the Council of Birmingham. A Jew was elected Mayor of Rochester in 1857; David Salomons was elected Lord Mayor of London in 1855. There had been a Jewish sheriff of the city of London as early as 1837, and a Jewish alderman in 1847. Moreover, Jews had been elected (returned) to Parliament by various constituencies throughout the fight for political emancipation. David Salomons, the future Lord Mayor of London, was so elected in 1851. Finally, it is curious, as Roth suggests, that, exclusion from Parliament notwithstanding, Jews "were permitted to act on behalf of the government abroad: John Jacob Hart was Consul-General in Saxony c. 1836-42."[67] All this occurred at a time when Jews could not legally enter public life.

The Test and Corporation Acts, enacted at a time when Jews could not conceivably take part in these activities, excluded them from participation in civic government, the judiciary, and education.[68] The reason was that full rights, including of course political ones, were allowed only to those who belonged to the Anglican Church. Initially there was a firm adherence to this policy of exclusion. Eventually, however, and with the significant help of Anglicans, other religious groups were recognized by and accepted into the English government. In 1829, when the Emancipation Acts placed Catholics on a par with Anglicans, serious religious discrimination existed against only one minority in England: the Jews.

There are two aspects to the political emancipation of English Jewry insofar as philo-Semitism is concerned. The first, and technically most significant, was the struggle of the friends of the Jews within Parliament to secure a change in the oath so that Jews could be seated. But it must also be recognized that Jews were elected to their posts by non-Jews. Those districts that elected and reelected Jews to Parliament did so with the full knowledge that until the rules were amended they would not be represented. Without the support of these people, the question of seating a Jewish M.P. would have been merely an academic exercise. It was specifically because people in these districts did support Jewish candidates that the question became both significant and immediate. Jews in England, at least insofar as political emancipation is concerned, could not have achieved their position without the support of what is usually termed "the common man."

Today there are more than five times as many Jewish M.P.s as their proportion of the population would suggest. If Jews are not chosen for or despite their Jewishness, they surely are not rejected because of it. This might be contrasted with the situation in Poland in 1912, when Jews, by virtue of their numbers, could have elected a coreligionist to the Duma but did not do so for fear of offending the Poles. The situation in England is all the more significant because Jews there have never been particularly influential in terms of either wealth or voting power; the "Jewish vote" as such does not exist there.

As early as 1820, John Hobhouse (later Lord Broughton de Gyfford) introduced a resolution in the House of Commons that would place English

Jews on a par with Anglicans. To all intents and purposes, however, this was an academic exercise. More potent was the repeal of the Test and Corporation Acts in 1828, which if its original idea had been carried through, would have eliminated political discrimination against Jews. It was already implied that the struggle for political emancipation of Roman Catholics would lead to a similar change in the status of Jews. Thus the English government, or at least specific members of the government, was ready to reconsider the political status of English Jewry. Beginning in 1830, serious attempts to attain political emancipation for Jews began. Several emancipation bills in varying forms and designations aimed at admitting Jews into Parliament were passed by the House of Commons in 1833, 1834, and 1836 but were consistently rejected in the House of Lords.[69]

The first bill specifically aimed at securing Jewish political emancipation was introduced into the House of Commons on April 5, 1830, by Sir Robert Grant. This bill would have given Jews all of the rights that had been given Catholics in 1829. A second petition came from the renowned socialist and philanthropist, Robert Owen. In 1833, when the Reformed Parliament met, Grant, on April 17, once more requested that the House form a committee to consider the political status of English Jewry. He reintroduced this bill again in 1834. It passed in the House of Commons and was rejected in the House of Lords.

The supporters of Jewish emancipation were, among others, Grant, Hume, Daniel O'Connell, Thomas Babington Macaulay, Lord John Russell, and Lord Henry Peter Brougham. Robert Peel, the head of the House of Commons, opposed the measure. When the first bill was introduced in 1830, and although praising the character of Jews—their behavior, he remarked, is "beyond reproach"—Peel felt duty bound to ensure that the Christian principles of the English constitution remained intact. For this reason English Jewry would continue to be denied full participation in the political sector.

This reasoning, however, was not accepted without a fight. Brougham, among others, attacked Peel's "hypocrisy," and at least on one point he was correct: "Let a Jew come here and take the oath—which now excludes him from the Chamber—and he would be welcomed with open arms by the same assembly of Christians which today applauded so ardently the wildest anti-Christian principles and feelings that were ever uttered in a civilized country."[70] This logic did not persuade the members, however; on May 17, 1830, a majority of the House of Commons opposed the bill, 228 to 165.

The second bill, introduced in 1833 by Robert Grant, the unflagging champion of Jewish rights, passed in the House of Commons but failed to pass in the House of Lords.[71] The same thing happened in 1834. In this instance some twenty-four thousand signed the petitions of Christian merchants of London and over six thousand signed the petitions of Christian merchants of Edinburgh, endorsing political emancipation of English Jewry.

Up to this time no Jew had successfully run for election to Parliament. In 1847, however, Lionel de Rothschild ran for office and, after a lively political contest, was elected a representative of the city of London. A touch of drama was in the offing, for Rothschild went to the House of Commons to be sworn in. However, religious convictions prevented him from taking the oath, and the House of Commons decided to consider his case and requested that he leave while it did so. A struggle had begun that would last a full eleven years.

Shortly after Rothschild left, at the direction of John Russell, the Prime Minister, the House formed a committee to examine the political situation of English Jewry and to discuss the means of removing any disabilities that they suffered. The bill that came out of the committee, the Jewish Disabilities Bill, was introduced early in 1848. The bill placed Jews in the same position as Roman Catholics. Unlike the bills of the 1830s, however, this one dealt with admission to Parliament and little more. Roth suggests that it was because of the small amount of change involved that the opposition was intransigent. That is possible; what is sure is that the debates concerning the bill "were remarkable in the annals of parliamentary eloquence."[72] Russell once again voiced his support for Jewish emancipation, reasoning that each Englishman deserves the full benefits of the British Constitution. Moreover, English Jewry had now found new friends in Peel and William Ewart Gladstone, both of whom had earlier opposed Jewish emancipation.[73] The bill passed in the House of Commons but failed in the House of Lords. In 1849 a somewhat modified Parliamentary Oaths Bill fared similarly. During this period Rothschild ran for reelection and won.

In 1851 a new bill, the Oath and Abjuration Bill, was introduced with the same results. While Parliament was considering this bill, a second Jew, Salomons, had been elected to the Commons. Salomons was not Rothschild:

> The action of the Lords convinced him that the constitutional method hitherto followed could lead to no useful result, and that a different policy was required to force the problem on public attention. Accordingly, the day after the rejection of the Bill, he attended at the Table of the House of Commons and asked to be sworn. Instead of giving up the battle when he arrived at the Oath of Abjuration, as Rothschild had done, he recited it without the words to which he objected, and then took his seat on one of the ministerial benches, ignoring an order to withdraw.[74]

He was (peacefully) removed from Parliament by the sergeant-at-arms and fined.

Attempts at securing admission of Jews to Parliament continued in 1853 under Russell's leadership. The new Jewish Disabilities Bill was passed in the

House of Commons and defeated in the House of Lords. A second attempt based on a new Parliamentary Oaths Bill, which merely removed the words "on the true faith of a Christian," suffered the same fate. In 1858 Milner Gibson introduced a bill that simply eliminated the Oath of Abjuration itself. Viscount Palmerston's government supported it. This bill also passed through the House of Commons but failed in the House of Lords. It should be mentioned here that in 1857, for the fourth time, Rothschild was reelected. For ten years his constituents in London deliberately endured partial disenfranchisement.

Finally, in 1858, a compromise was reached. Lord Lucan, an opponent of the earlier bills, suggested that Commons and Lords determine for themselves the oath each would use to admit a Jew to their respective Houses. One week later a bill following Lucan's recommendation was introduced; the bill passed. On July 26, 1858, eleven years after his first election, Baron de Rothschild was finally seated in the House of Commons.

Final and true emancipation of English Jewry came eight years later in 1866 when the Parliamentary Oaths Act was adopted. This act, in addition to simplifying the oath for both houses, omitted the phrase that had delayed the emancipation of English Jewry for so long. All remaining disabilities were erased in 1871 with the passage of the Promissory Oaths Act.[75]

A somewhat absurd although not altogether unfitting footnote to all of this is mentioned by Roth: "Notwithstanding all of his [Baron Lionel de Rothschild's] efforts to enter the House, he is not once recorded to have opened his mouth in debate during all of the years he sat there."[76]

Throughout all this, no Jew pleaded the case for Jews before Parliament because no Jew was an M.P. The support of the right of English Jewry to be full Englishmen came, as did the support of French Jewry to be full Frenchmen, from Christians. In 1871 Sir George Jessel became the first Jew to become a Minister of the Crown when he was appointed Solicitor-General; in this year Jews were also admitted to the degree in both Oxford and Cambridge. More than this, "Since 1871 professing Jews have served as Judges (1873), Privy Councillor (1873), Colonial Governor (1900), Cabinet Minister (1909), Lord Chief Justice (1913), Secretary of State (1916), Ambassador (1918), and Viceroy of India (1920)."[77] But these successes were anticlimatic. English Jewry had achieved its place in English society in 1858.

Analysts have persuasively argued that in England social acceptance of the Jews was a significant factor in their emancipation. Roth, for example, in noting the social mixing of influential Jews with equally or more influential Christians, comments that "this could not fail to have a profound influence in completing the social emancipation which was the necessary prelude to the removal of political disabilities."[78] This is undoubtedly true, but it is not indicative of anything more than the degree of friendship offered Jews by

Christians. That English philo-Semites could be and were so outspoken suggests not only the significance of philo-Semitism for the political and social emancipation of English Jewry, but also the significance of philo-Semitism in itself.

## EMANCIPATION THROUGHOUT EUROPE

### The Aftermath of the French Revolution

When monarchs fight monarchs during an era of revolution, they cannot be too harsh in victory because they have more in common with one another than with their subjects. No monarch can afford to support a revolution in another country, lest it suggest to his own subjects that revolution is feasible and support is available. By the same token, if a revolution is aborted, it is in the interest of other monarchs to support reinstatement of the king. Thus the participants in the Congress of Vienna, which followed the Napoleonic Wars and was charged with resettling Europe, wanted only to return that Continent to the pre-French Revolutionary status quo. The Congress of Vienna was, in fact, completely reactionary.

However, the French Revolution had unalterably affected Europe. The spokesmen for the ideals of the French Revolution had become a force that would not be silenced. The policies established by the French during the revolution and those that were continued by Napoleon set the tone for the way in which nations would analyze the "Jewish Question" thereafter, no matter how much of an attempt was made to stifle them. Despite the reactionary ideology of the Congress of Vienna, the coming decades would witness the emancipation of Jews in more and more European nations.

It is true that the Congress of Vienna aborted most of the gains made by the Jews in Europe (although not in France); but it is equally true that the members of that congress were not particularly anti-Semitic—they simply did not think their main charge was to settle the "Jewish Question." Pragmatic men, Prince von Metternich and his colleagues worked to restore the world as they had known it before the French Revolution; nevertheless, it was at the Congress of Vienna that the "Jewish Question" was first regarded as a topic of significance for European politics in general. The Revolution was a fact, and it was also a fact that the time had come for a reevaluation of the position of Jews in Europe; another fact was that the position of the Jews had changed. Katz is correct in his assessment: anti-Semitic arguments could not eradicate Emancipation in those nations in which it had become a reality, nor halt the coming Emancipation in those nations in which the movement toward that goal had begun.[79]

By 1819, four years after the Congress of Vienna, some important changes were already becoming manifest. The universal restrictions placed on Jews were gone, and opportunities that had previously been denied them appeared, although some of their rights were still qualified.

The spirit of the French Revolution/Enlightenment, that is, the spirit of freedom and fraternity, increasingly pervaded Europe; the ideas debated in France took root in other nations, to the benefit of virtually every group, save perhaps the aristocracy. It is unlikely, however, that any other group bene-fited as much as the Jews. As the ideals of the Revolution were recognized— and they were, despite the efforts of some who sat in the Congress of Vienna—the Jews of the nations of Europe achieved their freedom. Changing moralities helped to tear down the ghettoes of Europe, and Jews began to attain full citizenship because of the social changes of the times and, more potently, because they had the help of Christian spokesmen.

Indeed, this was predictable from actions at the Congress of Vienna itself, where men such as Karl Hardenberg, the Prussian Chancellor, and Wilhelm von Humbolt, the Prussian Education Minister, spoke in favor of Jewish emancipation. With the backing of Metternich, an article favorable to Jews was secured in the constitution of the Germanic Confederation.[80] Through-out Europe, Jews began to receive Christian support for, and consequently admission to, full citizenship in society.

### The Continuing Emancipation

It is unnecessary to detail the process of the emancipation of Jews in every European country or to cite all of the Jews' Christian supporters, but it is reasonable to outline that process. To repeat the central point: in every country where emancipation was achieved, the Jews necessarily had their champions. If those champions' arguments varied somewhat, their tenacity and ideals were unfailing.

In the Dutch National Assembly, Jacob George Hieronymus Hahn argued from a humanistic position for the equality of Jews: "Who will contest that the Jews are human beings and that they and the non-Jews are brethren in nature in the full sense of the word." He added to this a standard argument based on national expediency: allow Dutch Jews to become Jewish Dutchmen. "Make [the Jews] happy by the elevation to full dignity of man and citizens and to arouse in the heart of the Dutch Jews a genuine national enthusiasm."[81]

Hahn and the other supporters of Dutch Jewry were eminently successful. After the fall of Napoleon, the Netherlands alone continued the Jewish emancipation imposed by the French. Well before that point, in fact, Jews had achieved positions of prominence in the Batavian Republic, where as early as 1798 Jews had been appointed and elected to important government posts. When the Netherlands was divided into Holland and Belgium in 1830, the rights of Dutch Jewry were not interrupted, and Belgium maintained its policy of toleration.

In Italy emancipation came with the Risorgimento. In 1848 the condition of Jews there was worse than in any other European country; by 1860 it was better than in any other European country—and stayed that way. The emancipation of Italian Jewry, as Frederick M. Schweitzer notes, was real.[82] This was especially due to the efforts of Camillo Bensodi Cavour, who was explicit and unyielding in his demands for Jewish emancipation and whose pro-Jewish views were supported by the Italian people.

In Scandinavia the stages of emancipation varied. The small Jewish community in Denmark had enjoyed a considerable degree of freedom well before the general movement of Jewish emancipation began throughout the Continent. As early as 1814, Kind Frederick VI had granted Jews the right of residence in Denmark under the usual condition that they, in effect, become Danes; they agreed to do so. Full emancipation came in 1849. In Sweden and Norway, despite supporters such as King Charles XIV of Sweden and Henrik Arnold Wergeland, the Norwegian poet and member of Parliament, the progress of the Jews was slow and painful. It was not until 1870 that Jews in Sweden were permitted to hold office (a restriction that had applied to Catholics as well). Jews in Norway did not become full citizens until the twentieth century. However, social emancipation, the right to live and work, had come much earlier in Sweden and Norway (in 1853 and 1855, respectively).

Of special interest was the situation in Bulgaria. That country was under the influence of Russian anti-Semitism. The granting of equal civil rights to Jews in Bulgaria came as a result of Bulgaria's acceptance of the resolution of the Congress of Berlin (in 1878). Bulgaria (and several other Balkan states) were offered autonomy if they agreed to conditions imposed by the Congress, among which was emancipation of Bulgarian Jewry. Despite the fact that Jewish emancipation in Bulgaria was externally decided, that emancipation saw the election of several Jews to political office, indicating that the citizenry of that nation not only tolerated but accepted Jews.

Contrast this with the situation in Switzerland. When a referendum was introduced (in 1862) concerning emancipation of the Jews in the canton of Aargau, and when a law affirming that had already been passed, the general vote was against the law. As a result, Jewish emancipation in Switzerland was abolished in June 1863.

Emancipation of German Jewry had long been debated. Although in fact the "Jewish Question" had been at issue since 1786, when Frederick II died, the first major battle was fought in the post-Napoleonic era, primarily by representatives of the three progressive communities in Prussia: Berlin, Königsberg, and Breslau.

The initial phase of the struggle (1808-1812) was fought by men like Brand, an official from Königsberg, who had a long record of supporting equal rights for Jews; Wilhelm von Humboldt, a supporter of the liberal tradition in Europe who was then director of the Ministerium of Education in Prussia; and Hardenberg, who in 1810 had become chancellor of Prussia.

In 1812 Prussia granted Jews partial emancipation, and the decree of 1812 gave impetus to a new outlook: each state was willing to tolerate Jews who had lived in it prior to or at the time of the revolution or reform. More significantly, Jews were now legitimately (that is, legally) recognized as a part of the nation. Some still thought the Jews were in need of change, but they were no longer a foreign element subject to capricious ejection.[83] Other German states followed along similar lines; for example, in Mecklenburg Jews were granted equal social (but not political) rights in 1813. This, in large measure, was brought about by the efforts of Tychsen, a professor at the University of Rostock.

Similarly, Baden accepted the hereditary citizenship of Jews if they were gainfully employed. A trend was developing throughout Germany, but it was not to last. In 1815 the emancipation edicts were rescinded, and the struggle for emancipation had to begin again. Progress was slower this time, but it was also surer. Total civic equality was granted the Jews in Kassel in 1833 and in Brunswick in 1834, and limited equality was granted to Jews in Prussia in 1847. The granting of limited equality in Prussia was partly brought about by requests from both Jews and Christians. Similar resolutions were passed in Silesia and Poznan.

Other battles for Jewish emancipation occurred throughout the German states. The supporters of emancipation initially concentrated on the legislatures in the independent areas, the *landtags* and senates. As early as 1824 and 1828, respectively, the legal status of Jews in Frankfurt and the county of Württemberg improved substantially. In Bavaria, where an exceptional struggle was taking place, one speaker after the other supported equal rights for Jews. One deputy, Kulman, demanded that the constitution be made "lawful." The Bavarian Landtag passed the emancipation resolution of Dr. Lang in 1831.[84] At the same time, in Cologne, the burghers sent a petition to the Landtag requesting that it speak out against "the oppression of Jews." It also requested that the Landtag intercede "with the king to grant equal political and civil rights to Jews."[85] This, of course, represents a marked change from the former attitude of the Jews' competitors.

Throughout Germany a shift in public opinion in favor of emancipation was discernible between 1843 and 1847. It was not until 1848-49, however, that an all-German assembly in Frankfurt approved the principle of equality for Jews, a principle that became a basic constitutional right. It is important to note that Jews were members of that assembly, and that, further, Gabriel Riesser, a Jew, acted as vice-president. Full emancipation in Germany came in 1871, when the German Imperial Constitution abolished all restrictions based on religious convictions. Even before this, however, full and final emancipation had been granted to Jews in Baden (1862) and Saxony (1868).

The reason for the emancipation of German Jewry was a complex mixture of nationalism, which at the time was inseparable from liberalism; nationalistic philo-Semitism; and humanism. The issue of expulsion did not arise; it was accepted that a number of Jews had been granted the right of presence. The problem was how to go on with that presence, since a nationalistic ideology precluded the existence of an alien state within the state.[86]

The only viable alternative at the time seemed to be to make German Jews into Jewish Germans. This is nowhere stated more clearly than in the words of Hardenberg: "I will not vote for any law pertaining to Jews, that will not include these four words: 'equal rights, equal responsibilities.' "[87] Jews would be full members of the state with full obligations to, and full privileges from, the nation.

Yet in addition to those who gave this nationalistic reason for acceptance of Jews, liberal and humanistic voices were heard that preached that same acceptance. These rejected the separateness of Jews, not for nationalistic motives, but for reasons of humanity. Consider, for example, the argument of Christian Wilhelm von Dohm: "These principles of exclusion, equally opposed to humanity and politics, which bear the impress of the dark centuries, are unworthy of the enlightenment of our times, and deserve no longer to be followed."[88] It was, then, a combination of nationalism and humanism that brought about the emancipation of German Jewry.

Unlike Jews in most central European countries, by the nineteenth century the Jews of Hungary were not ghettoized; it is not surprising, then, that Jews and Christians in Hungary supported Jewish rights and had done so for some time. Pressure to secure these rights increased after a liberation movement in 1830, the movement that led to the 1848 revolution. This revolution failed, however, when in 1849 Russia accepted the surrender of the Magyars and gave Austria the chance to crush the Hungarians. The aborted revolution was as unfortunate for Hungarian Jews as it was for Christian Hungarians. Louis Kossuth's revolutionary government had granted emancipation to Hungarian Jewry, and when the revolt was crushed and the struggles in other areas of Austria faded, the movement toward full emancipation was halted. Yet full restrictive policies did not return, so that to some degree Hapsburg Jews benefited.

Emperor Franz Joseph of Austria ruled Bohemia, Moravia, Slovakia, Hungary, and Galicia. In 1867 he issued a new constitution granting citizenship to all people who were subjects of the Hapsburg Empire. The constitution also guaranteed that Christians, Jews, and Moslems would be equal before the law. Half a million Hapsburg Jews were thus emancipated, and an autonomous Hungary now had to consider the situation of the Jews within its borders. When it did, Jews found a powerful ally in Francis Deak, the creator of the Hungarian constitution. In the Diet, Deak argued in favor of equal rights for Jews. He reasoned that Hungary must attract Jews and that to do so it must grant Jews the same rights they had in other European states. His arguments were clearly persuasive. Both chambers of the Diet voted to include in the Hungarian code of laws a statute granting Jews equal rights. It was not, however, until the 1890s that the Hungarian government, through the efforts of numerous Christians, in effect legalized Judaism. The government of Wekerle submitted a bill to the Parliament in 1893 that guaranteed Jews the rights already enjoyed by members of the Catholic, Lutheran, and Greek Orthodox faiths. The bill passed.

Part of the continuous support for Jewish emancipation in Hungary was based on political expediency. The reactionary Hungarian nobility was anti-Semitic, making liberals and Jews natural allies. In the late nineteenth century, governments in Hungary were generally liberal. Deak, Kalman Tisza (Prime Minister from 1875 to 1890), and others, although not particularly sympathetic to other minorities, were willing to defend Hungarian Jewry, partly on this basis.

More than this, however, many Hungarians felt that the Jews had earned emancipation. For example, in arguing in favor of emancipation, Moritz Jokai, an author, pointed out that in the battle for Hungarian independence in 1848, he had fought side by side with Hungarian Jews loyal to the nation. And it should be recalled that the short-lived liberal ideologies in Eastern Europe during the late nineteenth century were coupled with ideologies of toleration and humanism. While political expediency and the contributions of Hungarian Jewry to Hungarian independence were significant factors in bringing about Jewish emancipation, the then-prevalent liberal ideology was of considerable importance as well. Even in Poland, for similar reasons the short-lived revolutionary government of the 1860s granted full rights to Jews.

Only in the east, in Russia, was the situation of the Jews as difficult as ever. So disjointed was the czar, Nicholas I, concerning Jews that fully 600 legal enactments dealing with Jews were issued during his thirty-year reign (1825-1855). The overall purpose was to Russify the Jews living within the Pale, but "Russify" meant "destroy as Jews." Thus the enactments covered a variety of areas: extension of the length of conscription of Jewish youth to twenty-five years, banishment of Jews from villages near the western border, censorship of Hebrew books, forbidding of construction of synagogues near churches, special taxations, and reduction of the size of the Pale, among others.

The motivation for all this was to destroy the spirit of Russian Jewry—to force the Jews to assimilate or migrate. In this the enactments were partially successful. The full force of Russia's pernicious actions would be felt in the form of the pogroms of the late nineteenth and early twentieth centuries.

These would result in mass migration of Jews to the west and especially to the United States.

## INTERNATIONAL PHILO-SEMITISM

It is possible that the greatest demonstration of the ideals of the French Revolution, the Enlightenment (and not, incidentally, the changing sociopolitical structure of Europe), was the development of international actions aimed at protecting Jews in areas where they had no protection.

The nineteenth century saw the culmination of the rise of the nation-state; feelings of national unity and international rivalry became increasingly apparent. After the French Revolution, philo-Semitism became increasingly international, political, and worldwide in its scope. Indications of international philo-Semitism came even earlier. In 1745 Empress Maria Theresa, the mother of the Hapsburg Emperor, expelled the Jews of Bohemia. This led to a multitude of protests from various nations, especially England and Holland. Within one year the edict was rescinded. Such actions became increasingly manifest in the nineteenth century. Until 1824 Austria, Prussia, England, and—amazingly—Russia did not stand idly by when Jews in some German states were being persecuted, but protested and occasionally intervened in behalf of the Jews. The security of the Jews of Belgium was protected, probably unnecessarily, by an international guarantee when that nation was formed.

The basis of all of this was pressure born of liberal, humanistic, and religious philo-Semitism. There were also pressures from Jewish groups in the various countries, although these groups did not have overwhelming influence. Moreover, the governments of the countries that did aid Jews in foreign lands were, in the main, receptive to those pressures. Thus, for example, Roth, in speaking specifically of the attitudes of the English, comments that "although the British government seldom acted consistently on the principles of 1745, it never quite forgot them. Its abhorrence of Jewish persecution was never concealed, and sometimes vigorously expressed."[89] In the nineteenth century, then, the problems of Jews in any European nation became the concern of many Christians in other nations.

Among the most famous examples of nineteenth-century Jewish persecution was the Damascus Affair of 1840 in Syria, in which Jews were falsely accused of murdering a friar. Over one hundred people were imprisoned, and doubtless the situation would have worsened had not the American, British, and Austrian governments interceded to prevent the continuance of the cruel charade.[90] Even Metternich spoke out on the Jews' behalf in this affair. An interdenominational meeting was held in London at the Mansion House to protest the Damascus Blood Accusation. A similar London meeting was held forty-two years later, in 1882, to protest the persecution of Jews in Russia. The latter meeting was endorsed and supported by such luminaries as the Archbishop of Canterbury, Cardinal Henry Edward Manning, and Charles Darwin, as well as eighteen members of Parliament.

The reasons for these actions by the English were, to some extent, based upon religious philo-Semitism, that is, on a feeling of kinship with the people of the Old Testament. In the main, however, the cause was humanistic philo-Semitism. This was the basis of the protests throughout Europe, but nowhere so much as in England. For instance, "the Chairman, Thompson," began a London meeting held to consider the problem with these words:

> The Jews of Damascus are as worthy of respect as those who dwell among us in England. And of those I permit myself to say that none of our fellow-citizens are more zealous in the spread of humanity, in aiding the poor and oppressed, in protecting the orphan and in promoting literature and knowledge than they are, and that their benevolence is not only extended to the people who belong to their own religion, but also to Christians, equally with members of every creed.

Another man suggested that

> In the past times they were men who led the way in educating the human race, and granted to others that very civil and religious freedom which at the present time they demand for themselves. This nation has been given the best proof of the value it sets upon freedom, seeing that by its own example it has shown how greatly it was actuated by this principle in its conduct towards others without distinction of creed: it therefore has a claim to the highest tolerance.[91]

An indication of the British position on world Jewry may be seen in a dispatch sent to Bucharest in 1867: "The peculiar position of the Jews places them under the protection of the civilized world."[92] For reasons of humanity, England and others accepted this responsibility. Indeed, Roth notes that, from the time of the Damascus Affair, the British government "except when urgent political considerations made action inadvisable . . . could generally be relied upon for diplomatic support if conditions for Jews abroad became intolerable," a position Roth terms, with reason, philo-Semitic.[93] This attitude was shared for similar reasons by other nations, especially those nations in which the way had been paved for continental Jewish emancipation. When Isaac Crémieux appealed to King Louis Philippe of France regarding the Damascus Affair, Louis responded: "I do not know anything about the occurrence; but if anywhere there are unfortunate Jews who appeal to the protection of my government, and if anything can be effected by its means, I will conform with your wishes."[94]

Until international pressure by the United States, France, and England forced the issue, the Swiss government held firmly to a policy of not admitting any Jews to certain cantons. It was only in 1866, after considerable pressure from other nations, that all of the cantons admitted Jews. Some eight years later a proclamation of full religious liberty for all Swiss citizens was announced. Before most of the nations that brought pressure to bear on Switzerland had stepped into the situation concerning Swiss Jewry, France had its say, severing the treaty it had signed with the canton in Basel in 1835 on the grounds that Basel refused admission to French Jews. Similarly, in 1863 Holland declined to enter into a trade agreement with the Swiss because Dutch Jews were denied the right to live and trade in Switzerland.

The basis of these protests was a combination of philo-Semitism, nationalism, and national self-interest. The Jews of France, Holland, and England were, respectively, French, Dutch, and English. Refusal to admit Jewish agents, representatives, or businessmen into Switzerland was insulting to the homelands of those Jews. Moreover, and in England, Holland, and France especially, certain Jews were influential and could pressure their governments to protest the situation in Switzerland. Finally, as suggested, humanistic concerns were not absent.

Switzerland was subjected to similar internal pressures. For instance, when the issue of Jewish emancipation was first being discussed, Keller, a liberal deputy, responded to an anti-Semitic petition with these words: "The petition complains that Jews do not pray together with us. Yes, my sires—but we pray together with them: after all, we chant their magnificent Psalms in the church, in school and at home."[95]

Switzerland had to concede, however reluctantly. And as Dubs, the president of the Swiss Confederation, argued, it was not economic sanctions alone that caused the decision. "We have to admit, with a sense of shame, that on the Jewish question we stand alone, isolated—or rather we are in a company that is even worse than isolation [a reference to Russia]. We have become the laughingstock of European society, and we are no longer respected."[96]

These were not the only instances in which governments reached out to protect the rights of Jews in other nations. There were similar occurrences in Tangiers in 1863, in Russia during the pogroms of 1881 and 1903, in Romania in 1920, and of course during the 1930s and 1940s in Germany and during the resurrection of the State of Israel in 1948.[97] The "Jewish Question" had become one of international significance; Jews subjected to anti-Semitic acts found they had among their allies both Jews and Christians in foreign lands.

By the nineteenth century the changed status of European Jewry was astounding. At one time Jews could only flee persecution, which they did. By the nineteenth century, however, there existed a real possibility that nations outside the one permitting the persecution would come to the Jews' rescue. European governments no longer considered the Jews to be subject to mob rule or rule by a single ruler, as they had been in the Middle Ages. Jews were now subject to rule by law, as was everyone else, and the humanity and spirit of the French Revolution—of liberty, equality, and fraternity—dictated that this apply everywhere, at least in principle. With the beginning of the nineteenth century, philo-Semitism was essentially focused on a concern that the rule of law be followed, that the ideology of equal justice be implemented in practice. While this was being realized in some nations, those same nations watched to ensure that it occurred elsewhere as well.

## SUMMARY OF EUROPEAN EMANCIPATION

Despite Hannah Arendt's assertion that the Jews remained a pariah people even when emancipated,[98] Jews in Europe throughout the nineteenth century—certainly within specific countries—were increasingly accepted as members of society. The advances made in individual countries and the protection enjoyed by Jews through the actions of various governments were in a large part brought about by the efforts, concern, and humanity of Christians. It cannot be charged that these governments acted because of the influence of Jews in their countries. Jews had little political power and less economic influence. The actions taken in these countries by Christians reflect not the pressures of pragmatic Jewish persuasion but a desire on the part of many to see Jews take their rightful place in all societies. Given the history of Jews in Europe, the assumption that they could and would be part of every nation in the fullest possible sense, was itself a major change.

The governments that interceded in the internal affairs of other governments on behalf of Jews did so because of a fundamental humanity. Though Jews were often held back because of numerous Christians, when the time came for them to advance, they did so because of numerous Christians.

## GERMANY AND WORLD WAR II

By the mid-twentieth century it was assumed that not only the right of presence but the right of membership for Jews had been irrevocably established throughout Europe. This was, of course, an error. History, at least in this case, is not at all linear. The apparent progression from right of presence to right of membership had been illusory. Indeed, not only were presence and membership now to be denied Jews, but existence itself. The "last great pogrom," which occurred during the Hitler era in Germany, was intended to annihilate European Jewry.

There are two major reasons why a part of European Jewry survived the German Holocaust. The first is that the systematic murder of millions of people requires an enormous amount of time, money, and resources and the invention of new methods of slaughter. Along the same line, the Germans (or at least a portion of them) wanted to use the labor of healthy Jews for war purposes and to help in their own liquidation. Moreover, the mass murder of Jews, as well as Slavs, Gypsies, Seventh-Day Adventists, the mentally unfit, and so on, required resources that are scarce in times of war. Also, the final decision to mass-produce murder came relatively late, and military defeat interrupted the process when it was reaching its peak.[99]

A second reason, and the one with which this book is concerned, is the contribution of numerous philo-Semites to the survival of European Jewry throughout the Holocaust. Without the help of numerous Christians, the horrific butchery in Germany and Eastern Europe would have been worse.

## Philo-Semites and the Holocaust

Every individual even remotely concerned with European Jewry looked with consternation at the situation in Germany during the 1930s and early 1940s. Given the thoroughness with which the Germans slaughtered millions of people; given that at one point "German troops . . . stood guard from the Norwegian North Cape on the Arctic Ocean to Egypt, from the Atlantic at Brest to the southern reaches of the Volga River on the border of Central Asia;"[100] and given that one of Hitler's avowed major aims was to make Europe *Judenrein* ("Free of Jews"),[101] it is less remarkable that 6 million Jews were systematically butchered by the Germans and by some of their Polish, Ukrainian, and Romanian helpers than that some 3 million Jews survived, 1 million in areas occupied by the Germans.[102] There can be no doubt that many of those 3 million Jews who survived did so because of the work, self-sacrifice, and mortal risk undertaken by Christians. That some Jews survived in every European country is testimony to the fact that in every country courageous individuals actively helped them.

It is astounding, for example, that some five thousand Jews were found alive and comparatively well in Berlin when the war ended and that some twenty-five thousand were alive in West Germany and ten thousand in Austria.[103] These Jews, like others throughout occupied Europe, were hidden in "bunkers," fed, and sheltered by Christians. Other Jews were helped by Christians in their rush to enter neutral countries. Those who sheltered Jews not only denied themselves the rewards offered by the Germans for turning in the fugitives, but risked imprisonment, torture, and death; sometimes the punishment was worse.[104] The chance of being found out by the Germans was great and the risk made more perilous by the possibility of anti-Semitic native informants, a problem that existed throughout Europe in some degree and was especially prevalent in the east.

The individuals who heroically defied the German slaughter machine are honored in Yad Vashem, the Martyrs and Heroes Remembrance Authority, in Israel.[105] Should one ask for clarification of the term "heroes," Philip

Friedman offers an excellent definition: "We are willing to call them heroes if they saved even one human life."[106] As of January 1, 1975, the records of Yad Vashem cited over 2,270 persons, including more than 500 Dutch, more than 300 Poles, and nearly 100 French and 100 Belgians, under the title of "Righteous among the Nations."[107]

It is probable that no single group of people did more to rescue European Jewry than the clergy. With the exception of the German clergy, most of whose members not only condoned the anti-Jewish acts but contributed to them,[108] Protestant, Catholic, and Greek Orthodox clergymen and clergywomen regularly defied the Germans and struggled to save Jewish lives.

In Germany itself neither the Protestant churches nor the Catholic Church acted to prevent the catastrophe. Indeed, they rarely protested the increasingly tragic events except when the authorities classified Jewish converts to Christianity as Jews and treated them as such. William L. Shirer argues, for example, that even Crystal Night (Krystallnacht) brought no formal protest from the German clergy.[109] As late as December 1941, German Jews were attacked from the pulpits of religious institutions. Despite attempts by some to apologize for the Confessing Church (Beisennende Kirche) and the Catholic Church, perhaps the two major religious institutions in Germany at the time, it remains true that these churches were in fact intolerant of Jews at best and often overtly anti-Semitic. Indeed, the attitudes and actions toward Jews of the Protestant and Catholic churches in Germany stand in marked contrast to the efforts of their counterparts in other countries.[110]

It should be pointed out, however, that individual members of both the German Confessing Church and, rarer, the German Catholic Church not only protested the anti-Semitic acts of their government but worked to save Jews. Of particular note here are Pastor Dietrich Bonhoeffer, Michael Cardinal Faulhaber, and Pastors Julius von Jan and Hermann Maas. These men were not the only courageous and humane members of the German clergy, although the list is small.[111] In other European countries the Catholic and Protestant churches acted institutionally and with great courage to defy the Germans.

Bishops in the west whose nations were occupied by the Germans, most notably those in France, Belgium, and Holland, helped Jews even at the risk of their own lives. They not only spoke out against the more obvious horrors, but they sheltered Jews and refused to allow the sanctity of their churches to be defiled. As early as 1934 the Dutch church prohibited Catholics from participating in the Dutch Nazi movement. In 1942, when the first deportations of Dutch Jews occurred, the church protested publicly and immediately. Moreover, loss of jobs notwithstanding, the Church prohibited Catholic policemen from hunting down Jews. Members of the Belgium Episcopate worked to help the rescue efforts of the clergy in that country, efforts that saved the lives of hundreds of Jewish children. The leaders of the

Church in France regularly and vociferously denounced both the deportation of Jews and the barbarous treatment to which they were subjected.[112] Similarly, the Greek church opposed the anti-Semitic laws and used its influence to aid and rescue Jews.

Specific examples are plentiful: Jews were smuggled into Spain by Father Marie Benoît, a Capuchin priest, and Father Charles Devaux of the Pères de Notre Dame de Sion is credited with saving more than one thousand Jewish lives. Sandor Ujvary, operating through Monsignor Angelo Rotta, carried food, medicine, and safe conduct passes to Jews who desperately needed them. Bishop William Apor of Gyor, as well as hundreds of priests and nuns, worked unceasingly to help Jews. Archbishop Theophilos Damaskinos contributed greatly to the saving of Jewish lives, and Monsignor Angelo Roncalli, "the stocky son of peasants" who eventually inherited the Shoes of the Fisherman as Pope John XXIII, "fought for the lives of the Jews, for they, as all men, were precious to him."[113] There is evidence that some priests instructed children in Judaism and that at least one, Father Joseph André of Namur, conducted Seders. The list is lengthy.

It was not, of course, only the clergy who risked so much on behalf of Jews. They had the support and the active cooperation of numerous individuals throughout Europe, which contributed in no small degree to their effectiveness. Gunter Lewy correctly remarks that "the concern of the Gentile population" in France, Holland, and Belgium "for their Jewish fellow-citizens was undoubtedly one of the key factors behind the bold public protests of the French, Dutch, and Belgian bishops."[114]

More than simple humanity, helping Jews in France, Belgium, Holland, and other western countries was regarded as patriotism. This is why the Germans had to rule most western countries directly. In Holland and Belgium the local Nazi leaders were so loathed by the rest of the population that they were unable to run their governments. This also explains why there were no concentration camps in the west (and by implication why there were concentration camps in the east).[115]

This contrast between east and west is, however, one of degree, albeit a substantial degree. In every country of Europe some people risked their own lives to help Jews.

In the occupied countries most of the activities of these people consisted in defying the deportation orders and getting Jews into the safe areas of Europe: Sweden, Switzerland, European Turkey, Portugal, and Spain. Although Bulgaria, Finland, and Hungary sided with Germany during the war, they each played an important role in protecting the Jews. Finland would not give a single Jew to the Germans despite threats and in fact was a refuge for Jews. Similarly Bulgaria, which Roth considers as having a "relatively long philo-Semitic tradition," refused to turn a single Jew over to the German slaughterhouses. Indeed, Bulgaria had perhaps the most successful record of rescue activities in Europe.[116] Hungary managed to delay the deportation of Jews; and it must be recalled that by 1944 Hungary's prewar Jewish population had doubled because of refugees entering that country. The struggle against deportations continued until the Nicholas Horthy regime was replaced in 1944.[117]

In Germany itself, very limited protest against the barbarism was heard, and generally this was unorganized, coming only from outraged individuals.[118] It was only in Berlin that a comparatively large number of Jews could secure sanctuary with friends, heroic people who were mainly from the working classes. At least one protest organization did exist in Germany, however briefly. The "'White Rose', an organization made up of a group of students and a professor of philosophy at the University of Munich, distributed leaflets telling of the murder of 300,000 Jews in Poland and asking why the German people were being so apathetic in the face of these revolting crimes." Their question went unanswered.[119]

Germany's two other political allies, Spain and Italy, also protected Jews. Generalissimo Francisco Franco, who is rumored to have been of Marrano descent, had previously indicated a friendly attitude toward Jews. In the 1930s, for example, an advertisement appeared in the Jewish newspapers in the United States inviting Jews to return to Spain. However, Franco manifested his strongest philo-Semitic tendencies during the war. He successfully developed and implemented a program to save Jews from the German pogroms, allowing Spain to become a sanctuary for them. Franco has been personally credited with saving perhaps sixty thousand Jews.[120] Portugal and Switzerland also offered sanctuary to those Jews who could reach their borders.

The Germans not only failed to receive assistance from Italy, but were effectively hindered there. Benito Mussolini, who after all was an "ally" of Hitler's, flatly refused to take part in the "final solution." Nearly 90 percent of Rome's Jews found shelter, most in "the numerous monasteries and houses of religious orders in Rome" and a few within the Vatican itself.[121] The rest were taken in and protected by their neighbors; in Italy the anti-Jewish policy of the Fascists had never been popular. Mussolini, in fact, offered Jews in Greece, Croatia, and Southern France sanctuary if they could find their way into territory controlled by Italy, and when Yugoslavia was invaded, Jews did seek refuge in the Italian zone of occupation. During the occupation of France, Italians undermined German efforts to deport Jews, and Jews imprisoned in Grenoble and Annecy were released by the Italians. Vichy police were warned to behave humanely when dealing with Jews, and Jews were surreptitiously moved from the German zone of occupation to the Italian zone.

Perhaps the greatest number of Jews were saved by the Russians, who permitted as many as possible to enter their country when the war began.

Even as the Russian armies retreated, they saved as many people as possible, and they did not distinguish between Jews and Gentiles in their rescue efforts, a clear reversal of their historical tendencies (which were soon readopted). Protection was also offered in Russia when that country was occupied. In Byelorussia, specifically, there were several instances in which individuals risked their lives to help Jews.

Poland, too, despite its profound anti-Semitism, was not without some individuals who helped save Jews from the German butchery. The home of one Polish worker, to offer a single example, was a way station for Jews escaping from the ghetto.

England, beleaguered by the German war machine, did what it could. Early in the war over two hundred organizations in England demanded action by the United States and Britain to support the Jews. These organizations represented virtually every segment of England's population. On December 17, 1942, the House of Commons rose in homage to Jewish suffering, an event unique in the history of that honored House. More pragmatically, prior to the outbreak of the war when the situation of the Jews in Germany was already oppressive, "England welcomed more than nine thousand German children, nine-tenths of whom were Jewish. They were without parents or possessions and this was an England in imminent danger of attack, a nation undergoing economic hardships, an island which had never been able to grow enough food for its population."[122]

In several countries demonstrations against deportations took place, and in Belgium, Holland, and France flaunting the Jewish badge was considered to be a patriotic gesture.[123] In France the saying was that "every Catholic family harbors a Jew," and because popular resistance was strong, numerous people exerted every effort to save Jews, especially Jewish children. French resistance to the deportations extended from the peasantry up to Vichy Premier Pierre Laval, who is credited with saving more than two hundred and thirty-five thousand lives by interceding when French Jewry was scheduled to be given over to the Germans. He did this despite numerous threats. This resistance explains why about 75 percent of the Jews in France were saved, a higher percentage than in any other country controlled by or cooperating with the Germans except Bulgaria, Denmark, Finland, and Italy.[124]

Public demonstrations of solidarity with the Jews took place in the three occupied countries of the north, Denmark, Norway, and Holland. There was a general strike in Holland in February 1941, a temporarily successful attempt to halt the mass deportations. In Amsterdam perhaps half of the people wore the yellow badge when the Germans reintroduced it. Earlier, in 1938, reflecting the traditional compassion, humanity, courage, and integrity of its people, the Dutch government had continued to offer itself as a country of temporary safety, even though it had already accepted twenty-five thousand Jewish refugees. During the war some forty thousand Jews were hidden in Dutch homes.[125] A similar situation prevailed in Norway, where in spite of Quisling's infamous rule, the people managed to help Jews there escape to Sweden.

Attention must also be paid to the extraordinary courage shown in Yugoslavia, Greece, and again Bulgaria, "whose peoples put the principle of human dignity above safety and expediency."[126] Yet it is possible that the most effective opposition to the policies of the Germans in any of the occupied countries was to be found in Denmark, where the people simply would not condone or support discriminatory regulations. Virtually all of Denmark's Jews were smuggled into Sweden before the Germans could capture them. And it must be remembered that, like Holland, Denmark was occupied early in the war and had taken in a disproportionate number of people fleeing Germany. Christian Danes are credited with saving not only their own Jews but those of other countries.

Certain individuals were in a position to do a great deal of good and did, in fact, save numerous lives through acts of singular courage, dedication, perseverence, and intelligence. For example, Raoul Wallenberg, a Swede, saved many Hungarian Jews and inspired other countries to accept Jewish refugees. Red Cross delegate Georges Dunard carried funds to Jews who were hiding in Slovakia, risking his life by doing so, and near the end of the war a second delegate named Hoeflinger saved some forty thousand Jews who would have been entombed in the underground aircraft factories of Mauthausen Concentration Camp had he not dissuaded the commandant from blowing it up. Prince Johannes Schwarzenberg, an Austrian anti-Nazi aristocrat, led a campaign that clearly saved thousands of lives.

Two other individuals warrant special mention. Philip Friedman comments that "Jews throughout the world have praised both [Count Folke] Bernadotte and [Dr. Felix] Kersten" for their work, which saved countless numbers of Jews.[127] Both men negotiated with Heinrich Himmler who took over the German government after Hitler's death, and Kersten, Himmler's personal physician, dissuaded the authorities from destroying the concentration camps and the Jews within them in March 1945.

Throughout the west, Germans found virtually no sanction for their genocidal policies. Only in the east did they receive support, and even assistance, for their work.[128]

## NOTES

1. Quoted in Katz (1973), p. 72.

2. Necheles (1971), pp. 129-30. Grégoire, however, was not supportive of Protestants, and it should be noted that Protestants, like Jews, were initially excluded from the Declaration of the Rights of Man.

3. Hertzberg (1968), p. 337. See also Katz (1973), p. 72. Necheles (1971, p. 122) notes that "Grégoire was attracted to the ethical rather than to the economic side of

the Jewish controversy." This, she suggests, was caused by more than humanism; it was a function of Grégoire's unorthodox and eclectic theology.

4. Mirabeau, for example, was a friend of several influential Jews, and both Moses Mendelssohn and Henrietta Herz were friends with several important Christians.

5. Katz (1973), p. 73. Indeed, it took a great deal of work merely for a memorandum stating their wishes to be read at the meeting.

6. The Church, however, was not uniformly anti-Jewish. Hertzberg (1968, pp. 8-9) comments that "even the Church was divided," although he adds that "here the pro-Jewish elements were very small indeed."

7. Cited in Dubnov (1971), vol. 4, p. 506.

8. Cited in Dubnov (1971), vol. 4, p. 507.

9. Graetz (1895), vol. 5, p. 439.

10. Again, Protestants, too, needed a separate decree for full equality.

11. Necheles (1971), p. 132. See also Dubnov (1971), vol. 4, pp. 507-8.

12. Dubnov (1971), vol. 4, p. 512.

13. Apologies were offered, for example, for Jewish involvement in usury.

14. Quoted in Dubnov (1971), vol. 4, pp. 520-21. Also see Graetz (1895), vol. 5, pp. 442-43.

15. Quoted in Graetz (1895), vol. 5, p. 444.

16. Quoted in Graetz (1895), vol. 5, pp. 447-48. Also see Dubnov (1971), vol. 4, p. 531.

17. Graetz (1895), vol. 5, p. 448. As stipulated in the decree, Jews gave up any special advantages they had enjoyed. See Dubnov (1971), vol. 4, p. 531. Final and complete equality came in 1831, when Judaism was placed on a par with other religions "by the granting of state support to the synagogue and the Jewish ministry" (Margolis and Marx, 1969, p. 642).

18. H. M. Sachar (1958), p. 64. See also Margolis and Marx (1969), p. 615, and Grayzel (1968), p. 496.

19. Hertzberg (1968), p. 2; Roth (1970), p. 323; H. M. Sachar (1958), pp. 65-66; and Dubnov (1916), vol. 1, p. 198.

20. Gottschalk (1929), p. 353.

21. Gershoy (1964), p. 467.

22. H. M. Sachar (1958), p. 64. Also see Parkes (1962), p. 135, and A. L. Sachar (1965), pp. 283-84, for a discussion of the effects of Napoleon's policies vis-à-vis Jews in the German states.

23. A. L. Sachar (1965), pp. 283, 293.

24. Napoleon's emissary bluntly told the Jewish leaders: "Sa majesté veut que vous soyez français."

25. Glazer (1957), p. 26. But see Dubnov (1916), vol. 1, p. 298.

26. A. L. Sachar (1965), p. 284.

27. Dubnov (1971), vol. 4, p. 646. Napoleon's undiplomatic comments reflected his attitude toward all religions. See Gershoy (1964), p. 467.

28. It is well to remember that the affair began less than twenty-five years after France's defeat in the Franco-Prussian War.

29. Marrus (1971, p. 41) notes that "there were Jewish army officers, five listed as generals in 1889, Jewish municipal councillors in Paris, Jewish deputies, Senators, and

important civil servants." Yet at the same time, as Lewis (1973, p. 21) points out, anti-Semitism had become "particularly ferocious in the Second Empire when Napoleon III granted railroad licenses to his Jewish banker friends."

30. Byrnes (1969), pp. 114-15. See ibid., pp. 115-25, for an analysis of this leftist anti-Semitism. See also Katz (1973), p. 200.

31. Drumont was anti-Protestant as well. In fact, he combined his prejudices nicely: "Every Protestant was half-Jew" (Byrnes, 1969, p. 138). Byrnes also notes (ibid., p. 224) an "anti-Protestant bias of the anti-Semitic campaign." This was not unusual. Halasz (1955, p. 121) points out that "in the eyes of the nationalists, the Protestants stood outside of the nation. To be faithful to France in the mere world of intellect was not enough. The Protestants, unlike the Catholics, would never be part of that physico-mental continuum which mystically encompassed the nation."

32. Byrnes (1969), p. 320. He notes, retrospectively, that this was a dangerous policy. Until the Dreyfus Affair, however, Drumont's paper had not had anything at all approaching a wide circulation. It had been, in fact, steadily declining in readership. The affair changed this.

33. Halasz (1955, p. 125) notes that Jews "wished to remain unnoticed" and attacked revisionists. Also see Lewis (1973), p. 60, on French-Jewish leaders' acceptance of the verdict, and Marrus (1971), pp. 208-9, for a discussion of anti-Semitic riots.

34. Byrnes (1969), p. 42.

35. Perhaps the most influential of the leftists to eventually support Dreyfus was Jean Léon Jaurès. A Catholic colonel, Georges Picquart, jeopardized his own military career by calling attention to evidence that seriously questioned Dreyfus's guilt.

36. Halasz (1955), p. 108. Zola, it should be noted, was an assimilationist who accepted the view (as he wrote in Le Figaro in 1896) that "if the Jews still existed it was the fault of the anti-Semites. Left alone the Jews would have vanished, dissolved, become, in fact, Frenchmen like all others" (quoted in Marrus, 1971, p. 171).

37. See Halasz (1955), pp. 128-29. Dimont (1962, p. 326) states that Zola's essay "had broken the back of the anti-Dreyfusards."

38. Arendt (1958), p. 118.

39. He had been invited to do so twice before, but international conditions (wars) had prevented the journeys.

40. Cited in Roth (1962), p. 94.

41. Roth (1962), p. 95. The speech of Cromwell, unfortunately, is not available; in fact, the details of the whole debate were published on "a single sheet of paper," and that paper itself is very rare. See Tovey (1967). It was said by Sir Paul Rycant, who was at the debates, that Cromwell "never spoke better" than in his defense of Jewish readmission.

It has been suggested that the conversionistic tenor of Cromwell's arguments was directed toward the English clergy in an effort to persuade them to support the readmission. See Rosenberg (1960), pp. 317-18.

42. Quoted in Roth (1962), p. 95.

43. Roth (1962), p. 96.

44. Dubnov (1971), vol. 4, pp. 263-64. Calish (1969, pp. 87-88) names several of the supporters of Jewish readmission to England.

45. Cited in Dubnov (1971), vol. 4, p. 264.

46. Roth, "The Jews of Western Europe," in Finkelstein (1974), p. 265.

47. Roth (1962), p. 167.

48. See Roth (1962), p. 46.

49. Roth (1962), pp. 10-11.

50. H. M. Sachar (1958), p. 44. See also Margolis and Marx (1969), pp. 491-92.

51. Bermant (1971), p. 9.

52. A. L. Sachar (1965), p. 23; Roth (1962), p. 93.

53. Roth (1962) pp. 13, 15. It might be noted that the English financial system was built up by Scots, Huguenots, and Quakers, not Jews.

54. Kohn (1967), p. 125.

55. Kohn (1967), p. 168. See also Roth (1962), pp. 12-13, and Poliakov (1965), pp. 198, 208.

56. Weber (1958a), p. 270.

57. Poliakov (1965), p. 204. He suggests that this has continued to the present day.

58. A. L. Sachar (1965), p. 23. See also Ettinger (1961), p. 202.

59. Roth (1962), p. 15.

60. Roth (1962), pp. 11-12.

61. Roth (1962), pp. 87-88.

62. See Roth (1962), pp. 3-4.

63. Blake (1967, p. 10) points out that converted Jews were seated without incident.

As early as 1770 Sampson Gideon the younger, who later became a peer, was returned for Parliament. Sir Manasseh Lopes entered the House in 1802, Ralph Bernal in 1818, and, most famous of all, David Ricardo, in 1819. All four were members of the Anglican Church, but their racial origin was well known, and it was evidently not an insuperable bar.

Roth agrees (1964, p. 292n) that Jews were not admitted to the House solely because of religion.

64. See Blake (1967), p. 258. However, Dubnov notes (1973, vol. 5, p. 236) that within the church there was a lack of unanimity on the issue.

65. Roth (1962), p. 256.

66. As early as 1779 the University of Edinburgh had graduated a Jewish physician, and in 1836 a Jew was admitted to Trinity College in Dublin. See Roth (1964), p. 293n.

67. Roth (1964), p. 293n.

68. These acts were repealed in 1828; bills removing the words of the oath that prohibited Jews from taking office were first introduced in 1830.

69. Roth (1964, p. 253) argues that the passages in the House of Commons indicate that "the now dominant middle class was antagonistic to the continuance of religious disabilities."

70. Quoted in Dubnov (1973), vol. 5, pp. 234-35.

71. This despite a flood of petitions urging equal rights for Jews from both "Jewish communities and Christians from many cities" (Dubnov, 1973, vol. 5, p. 235). The vote was 104 against, 54 in favor.

72. Roth (1964), pp. 260-61.

73. Disraeli, too, spoke with passion in favor of the bill; so did Lord George Bentinck. See Roth (1964), p. 261; Roth (1962), p. 279; and Blake (1967), p. 261.

74. Roth (1964), p. 262.

75. There are still some rather minor restrictions, however. Jews still cannot "exercise ecclesiastical patronage attached to any public office they may happen to hold," and it is unclear whether they can be "keeper of the King's conscience," that is, Lord Chancellor (Roth, 1964, p. 268n).

76. Roth (1962), p. 281.

77. Roth (1964), p. 268n.

78. Roth (1964), p. 243. See also Roth (1962), p. 286, for examples.

79. Katz (1973), p. 200. It should also be noted that to many people the Revolution was linked to Jewish emancipation, and they extended opposition to the Revolution to opposition to Jews. The defenders of reaction, the *ancien régime*, became anti-Semites. Joseph Arthur Comte de Gobineau, Joseph de Maistre, and others prepared the ground for a new nationalistic, reactionary, and pseudoscientific anti-Semitism.

80. Metternich, however, was not willing to free Austrian Jewry.

81. Quoted in Katz (1973), p. 74.

82. Schweitzer (1971), p. 198. See also H. M. Sachar (1958), p. 113. The unhappy condition of Italian Jews before their emancipation was largely caused by the fact that the Church had become and stayed reactionary after the Reformation.

83. Katz (1973), p. 170.

84. For a discussion of Jewish emancipation in Bavaria see Dubnov (1973), vol. 5, pp. 52-55.

85. Dubnov (1973), vol. 5, p. 52.

86. Of course, that same nationalistic ideology would be a major cause of political anti-Semitism.

87. Quoted in Dubnov (1973), vol. 5, p. 611.

88. Quoted in Graetz (1895), vol. 5, p. 351.

89. Roth (1962), p. 19. Also see Parkes (1962), p. 128.

90. Sir Moses Montefiore went to Turkey to help settle the problem, with the full and consistent support of the British government.

91. Quoted in Graetz (1895), vol. 5, p. 656.

92. Graetz (1895), vol. 5, p. 20.

93. Roth (1964), p. 257.

94. Quoted in Graetz (1895), vol. 5, p. 645.

95. Quoted in Dubnov (1973), vol. 5, p. 379.

96. Quoted in Dubnov (1973), vol. 5, p. 381.

97. The issue of Germany will be discussed below.

This is not the place to detail the long struggle for the rebirth of Israel or document the support that Zionism received from Christians. Yet some indication of that support should be recorded here. Pro-Zionism in nineteenth-century England was an influential force, and this tendency extended into the twentieth century. It has long been recognized that Lord Arthur James Balfour had a "deep admiration for the achievements of the Jewish people and sympathy with their suffering," and there should be no doubt that "it was the Protestant allies of Zionism who helped the Balfour Declaration to prevail" (Bermant, 1971, p. 262).

The support Jews received from some of their Christian allies in recreating Israel took numerous forms and occurred in numerous places, from the transport of arms with which Israel defended itself to the training of Israel's soldiers and pilots. Christians also fought and died for Israel's survival. Some battled the American embargo on arms to Israel politically, others were involved in arms smuggling. Immediately after the war millions of Jews were imprisoned in displaced persons camps and needed assistance in getting to Israel. Few governments had much sympathy with British colonial policy, and hardly any had sympathy with the White Paper that limited Jewish immigration to Palestine. On numerous occasions governments unsympathetic with these policies provided the Mossad with tide tables and navigators to help Jews sail.

The complete story of Christians' help in reestablishing the state of Israel has yet to be told. It should be. See Lebeson, in Finkelstein (1974), p. 574; Slater (1971), pp. 271, 309; Postal and Levy (1973), p. 373; H. M. Sachar (1958), pp. 467, 469.

98. Arendt (1958), p. 117.

99. It might be more accurate to say that the *implementation* of Germany's program of mass murder came late in the war. The decision to slaughter millions of innocent men, women, and children was voiced publicly as early as 1938. William Stevenson, in his excellent and exciting study, *A Man Called Intrepid* (Ballantine Books, New York, 1976), points out (p. 385) that "in November 1938, the SS newspaper *The Black Corps* called for 'the extermination with fire and sword, the actual and final end of Jewry in Germany.' Hitler made speeches in that month attacking Jewry, prophesying the annihilation of the Jewish race."

100. Shirer (1960), p. 914.

101. See Dawidowicz (1975), passim.

102. The figures come from Grayzel (1968), p. 67. Also see Roth (1970), p. 408; Dimont (1962), p. 373; and Philip Friedman (1957), p. 13.

103. H. M. Sachar (1958), p. 489. Also see Cecil Roth, "The Jews of Western Europe," in Finkelstein (1974), p. 296, and Schulweis (1962).

104. Friedman (1957, p. 73) tells of Edoardo Focherini of the Bologna Catholic daily *Avverire d'Italia*, whose seven children died in a concentration camp because of his efforts on behalf of Jews.

105. The *Encyclopedia Judaica*, vol. 16, p. 698, notes that "the department for Righteous Gentiles . . . was set up to award honors to persons recognized as belonging to *Hasidei Ummot ha-Olam*, who risked their lives to rescue Jews in the holocaust."

106. Friedman (1957), p. 38.

107. From a private letter to the author dated 25 May, 1975, from Donia Rosen, Head of the Department of the Righteous, Jerusalem, Israel. It is important to note, quoting from the letter, that "the commission must be convinced that the Gentiles were not motivated by financial considerations or religious conversion considerations."

108. For example, the German clergy "readily provided" the authorities with church registrars to facilitate determinations of Aryan descent. Gutteridge (1976), p. 153. Also see Lewy (1964b), passim.

109. Shirer (1960), p. 435. This is not really true. The Confessing Church issued a statement of "protest" that began: "As justified as the political measures against the Jews may be . . . " Quoted in Gutteridge (1976), p. 182. See also ibid., p. 231.

110. See, for example, Ritter (1958), who consistently apologizes for the German clergy. Yet not once is he able to point to the religious institutions in Germany saving

Jews as Jews, or even publicly protesting against the horrors they witnessed. Helmreich (1979, p. 277), speaking specifically about the German Catholic Church, points out that it "drew a line between religious Jews and converted Christian Jews. It was the Church's duty and obligation to look after the latter; the former could take care of themselves." This was also the policy of the German Protestant churches. Soon after the war ended Karl Barth suggested that the Confessing Church did as much as possible to help the Jews. This simply is not true. Martin Niemoeller admitted as much in August 1945, and in the Stuttgard Declaration of October 1945 Bishop Theophil Wurm, Niemoeller, and other leaders of the Confessing Church acknowledged their failed responsibility. However, they did not bother, even then, to deal directly with the issue of Jews or anti-Semitism. Their "apology" was theological, not humanistic. See Gutteridge (1976), p. 267; and Spotts (1973), p. 119.

111. According to Friedlaender (1969, p. 38), Bonhoeffer was the only leader of the Confessing Church to ask that institution to help the Jews. They declined to do so. Bonhoeffer was executed in Germany during the war. Lewy agrees (1964a, pp. 29-30) that few Jews in Germany were helped by the German clergy. However, he does point out that Gertrud Luckner aided Jews in several important ways and that Provost Bernhard Lichtenberg regularly offered prayers for them. Recognition should also be given to the efforts of Heinrich Grueber, Werner Slyten, Clemens August von Galen, Hermann Mullert, Ernst Fuchs, Ulrich Bunzel, Friedrich Middendorf, and Georg Althaus, among others. See Gutteridge (1976), pp. 160-61.

112. See Lewy (1964a) p. 29.

113. Morse (1967), pp. 259-60. See also ibid., pp. 61, 296-97, and Philip Friedman (1957), pp. 106-9.

114. Lewy (1964a), p. 29.

115. Suhl (1975), p. 305. See ibid., p. 283, for a discussion of the differing attitudes of east and west toward Jews and the significance of this difference.

116. Cecil Roth, "The Jews of Western Europe," in Finkelstein (1974), p. 296. Also see H. M. Sachar (1958), p. 451; Flannery (1965), p. 223; Schweitzer (1971), p. 225; Morse (1967), p. 260; Philip Friedman (1957), p. 104; Suhl (1975), pp. 275-79; and Oren (1968), passim.

117. Morse (1967), p. 281; Flannery (1965), p. 224; and Kirchen (1968), passim. McCagg (1972, p. 200) points out that "it was not until the 'Jewish Laws' of 1941 that the Jews of Hungary were systematically subjected to persecution, and they retained until 1944 civil rights which had long since disappeared everywhere else in German-dominated Europe."

118. See, for example, Lewy (1964a), pp. 23-25, who notes the efforts of Franz Steffen, Felix Langer, and Waldemar Gurian.

119. Lewy (1964a), p. 27. Also see Shirer (1960), pp. 1022-23; Ritter (1958), pp. 235-36; and Gutteridge (1976), p. 250. Gutteridge (1976, p. 304) suggests that the main tragedy of the Hitler era in Germany is that there was no "spontaneous outburst at any point by ordinary decent Christian folk."

120. Birmingham (1972), p. 281.

121. Lewy (1964a), p. 32. Flannery (1965, p. 226), in speaking of Pope Pius XII, comments: "The Pope's aid to Jews, both financial and organizational, saved thousands of lives and earned the praise of many Jewish leaders and groups." However, Flannery's assertion is subject to debate. Morse (1967, pp. 17-19), for example, is

highly critical of the Pope's "apathy" and argues that Pius never spoke out against German atrocities. The contributions of Pope Pius XII—or the lack of contribution—to the saving of Jewish lives during World War II is, at the very least, too complex an issue to be settled here. However, the evidence seems to support Morse's position; at best Pope Pius XII contributed too little, too late. See Falconi (1970), passim; Lewy (1964a), passim; Lewy (1964b), passim; and Gutteridge (1976), pp. 305-6.

122. Morse (1967), p. 138. He notes that "more than one thousand of these immigrants eventually served in the British armed forces, a record no doubt noted and approved by that nation's patriotic societies."

123. On the Jewish badge and various nations' reactions to it see Philip Friedman (1957), pp. 34-42.

124. H. M. Sachar (1958), p. 450. See also Friedman (1957), p. 44; Eligulashvili (1967); and Atchildi (1967). It should be noted, however, that Laval's concern for Jews did not extend past France's borders, and there are those who suggest that even within those borders his efforts were less than might have been hoped for.

125. Friedman (1967), p. 62. Also see Lewy (1964a, p. 33), who points out that the Dutch Catholic Church refused to cooperate in any way with the deportation of the Jews in 1942.

126. Dimont (1962), p. 387.

127. Friedman (1957), p. 179.

128. But see "Polish Catholics and Jews," in *America*, February 13, 1943. This article, gotten via the underground, attacks the charge that Polish Catholics in German-occupied Poland were indifferent to German persecution of Jews. Also see Berenstein and Rutkowski (1960) and Heiman (1961).

# TOWARD AN UNDERSTANDING OF PHILO-SEMITISM

7

## ON PREJUDICE

It is well accepted in the social sciences that prejudice, both pro- and anti-, is not inherent. Infants are not philo-Semitic or anti-Semitic; they are a-Semitic. Prejudicial attitudes are *instilled* in children (and adults). Gordon Allport notes that it is not necessarily or even usually the parents who are the instructors in prejudice. In fact, he says, prejudice is not taught by anyone; it is "caught . . . from an infected atmosphere." "No child is born prejudiced. His prejudices are always acquired. They are acquired chiefly in fulfillment of his own needs. Yet the context of his learning is always the social structure in which his personality develops." It follows that "tolerant thinking about ethnic groups is, no less than prejudiced thinking, a reflection of a total style of cognitive operation."[1]

One can surmise by extension that the same applies to favorable perceptions of ethnic groups. If this is correct, then "atmosphere" and "social structure" become crucial elements in determining not only the prevalence of anti-Semitism but of philo-Semitism as well. Yet anti-Semitism and philo-Semitism are determined by the perceptions of individuals, which are both psychologically and sociologically controlled by the ideology prevalent in a society. That ideology, in turn, is supported and sustained by the dominant institutions of that society. An individual acts prejudicially "because he perceives the object of prejudice in a certain way";[2] it follows that an understanding of prejudice necessitates an understanding of the causes of perception. One cannot simply suggest that group prejudice is based directly upon social, historical, cultural, or economic factors; it is the individual's *understanding* of these that is the key to understanding his attitudes. This is the significance of the "social structure" or "atmosphere," for these determine the perceptions that are defined as prejudice.

It follows that an individual's conduct is a result of his own *Weltan-schauung*; that is, "his response to the world conforms to his definition of the world."[3] Yet his *Weltanschauung*, his definition of the world and his values, is similar to prejudice in that it is not innate. Knowledge is a social product. This is one reason why socio-cultural norms play an immense part in the acquisition of prejudice.

If it is correct that prejudice is not innate but taught (or "caught"), then the idea of an innate "pure" prejudice must be meaningless. There cannot be, for example, a formless anti-Semitism, an anti-Semitism without cause, without some misconceived idea or ideology, without some reason for existing. To suggest that a pure (unmotivated or not causally linked to something else) attitude exists is to argue that, within the bounds of its formation, it is untouched by the world around it. The concept of "pure" prejudice suggests that attitudes can develop, be sustained, and perhaps become manifest in some specific discriminatory act without being formed by, accountable to, or relative within the social world. It implies that such attitudes are inherent and that there need not be any causal factor in attitude formation. Such a position is, quite clearly, untenable. This is no less true of philo-Semitism than of anti-Semitism; one will seek in vain for a "pure" form of philo-Semitism; the term itself is without meaning.[4]

The attitudes held by an individual cannot legitimately be separated from those forces within society, such as social, political, economic, and ideational influences, that contribute to the formation of these attitudes and sustain them. Even if one agrees with Freud that the deeper motives of anti-Semitism (and, one supposes, philo-Semitism) come from the unconscious,[5] the impossibility of separating them from environmental influences still obtains. The alternative would be to argue that the unconscious is unshaped or, at minimum, unaffected by the social world; this is equally unacceptable as a thesis.[6]

The significance of the social world has clearly and correctly been noted in terms of its effects on anti-Semitism. James H. Robb points out that "the two most important roles played by the social forces are the determination of the Jewish stereotype and the determination of the form of the anti-Semitic manifestations. The stereotype always reflects the main emphasis of the society to which the anti-Semite belongs."[7] The same factors are in effect in considerations and determinations of philo-Semitism.

"Philo-Semitism," as used by various scholars, is a vague, generalized term, usually applied descriptively to indicate the supposed attitude of specific individuals who, in the opinion of the scholar, benefit or assist Jews.[8] There have been few efforts to examine the term, to offer any detailed definition of it, or to analyze its causes or specific applications. Cecil Roth is unique in suggesting a basis for philo-Semitism, but he does not discuss what is meant by the term itself.[9] Moreover, Roth's analysis is limited, being concerned essentially with the period in English history when Jews were readmitted to that nation. There has been, in short, no systematic inquiry into the meaning, application, or types of philo-Semitism.

As has been noted earlier, ambiguities exist in discussions of anti-Semitism. One cause of these ambiguities is the multiple bases of prejudice; definitions of that attitude are inconsistent in terms of causes and, as a result, in terms of expression and degree. However, most scholars recognize various bases and forms of anti-Semitism, and if not all scholars recognize all of the underlying causes suggested by their colleagues, most agree on specific forms of anti-Semitism. With considerable regularity scholars point to economic anti-Semitism, nationalistic anti-Semitism, and religious anti-Semitism as being historically consistent and ubiquitous. There is less agreement on variations within these classifications and on other independent forms of anti-Semitism.[10]

Although it is difficult to impute causes to many of the forms of anti-Semitism, some in themselves suggest specific motives. In the case of the three forms mentioned above, for example, one can find underlying reasons for antipathy towards Jews by Gentiles. To illustrate: many burghers during the Middle Ages (and after) saw Jews as competitors and because of economic self-interest viewed them with hostility. The intense nationalism of the nineteenth century led to a xenophobic detestation of "outsiders"; in this case Jews were doubly damned as religious and national aliens. Some religious leaders viewed Jews as the killers of Christ and for that reason, among others, were hostile to them. There exists, then, along with the identification of several forms of anti-Semitism, a (perhaps tentative) designation of the motives underlying those forms.

Although it is rarely considered, bases also exist for philo-Semitism. Just as there are, among others, economic, nationalistic, and religious factors underlying anti-Semitism, so there are, among others, economic, nationalistic, and religious factors underlying philo-Semitism. Just as there are underlying motives discernible for anti-Semitism, so there are underlying motives discernible for philo-Semitism. Just as scholars have considered and discussed various forms of and motives for anti-Semitism, so an examination of philo-Semitism in its several aspects, consequences, and implications is equally possible and necessary.

## THE FORMS OF PHILO-SEMITISM

Chapters 3 through 6 of this book suggest several forms of philo-Semitism that are readily identifiable. These will now be reviewed briefly; each form of philo-Semitism considered here warrants extensive study in itself, and each is subject to various interpretations, especially as there is no absolute consistency within any single form.

If any continuum of motives can be imputed to the actions of Christians in accepting and protecting Jews, the absolute and unremitting greed of Christians, particularly that of the nobles and kings, would lie at one end of it. The other end would be a simple love of Jews, Judaism, or things Jewish. It is not impossible that both existed.[11] But pure motives in the sense of an individual's being uninfluenced by the world around him are unlikely. As the idea of a purely avaricious basis for philo-Semitism is discounted here, so, too, is the idea of a purely beneficent philo-Semitism.

The forms of philo-Semitism that follow, in no particular order, have been the most prevalent and consequently the most effective for European Jewry. They constitute, therefore, the most important types of philo-Semitism. Each form has varied in intensity throughout history; at various periods one or another would become dominant, with the others of relatively minor importance. Two forms of philo-Semitism, however, the humanistic and the religious, appear to have been omnipresent in European history, although of course not necessarily dominant.

### Economic Philo-Semitism

*Economic philo-Semitism* implies that the dominant reason for the acceptance and protection of Jews is the real or imagined financial advantages that can be gained by offering Jews that protection and acceptance. One of the two most prevalent forms of philo-Semitism in the Middle Ages (the other was religious), economic philo-Semitism must be regarded with considerable caution. That it existed and was consequential is beyond dispute; however, where Jews were accepted and protected *solely* because of economic gain, it was not philo-Semitism; it was simply avarice.[12]

It will be allowed that favorable treatment of Jews for economic reason is actually philo-Semitism if, and only if, it coexists with one or more of the other forms of philo-Semitism.[13] Yet there are instances in which one can tentatively assume the existence of economic philo-Semitism. During the reign of Louis XIV, Jean Baptiste Colbert and Anne Robert Jacques Turgot struggled to bring Jews into France's economic mainstream. Arthur Hertzberg argues that "the whole process of the piecemeal readmission of Jews to France after 1500 had been rooted in mercantilist considerations, that is, in the idea that by allowing at least some Jews into the country France would increase its international trade." Yet in 1685 Louis had revoked the Edict of Nantes, with the result that over a quarter of a million Protestants (Huguenots) emigrated, "to the great harm of French commerce."[14] It made no economic sense to crush the most financially efficacious group in the country if Jews were being brought in especially to enhance the economy. Clearly the question of why Jews were accepted while Protestants were not is not answerable simply in economic terms.[15]

Economic philo-Semitism, then, suggests that while Christians believed there was financial value in having Jews within an area, other causes also favored their acceptance. At minimum, a second factor must be present. To illustrate this, consider the admission of Jews into Turkey after the Spanish expulsion, their readmission to England in the mid-seventeenth century, and their welcome into Poland during the era of the Black Death.

The acceptance of Jews into Turkey was based to some degree on the financial (and other) benefits that Jews could and did provide. However, the Jews in the Turkish Empire were also loyal to that empire, and part of their good fortune was contingent upon their loyalty (as well as upon a fundamental tolerance on the part of the sultans). The Jews' residence in Turkey was a happy one, but not simply because they offered economic advantages to the sultans. Their commitment to the empire and the sultans' recognition of that commitment were also of primary significance.

Similarly, loyalty was a factor in the regard for Jews of Henry IV of the Holy Roman Empire. Along with any economic benefits Jews may have brought to the Holy Roman Empire, loyalty was one reason for Henry's protection of Jews during the First Crusade.[16] In neither the Turkish Empire nor the Holy Roman Empire under Henry IV, then, were Jews regarded merely as economic tools.

The readmission of Jews to England offers a parallel analysis. As noted, many scholars argue that Cromwell's acceptance of Jews was based on economic factors alone. Cromwell attributed Holland's financial growth to that country's acceptance of Jews and hoped that, through Jewish financial acumen, England's economic status would similarly improve. Yet beyond this, or perhaps in addition to it, Cromwell had a genuine regard and admiration for the people of the Book. It is not the case that his motive for accepting Jews was economic and his justification theological, as Katz suggests;[17] theological considerations were as much a part of his motives as were economic considerations. Moreover, numerous Englishmen recognized and supported the religious reasons for the readmission of Jews.

It is possible that the clearest illustration of economic philo-Semitism is found in the situation of Poland during the reigns of Boleslav and of Casimir the Great. Here, too, the acceptance and welcome of Jews was not based merely on economic considerations; there were humanistic and nationalistic aspects to their entry into Poland as well. Casimir took pains to facilitate and encourage the social intermixing of Christians and Jews. Beyond this, Casimir worked to make Jews part of the Polish Empire. It is indisputable that one reason for this was the economic advantage to be gained by having Jews as part of the Polish citizenry; however, there were humanistic motives for Casimir's actions, too, and these cannot be discounted. Poland under Casimir, like Turkey under the sultans and England under Cromwell, derived financial benefits from welcoming and accepting Jews into the nation. In none of these, however, were financial benefits the sole objective of that welcome and acceptance.

The economic philo-Semitism of the Middle Ages clearly helped Jews. It may be that this is one reason why there were no general attacks against Jews instigated by rulers and why rulers sheltered Jews in times of physical danger.[18] Yet it was not unusual for burghers—competitors of Jews—also to contribute to the latter's safety. This suggests that economic philo-Semitism is not simply a manifestation of Christian avarice, but that humanistic aspects were also present.

Economic philo-Semitism did not die immediately with the decline of the Middle Ages; with the growth and development of capitalism and changing ideologies, it evolved into other forms. This occurred partially because "capitalism bred free thinkers."[19] Concomitant or inherent within this, and nourished by the Enlightenment, was a growing liberal ideology that manifested itself, in part, in political-liberal philo-Semitism. Within the changing socioeconomic structure of Europe, the particular form of economic philo-Semitism of the Middle Ages was no longer relevant.[20]

### Religious Philo-Semitism

*Religious philo-Semitism* is the oldest form of philo-Semitism in Christendom; it dates from the beginnings of Christianity. Christianity recognizes and acknowledges, if occasionally with reluctance, that it began as a Jewish sect, that its early leaders were Jews, and that many of its symbols and feasts are reinterpreted Jewish symbols and feasts. (For example, Passover became Easter.) Christian religious leaders as well as Christian laymen acknowledge that the origins of Christianity are found in Judaism, recognize the Old Testament, and accept Judaism as the parent religion. Specifically because of the origins of Christianity, "the Jew [is] consistently relevant and visible in Christian teachings."[21] More than one scholar has noted the peculiar position of Jews in Christian theology.[22] Christians, as Poliakov comments, neither ignore nor disdain the heritage of Judaism; rather they claim it as their own.[23] Although this had, and continues to have, negative consequences for Jews, it also had, and continues to have, positive ones as well.

One result of the connection between Christianity and Judaism has been the willingness of Christian leaders to grant Jews the right of presence in Europe. It must be recalled that the right of presence was granted despite a strong desire for religious unity. Although the nations of Europe worked to achieve religious homogeneity within their borders, Jews were often excepted. The reason for the exception was usually theological.[24]

It is probable that no single institution has been examined as thoroughly in its relationship to Jews as the Catholic Church. Subject to only slightly less scrutiny has been the relationship between Protestantism and Jewry. These relationships explain the bases of both religious anti-Semitism and religious philo-Semitism in Europe. Studies of anti-Semitism rarely hesitate to note, explain, and document the religious causes of that prejudice; yet a theological philo-Semitism exists too, and its effectiveness cannot be disputed.[25] Religious philo-Semitism was the main reason, but not the only reason, why Jews were not annihilated within medieval Christendom, or, at minimum, why no crusade was instituted against them by a reigning pope.

It has often been argued that the Church did not throw its weight against the virulent anti-Semitism of the Middle Ages.[26] To some degree this is true, although care must be taken in evaluating this assertion. The attitude of the Church toward Jews at any given time depended on the reigning pope, and as noted earlier, the relationship between Jews and the papacy was not at all consistent. Yet beyond this, the Church did not systematically attack Jews at any time, regardless of who was pope. Moreover, only Jews enjoyed this papal acceptance. Further, there were numerous instances when the Church was protective of Jews. If at certain times that protection was less than what was needed, in the main it was effective. It need hardly be pointed out that the official Catholic acceptance of Jews in Christendom contributed to Protestant acceptance of Jews.

This is not to suggest that all religious leaders favored the Jews. Luther, for example, expected Jews to flock to Protestantism and initially was very sympathetic to them. When they continued to adhere to Judaism, he turned on them with an intense ferocity and became a virulent anti-Semite.[27] Similarly, various members of the lower clergy, for example the Franciscan monk John Capistrano, among others, were responsible for the deaths and forced conversions of numerous Jews. Various popes, as indicated, were definitely not contributors to the well-being of European Jewry, especially after the Reformation. Yet again, the ties between Judaism and Christianity prevented any major religious leader from suggesting or supporting a crusade directed against Jews. This refers only to Jews, however; attempts were made to annihilate *all* other religious groups within Christendom.

Religious philo-Semitism is particularly susceptible to the charge of conversionism, of seeking the conversion of Jews to Christianity through the mechanism of an assumed religiously based philo-Semitism. Many attempts at proselytizing did exist, and such a motive may have been in the minds of many who assisted Jews and Jewry, although it is of course impossible to know motives absolutely.[28] Without condoning this proselytizing, it should be noted that:

1. From the perspective of the Christian conversionists, their attempts were justified on the basis of the universalism of Christianity and because they were in their own context theologically correct; that is, the New Testament endorses such actions. (It should be recalled that initially both Christians and Jews were conversionists.)

2. The conversionists were, in the main, unsuccessful.

3. Jews as a whole continued to have official protection despite their resistance to conversion.

4. The conversionists generally rejected the use of force to attain their ends, and those Jews who were forcibly converted to Christianity were often permitted to return to Judaism.[29]

5. Even in their attempts to convert them, the Christian conversionists acknowledged and contributed to the unique position of the Jews.

In addition to being a basis for the protection of Jews and Judaism, for example from annihilation and from forced baptisms, religious philo-Semitism provided a mechanism by which to view Jews in a positive light. Many Christians have respect for Jews because of their religion.

Probably the most famous and perhaps the most significant illustration of Christian respect for Jews because of their religion was the welcome of Jews to England in the seventeenth century. And England was not alone in accepting Jews, in part because of religious philo-Semitism; this was also the case in Holland.[30] It is not unreasonable, then, to suggest that religious philo-Semitism was a significant factor not only in continuing to allow Jews the right of presence in medieval Europe, but in permitting Jews to gain admission into various countries.

Religious philo-Semitism and its effects diminished, but did not disappear, as religion itself faded as a significant force in Europe. As illustrated, religious philo-Semitism was a factor in the emancipation of European Jewry, although less so than nationalistic or liberal philo-Semitism.

The ties that connect Judaism and Christianity did not, of course, prevent the emergence of religious anti-Semitism; in fact, they contributed to it. However, these same ties prevented the convoluted logic of that form of anti-Semitism from arriving at a final commitment to annihilation. This is one reason why the Nazi movement is recognized as not only anti-Semitic but anti-Christian. The Nazis, as many others, recognized the connection between Judaism and Christianity and recognized further that there is inherent in the latter a commitment to the former, however ineffective that commitment has been at various times. This is not to deny that religious anti-Semitism was effective, but it is to charge that the established doctrine of Christianity was not and is not *necessarily* inimical to Jews and that, further, many Christians interpreted those doctrines in a way that was favorable to Jews.

It might also be noted that concomitant with religious philo-Semitism is a humanistic philo-Semitism. This will be discussed in a later section of this chapter.

### Nationalistic Philo-Semitism

It is probable that modern anti-Semitism has at its core the nationalistic theories embodied in its support and defense of the concept of the State, which is the movement toward and desire for national homogeneity. This was demonstrated not only in the struggles for Jewish emancipation but also in the Dreyfus Affair, in the attitude of numerous Germans toward Jews in the post-World War I era, and in the growth of modern pseudoscientific "racial" anti-Semitism, which suggests that Jews are biologically different from the hereditary citizenry of a given state. At the same time, however, the attempts and offers to assimilate Jews into the various European nations, particularly in the nineteenth century and especially in France, England, and Holland, indicate that to some degree the concepts of nationalism and national unity were conducive to favorable attitudes toward Jews on the part of at least some Christians. This is why Abraham Leon Sachar suggests that one reason for Jewish emancipation was "the need felt by European legislators and bureaucrats ... to create taut and efficient governments, to complete the process of state unification."[31]

Not all the citizens of the various European states accepted the admission of Jews as Jews into their culture. The citizens of several states attempted not only to enculturate the Jews but to Christianize them as well. In the long run, however, Judaism survived. Even in those societies in which reform and conservative forms of Judaism split from the orthodox branch, orthodoxy retained a degree of vitality. Although there is no doubt that many Christian leaders would have accepted a Christianization of Judaism, making the minority religion more and more like the majority religion,[32] their main concern was with eradicating sociopolitical differences between Christians and Jews and not religious ones. This is certainly clear in Rabaud St. Etienne's arguments for Jewish emancipation in France: "I demand liberty for the nation of the Jews, always condemned, homeless, wandering over the face of the whole globe, and doomed to humiliation. Banish forever the aristocracy of thought, the feudal system of opinion, which desires to rule others and impose compulsion upon them."[33] It is even clearer in the words of Thomas Babington Macaulay during his struggle for Jewish political emancipation in England: "What is proposed is ... that a legislature composed of Christians and Jews should legislate for a community composed of Christians and Jews."[34] No mention of the Christianization of Jews or Judaism is detectable; these men simply argued for the acceptance of Jews as part of the nation.

Although nationalistic philo-Semitism is, in the main, a modern aspect of Jewish-Christian relations, intimations of it existed before the nineteenth century. The Toleration Patent of Joseph II has already been discussed. Partially for humanitarian reasons and partially for nationalistic ones, Joseph tried to include Jews in his empire. And more than five hundred years before that, Frederick II (the Belligerent), Duke of Austria, had begun the Fridericanum of 1244 with these words: "We desire that men of all classes dwelling in our land should share our favor and good will, we do therefore decree that these laws, devised for all Jews found in the land of Austria, shall be observed by them without violation."[35] In neither case was the Christianization of Jewry suggested; both the Tolerenzpatent and the Fridericanum stress a desire for national unity and harmony while acknowledging religioethnic differences.

It is possible to argue, however, that nationalistic philo-Semitism had little to do with Jews, especially as this form of philo-Semitism was most manifest during the nineteenth century—the Fridericanum notwithstanding. One can suggest, that is, that the basis of nationalistic philo-Semitism was the logic of nationalistic universalism rather than concern for Jews.[36] Where the right of presence of Jews had already been accepted when the nationalistic movements became effective, there was little choice but to accept Jews into the state along with other minority groups.

The only viable point in this position, however, is that Jews were accepted along with other groups as being unlikely to subvert the state. It is clear that Jews were regarded as a unique entity and were considered separately, that is, not as one of several groups to be emancipated but specifically as Jews who could be emancipated. It is true, for example, that Jean Bodin argued for toleration as a general principle for a *raison d'état*; but it is also true that he singled out Jews for consideration and inclusion in the state. Moreover he did so for reasons that included, but were not limited to, nationalistic concerns. Bodin argued that "Jews had served as civilizing agents in all the lands of their dispersion." This clearly reflects his concern with the state. Beyond this, however, Bodin argued for emancipation of the Jews from a theological perspective: "Their presence in the Diaspora was a sign not of God's anger but of his favor."[37] And it is important to recognize that Bodin's influence at the time was extensive.[38]

In a similar vein, the Judenpatent, which Francis II of Austria wrote for the Jews of Bohemia at the close of the eighteenth century, was specifically concerned with eradicating sociopolitical differences between Jews and Christians. The reason for this, as suggested in the preamble to that document, was not simply nationalistic universalism; the Judenpatent was issued "to bring Bohemian Jewry closer to their civic destination for the benefit of the state and themselves."[39]

It is undoubtedly true that the universalisms of the time contributed to the existence of nationalistic philo-Semitism and thus to the movement toward Jewish emancipation; yet nationalistic philo-Semitism was a potent factor in that emancipation in and of itself. It may be that consistency of argument coupled with nationalistic universalisms prompted some automatically to include Jews as members of the state, but it would be wise not to overemphasize this: consistency of argument was no barrier to Voltaire, Denis Diderot, and other Philosophes arguing for the *exclusion* of Jews from French citizenship. This same disregard for consistency of argument explains, or at least helps to account for, the separate emancipations of Jews and Protestants in France and of Jews and Catholics in England. Groups were separately considered and separately emancipated, and in the case of the Jews a significant factor in their emancipation was nationalistic philo-Semitism.

One indication of the existence of nationalistic philo-Semitism was the acceptance of the entry of Jews into politics and the military, professions that, by their very nature, demand full loyalty to the state. It cannot be insignificant that in politics Jews were elected to office by non-Jews and that in the military they were usually appointed to their posts by an elite, nationalistic body of officers. That they could attain such positions is indicative of both their acceptance of membership in the nation and their acceptance, even if begrudgingly, by other members of that nation.

However, the clearest manifestation of nationalistic philo-Semitism remains the struggles by Christians to emancipate European Jewry. Ulterior motives may be attributed to economic and religious philo-Semitism, but it is difficult to imagine such motives in the battles to secure for Jews their place in society; in many instances those who fought for the emancipation of Jews actually did so at personal risk. The struggles to a large degree manifested the conviction that Jews could and should become citizens of the nation; Christians who fought for Jews did so for the good of the nation as well as for the good of Jews. That they equated the two is testimony at once to their nationalism and to their philo-Semitism.

### Intellectual Philo-Semitism

*Intellectual philo-Semitism*, which may be said to have begun during the Middle Ages, has continued to the present day and is currently the most prevalent form of philo-Semitism.[40] The bases of intellectual philo-Semitism are the historical affinity of Judaism with literacy, the disproportionately high representation of Jews in intellectual or scientific professions, and the contributions of Jews, well out of proportion to their numbers, to scientific and other forms of cultural innovation. These have led to a high regard for Jewish scholarship and intellect.

It must be made clear, however, that Christian regard for Jewish intellectualism is not in itself indicative of philo-Semitism. Many anti-Semites admit Jewish intellectualism, and this intellectualism may itself be a cause of anti-Semitism.[41] It is almost an axiom that "Jews are frequently thought to be especially intelligent and talented by persons who nonetheless dislike them."[42] Whether this is from jealousy, fear, or a combination of both is less important here than the fact of an intellectual anti-Semitism.

What distinguishes intellectual philo-Semitism from intellectual anti-Semitism is that the philo-Semite couples his respect with a manifest, untroubled admiration for Jewish intellectualism and, because of this admiration, an affection for Jews. C. P. Snow, for example, points out that "Jews have ... thrown out more ability in relation to their numbers than any group on earth." He adds that "in almost every sphere of human activity, the Jews have made contribution utterly out of proportion of their numbers." Snow regards himself as a friend of Jews and announces this openly: "While there is a single anti-Semite alive, we [Christian friends of the Jews] are proud to be on the other side."[43] This illustrates intellectual philo-Semitism.

Intellectual philo-Semitism was historically manifest in the employment of Jewish scientists, mapmakers, and translators during the Middle Ages as well as in the respect with which men such as Maimonides and Rashi were held. Yet well before the time of Maimonides and Rashi, as far back as the fifth century, Theodoric the Great asked Jews into Ravenna and Milan because of their contributions to business, to arts and crafts, and to the humanities. Several centuries later Jews were invited into Naples by Frederick II to work as translators and to instruct Christian scholars in Hebrew.[44] More significantly, intellectual philo-Semitism was implicit, and often explicit, in the actions of various popes and rulers who used the services of Jewish physicians during the Middle Ages. To a large degree it was because of their warm regard for their Jewish physicians that these popes and rulers were supportive of other Jews.

Intellectual philo-Semitism diminished in the later Middle Ages, when the ban on Jews entering universities was in effect and few Jewish scholars produced works of interest to those outside the Jewish community. With the coming of Emancipation, however, Jewish intellectualism and Christian regard for that intellectualism once more flourished. To at least one man, Mirabeau, it was in itself a reason for that emancipation. "There is only one thing to be lamented, that so highly gifted a nation should so long have been kept in a state wherein it was impossible for its powers to develop, and every far-sighted man must rejoice in the acquisition of useful fellow-citizens from among the Jews."[45] The continuing growth of a distinctive intellectual class, beginning in the eighteenth century and flourishing in the nineteenth, contributed greatly to intellectual philo-Semitism.

Perhaps the most singularly important consequence of intellectual philo-Semitism has been its effect on Jews. This form of philo-Semitism, more than any other, contributes to a favorable self-image of Jews, provides a motive for continuing whatever intellectualism (preeminent or not) that Jews have, and in an age in which brain is valued over brawn, makes all intellectuals, not least Jews, valuable in and of themselves.

### Democratic/Liberal Philo-Semitism

As the supremacy of religious ideology diminished, religious philo-Semitism similarly declined—although, like religion itself, religious philo-Semitism has not withered away completely. Taking religion's place was a secular, democratic ideology conducive to a democratic, liberalistic philo-

Semitism. Democratic-liberal philo-Semitism is a regard for Jews based on the idea that each individual is entitled not only to religious freedom, but to social and political freedom. In Cromwell's words, "liberty of conscience is a natural right,"[46] and Jews as Jews are entitled to and deserving of the same social, political, and religious considerations as any other group.

Because individual social and religious freedom is explicit in liberal ideology, that position necessarily supported Jewish emancipation. The revolutionary idea that every individual, regardless of religious convictions, should be a member of the state with full rights and responsibilities was at the heart of Jewish emancipation. This is the crux of liberal ideology.[47]

It is true that the causes of Jews and liberals coincided, so that liberals, in supporting Jews, supported their own ideals; but care must be taken not to overstate this. To charge, as Peter G. J. Pulzer does, that Christians served only their own interests by supporting Jewish emancipation does not denigrate that support, nor lessen the philo-Semitism that support manifested.[48] As "political power may be obtained or consolidated through the manipulation of prejudice" in a negative sense, so, too, may it be used in a positive sense.[49] If in the case of negative prejudice specifically directed against Jews, it is manifest anti-Semitism, where positive prejudice toward Jews is employed, it is manifest philo-Semitism—or at least this possibility must be seriously entertained. Although liberals supported Jews in furtherance of their own causes, they often continued to support Jews after these had been secured and when, in terms of their own self-interest, it was unnecessary to do so.[50]

One should also consider the possibility that the liberals' actions in support of Jews may have been based more on a logical extension of their prior arguments than on their concern for Jews. But as noted in the discussion of nationalistic philo-Semitism, this was not universally the case. The argument that liberals supported Jews only because of logical consistency does not obtain, although consistency of argument surely influenced some individuals and would be important for tolerance and acceptance of Jews.

The above notwithstanding, one cannot deny the possibility that liberals used Jews as tools, that is, that they used the "Jewish Question" for their own ends. Still, these liberals can legitimately be said to be philo-Semitic because the Jews gained benefits as great as did the wielders of the "tools." From the point of view of the Jews, their employment as tools, if such an assertion is justifiable, was not only tolerable but enthusiastically endorsed.

Yet it must be determined whether they really were the liberals' tools. If by securing for Jews a place in society, which they clearly wanted, the liberals enhanced their own position, is this using Jews or is it merely a manifestation of liberal Christian-Jewish cooperation for mutual benefit? The latter position seems reasonable, especially in light of the fact that Jews often asked Christians to plead their case.[51] It was hardly a situation in which Jews were unwilling or unwitting victims. Further, it must be recalled that in numerous instances philo-Semites undertook great risks and costs in supporting Jews. Beyond this, it cannot be discounted that liberal Christians saw Jews as potential members of society; this, virtually by the definition of the times, was philo-Semitic and was so viewed by Jews, anti-Semites, and liberals alike.[52]

It is possible to suggest, however, that liberal philo-Semitism is in fact a-Semitism, that liberals were not concerned with Jews as Jews, but only with Jews as one of many oppressed peoples. In some cases this may have been true. However, the depth, tenacity, and ferocity of the struggles undertaken by many Gentile liberals to support Jews—and if not only Jews, most dramatically Jews—in the struggle for emancipation precludes the conclusion that they regarded Jewish rights simply as an extension of universal rights without taking notice of these rights, at the time of the struggle, as the rights of Jews.[53]

In conjunction with the above, one should consider the support other minority groups gave Jews. In this case it is virtually impossible to judge whether or not the manifest philo-Semitism is genuine. Here alone, those who supported Jews had as much to gain by that support as the Jews themselves, although it is possible that the Jews found genuine allies among other minority groups, that is, allies truly concerned with helping Jews.[54]

## Humanistic and Social Philo-Semitism

Finally, one must consider humanistic and social philo-Semitism. *Humanistic philo-Semitism* implies a belief that all men are valuable in and of themselves and, therefore, that Jews are worthy of support, regard, respect, and consideration. Humanism is manifest in and contributes to the liberal/democratic, religious, and to a lesser degree, nationalistic forms of philo-Semitism. It is the one form of philo-Semitism that does not have a corresponding form of anti-Semitism. *Social philo-Semitism* is based on the idea that social intercourse between Christians and Jews leads to friendly, positive relations.[55] Humanistic and social philo-Semitism contributed greatly to the right of presence and, most especially, to the right of membership of Jews in Europe (Jewish emancipation).

During specific periods in the Middle Ages, such as the Little Renaissance of the twelfth century and the major Renaissance of the fifteenth century, humanism was a prevalent philosophy in Europe. Similarly, humanistic philosophy was a major contributor to the evolution of liberal and democratic ideologies.

Perhaps the strongest counterargument regarding humanistic philo-Semitism is that humanism, virtually by definition, is not specifically directed toward Jews. To some degree this is true, but while humanism suggests regard for all people, no group in Europe so benefited from that perspective as did Jews. Humanistic considerations were one of the reasons for the Catholic Church's tolerance of Jews, tolerance that was not always, or even usually, applied to others. Similarly, Protestantism often viewed Jews through religiously humanistic eyes. Oliver Cromwell, for example, expressed his concern for Jews in this way: "Great is my sympathy with this poor people whom God chose, and to whom He gave his law." Nor was he alone in such views.[56]

Although it may be true that humanism "was a pagan movement" because "it was anti-clerical,"[57] a good deal of humanism was expressed within the two main Christian powers of Europe. The ideology of humanism required toleration, and not only in the negative sense of that term, of Jews, the universal minority.

Humanistic philo-Semitism was particularly effective in conjunction with intellectual philo-Semitism or, in a different vein, in conjunction with intellectuals supporting a humanistic position. This was nowhere more apparent than in the struggles for Jewish emancipation. It was through intellectuals arguing a humanistic and philo-Semitic position that the initial support of emancipation was heard. This explains Katz's suggestion that the two "key words" in the process of emancipation were "*raison*" and "*humanité*." He is speaking here of France, but this was the case throughout Europe.[58]

Most obviously, perhaps, humanism was at the heart of Jewish emancipation in England. Macaulay's arguments offer a case in point:

> *Let us do justice to them.* Let us open to them the door of the House of Commons. Let us open to them every career in which ability and energy can be displayed. Till we have done this, let us not presume to say that there is no genius among the countrymen of Isaiah, no heroism among the descendants of the Maccabees.[59]

A similar position was taken by Hazlitt, who termed the emancipation of English Jewry "but a natural step in the progress of civilization." If we do not grant Jews emancipation, Hazlitt continued, it is because "we are intolerant. This, and this alone, is the reason."[60]

As suggested earlier, humanism was the catalyst for the international philo-Semitism that was especially manifest in the nineteenth century. While this expression of pro-Jewish bias encompasses humanistic, liberal, and religious philo-Semitism, none are as significant as the humanistic. This was clearly shown during the Damascus Affair in the mid-nineteenth century. Consider, for example, the way in which "a member of Parliament named Smith" regarded Jews during that time.

> A nation connected with us by everything that religion holds dear and sacred; a nation whose faith is based upon history, that awaits with unfaltering confidence its political and religious restoration; a nation closely bound up with the progress of trade and civilization through the whole world, and in friendly intercourse with the whole world.[61]

Again, while humanism rightly regards all people as invaluable, few have benefited so much from this philosophy as has European Jewry.

Numerous scholars have effectively argued that social intercourse between Jews and Christians was a prime factor in the assistance Christians offered Jews in the Middle Ages and later in Christian support for emancipation.[62] Indeed, this has been illustrated earlier. It has been pointed out, for example, that numerous Christian friends of Jews assisted them during the Crusades. Similarly, during the struggle for Jewish emancipation, Christian allies supported and defended Jews and their right of membership. The reasons are cogently offered by Howard Morley Sachar: "Jews were no longer strangers behind ghetto walls, abstract creatures to be pitied and indulged because of a doctrinaire humanitarianism. They were comrades in arms, flesh-and-blood people, who had fought the good liberal fight for several decades at the side of their Christian colleagues." He adds that Jews had proven themselves, they were "known to be trustworthy."[63] Sachar is speaking here about the post-1848 era. Similar situations obtained, *mutatis mutandis*, throughout history.

From the Middle Ages until the present day, social intercourse between Christians and Jews has not only reduced animosity on both sides, but has heightened friendship. One must acknowledge a loose social philo-Semitism based upon personal and friendly relations between Christians and Jews. It is possible to view this with skepticism, however, noting that it would involve only those with a propensity for friendliness toward members of another group. This may be true; nonetheless it is not the case that initial contact in all situations is voluntary. Often such contacts begin as secondary group affiliations and gradually emerge into primary relations. It seems reasonable to assert that personal contact was, and is, effective in reducing anti-Semitism and increasing philo-Semitism. If there is a psychologically based anti-Semitism formed on the basis of idiosyncratic personal problems, there can also be a psychologically based philo-Semitism. This may come to the fore through personal contact, although other factors, such as religion or liberalism, undoubtedly contribute to this.

A second factor that is linked to social philo-Semitism should also be noted here. This form of philo-Semitism can arise and be sustained through individual Jews and Christians having commitments to the same or similar values. This is of special significance in the intellectual community, where Jews are disproportionately represented and where Christian philo-Semitism is perhaps most clearly manifest; yet it can and does also extend to other areas, such as the arts, music, and sports.

A parallel interest in, and commitment to, a shared value may result in regular social intercourse and frequently does so. Moreover, the interest will often transcend the narrow, particularistic qualities that form interpersonal barriers. Factors such as ethnicity, religion, and nationality may then be superseded by mutual concerns and enjoyments. In addition, the existence of a mutual commitment by Jews and Christians to a value that leads or contributes to social philo-Semitism may transcend the value itself. The enjoyment and profitability (in a nonmaterialistic sense) of a mutual commitment may enhance the potential of any extant social philo-Semitism; it may, that is, increase the depth of the philo-Semitism that existed when that philo-Semitism was based solely on the shared values.[64]

With the exception of humanistic philo-Semitism, all forms of philo-Semitism have a parallel form of anti-Semitism. There is, however, a kind of anti-Semitism that has no converse form of philo-Semitism: the rise of "scientific" anti-Semitism is without direct philo-Semitic parallel.

Yet to some limited degree a form of scientific philo-Semitism may be said to exist. Almost simultaneously with the rise of biological, pseudoscientific anti-Semitism, there developed a rejection of this type of anti-Semitism. The argument that Jews (or any group for that matter) are inferior, immoral, or unethical because of genetic factors did not surface without a struggle; nor was that position propagated without opposition. Numerous Christians rejected the concept of Jewish racial inferiority, regarded it as specious, and came to the defense of Jews when the latter were attacked because of their "biology." Indeed, philo-Semites have long argued that the "problems" of the Jews resulted from their treatment at the hands of Christians. Thus repudiation of a genetic cause of the Jewish difference preceded arguments endorsing that view by several centuries. Counterattacks against arguments of Jewish "racial inferiority," however, were most widely heard in the late nineteenth and early twentieth centuries, when biological anti-Semitism was at its peak.

It is difficult to claim with any certainty that the repudiation of biological anti-Semitism was inspired by philo-Semitism. It is not at all impossible that those who rejected theories of racial inferiority were simply intellectually honest and recognized the absurdity of that idea. However, their counterarguments did blunt the charges of those who attacked Jews because of alleged biological differences. Therefore they manifested a form of philo-Semitism, if only in its weakest sense, as anti-anti-Semitism, whether or not they intended to do so.

## NOTES

1. Allport (1958), pp. 285, 307, 410.
2. Allport (1958), p. 203. See also ibid., p. 201.
3. Allport (1958), p. 210.
4. There are, of course, other meanings of the word "pure"; it might, for example, be used to describe absolute anti- or philo-Semitism. In this sense "pure" anti-Semitism and "pure" philo-Semitism might exist as a motive of individuals, but not as an essential, ahistorical form.

5. Freud (1967), p. 116.

6. Mannheim (1936, p. 31) succinctly explains this: "As a rule, human thought is not motivated by a contemplative impulse since it acquires a volitional and emotional-conscious undercurrent to assure the continuous orientation for knowledge in group life. Precisely because knowing is fundamentally collective knowing, . . . it presupposes a community of experiencing prepared for in the subconscious."

7. Robb (1954), p. 29.

8. See, for example, H. M. Sachar (1958), p. 55; Katz (1973), p. 15; Schweitzer (1971), p. 140; Arendt (1958), p. 57; Prinz (1968), pp. 154, 186, 195; Poliakov (1965), p. 197; Margolis and Marx (1969), p. 609; Necheles (1971), pp. 123, 129; Parkes (1962), p. 129; Sklare and Solotaroff, in Stember (1961), p. 9; and Cuddihy (1976), p. 79. The *Universal Jewish Encyclopedia* (index, p. 49) lists various "philo-Semites." Those included have "rendered particular services in behalf of Jews." Neither motives nor explanations in connection with this are discussed. One scholar does offer an explanation of philo-Semitism. However, his explanation is untenable for a variety of reasons. Bermant (1971) equates philo-Semitism with Zionism. While it is true that he is concerned primarily with English Christians who worked for the establishment of a Jewish homeland, this definition is clearly unacceptable. It is limited, in a broad sense, to the post-Emancipation era of Jews and, in a more restricted sense, to political philo-Semitism. Moreover, one cannot equate philo-Semitism and Zionism. Such an equation implicitly restricts the definition of "Jew" to that of a nationality and, further, ignores the manifestations of philo-Semitism in the religious, economic, and social spheres and in relation to the two major issues in Jewish history: genocide and emancipation.

9. Roth (1962), pp. 10-11.

10. On the various bases of anti-Semitism see Robb (1954), p. 35; Byrnes (1969), pp. 85-86; Arendt (1958), pp. 4-5, 9; Pulzer (1969), pp. 70, 80; Mayer, in Graeber and Britt (1942), p. 318; Hertzler, in Graeber and Britt (1942), pp. 62-100; Hertzberg (1968), p. 7; Blalock (1967), p. 41; Ray (1972), pp. 207-8, 211; and Loewenstein (1951), pp. 17, 21, 64-65, 79. The number of bases is apparently limitless. They range from a multitude of economic factors to nationalism, minority status, the "chosen people irritant," and ideology, through various religious causes, the unique social structure of the Jews, and numerous psychological issues, to, finally, pragmatic considerations.

11. That this would depend upon interpretation of available data is obvious. It might be suggested, however, that numerous expulsions and reentries into France, for instance, were based in a large degree upon the avariciousness of the king. Those Christians who converted to Judaism may indicate the opposite extreme.

12. Many scholars deny that economic motives can be philo-Semitic at all. They attribute Christian acceptance of Jews exclusively to economic considerations; that is, they are convinced that Jews as people were not considered, that Jews were accepted solely because of the supposed financial advantages they could offer the community or the rulers of the community. However, when Jews were expelled for economic reasons, such as pressure from the burghers, there is little hesitation on the part of scholars in labeling that anti-Semitism. Expulsions of this sort were not uncommon. To illustrate: Margolis and Marx (1969, p. 414) point out that "Albert II of Austria, for the consideration of nine hundred gulden, granted the city of Augsburg the permission to drive out its Jews (1439)." Most scholars regard Albert as anti-

Semitic; yet one can reasonably ask whether he was anti-Semitic, greedy, or both. See also Rose (1974), p. 113, and Rogow (1961), p. 73.

13. Pulzer (1969, pp. 267-68) points to an example of a non-philo-Semitic pro-Jewish act.

14. Hertzberg (1968), pp. 9, 13.

15. Hertzberg notes (1968, p. 28) that it was because the Huguenots were ousted that Jews were wanted. He adds: "Clearly economic considerations were paramount in permitting the marranos of the sixteenth and seventeenth centuries to come to the surface as Jews after two centuries of living clandestinely." This is true, but it does not refute the argument that the French preferred Jews to Huguenots. One possible motive for that preference is that the existence of Protestantism was perceived as a greater threat than the existence of Judaism. In any case, if economics had been the sole motive, the Huguenots would not have been expelled.

16. Keller (1966), pp. 170-71. See also Pulzer (1969), p. 8.

17. Katz (1973), p. 38.

18. This worked against Jews as well. Graetz (1894, vol. 4, p. 260) points to an instance in Breslau and Schweidnitz where "the majority of the nobility were among their [the Jews'] debtors, and several towns were either themselves debtors or had become security for their princes. Hence it is not unlikely that some debtors of rank secretly planned to evade their liabilities by ridding themselves of the Jews."

19. Rivkin (1971), p. 160.

20. Hertzberg (1968, p. 338) argues that the French Revolution contributed to the development of a modern economic system and because of this restrictions against Jews were abrogated. It is also possible that the economic interdependence of Jews and Christians made more and more Christians repudiate anti-Semitism.

21. Glock and Stark (1966), p. 65.

22. Küng (1976), p. 167, writes of the "special affinity" between Judaism and Christianity: "It is not with Buddhism, Hinduism and Confucianism, not even with Islam despite its influence there, but only with Judaism that Christianity has this unique relationship: A relationship of origin, resulting in numerous common structures and values."

23. Poliakov (1965), p. 158.

24. Katz (1973), p. 14. He argues (ibid., p. 14) that the Jews were to be kept in a subservient position in order to attest to the "truth" of Christianity. However, the Pauline influence should not be discounted.

25. Arguments supporting theological philo-Semitism can be found in the works of Eckhardt (1973) and Parkes (1969b), for example.

26. Elias Freeman, "The Motivation of Jew-Gentile Relationships," in Graeber and Britt (1942, p. 159), states: "There is no unequivocal evidence of any sustained effort by the church to throw its weight against anti-Semitism." Yet it is also true, as Flannery notes (1965, p. 274), that "the anti-Semitic tradition in Christendom . . . never became a universal dogmatic tradition, let alone a formal definition of the church."

27. On Luther as an anti-Semite see, for example, Marcus (1965), pp. 166-69. Also see Bainton (1956), p. 62. In 1523 Luther wrote: "I would advise and beg everyone to deal kindly with the Jews." And: "If we wish to make them better, we must deal with them not according to the law of the pope, but according to the law of Christian charity." But twenty years later, when it became clear that Jews were not flocking to

Protestantism, Luther wrote: "What then shall we Christians do with this damned, rejected race of Jews, . . . since they live among us and we know about their lying and blasphemy and cursing, we can not tolerate them if we do not wish to share in their lies, curses, and blasphemy."

It seems that all leaders of new religions, at least in the western world, want and anticipate the conversion of Jews. This was the case with Mohammed also.

28. There seems to have been an especially impassioned desire on the part of many Christian theologians to convert Jews. See Abbott (1947), vol. 4, pp. 51-52. Heer (1962, p. 253) notes that in thirteenth-century England "the Dominicans of Oxford regarded the conversion of the Jews as their special mission." They were not alone. Pope Gregory IX wrote (May 5, 1236): "Although we open the bowels of paternal compassion to all who come to the Christian faith, since the salvation of everyone is dear to us, nevertheless we cherish converts from Judaism with even greater affection" (Quoted in Grayzel, 1966, p. 233).

29. However, this permission was usually granted by lay rulers, not churchmen.

30. Katz (1973, p. 11) argues that the acceptance of Jews into Holland was based on economic considerations as well as on religious tolerance. However, that tolerance was limited to Jews. A. L. Sachar (1965, p. 230) reports that toward the end of the sixteenth century a small number of Marranos regularly met in a private home in Amsterdam to worship. In time they were discovered and "attacked by suspicious citizens who mistook them for Catholics. When the worshippers explained that they were secret Jews, the council granted them permission to remain." In 1602, five years later, "a synagogue was publicly dedicated." In 1615, to a large degree because of the efforts of Hugo Grotius, the eminent jurist and scholar, the government in Holland formally granted sanctuary and religious freedom to Jews. By the end of the seventeenth century, the Jewish community in Amsterdam numbered some ten thousand, the largest in western Europe, See Schweitzer (1971), p. 138.

31. A. L. Sachar (1965), p. 70.

32. But many would not.

33. Quoted in Graetz (1895), vol. 5, p. 439.

34. Macaulay (1967), p. 227.

35. Quoted in Marcus (1965), p. 28.

36. In a broad sense, nationalistic universalism means the treatment of all citizens of the state as legally and formally equal regardless of ethnic or national descent or religious preference. As with all universalisms, however, there is a particularistic facet to nationalistic universalism. To say that every nation subscribes to an ideal of nationalism that overshadows ethnic or religious differences and accepts a fundamental equality of its citizens is not the same as saying that all nations interpret each of these terms in the same way. National unity, national homogeneity, and nationalistic universalism are differently perceived in different nations. Universalistic nationalism, that is, is particularistic in practice.

Western European nations tended to follow a "true" universalistic nationalism. This is why Jews in the western nations were the first Jews to be granted citizenship. It is also why Jews in France, England, and Holland were accepted as Jewish Frenchmen, Englishmen, and Dutchmen, respectively, with comparatively little difficulty.

In the central and eastern European states, nationalistic universalism existed in a form similar to that found in the west. Yet its content was different. In central and eastern Europe many regimes attempted to force religious and ethnic groups to adopt the culture of the dominant group; this became a condition for equal treatment. These nations established criteria of citizenship beyond which one could not go. These criteria were not simply based upon national loyalty; rather, they rested upon conformity to the dominant culture. Each ethnic and religious group had to lose specific aspects of the ethnicity or religiosity that made them unique in order to conform to these standards. The growth and development of reform Judaism in Germany can be understood as an attempt to meet these terms. German reform Judaism represented an attempt to bend traditional Jewry into a nationalistically acceptable Germanic form.

37. Quoted in Hertzberg (1968), p. 31.

38. Hertzberg (1968, p. 22) notes .that Bodin was not only "widely read and revered" but regarded as "the new Aristotle of politics."

39. Quoted in Katz (1973), pp. 164-65.

40. See Veblen (1919); and Glock and Stark (1966), pp. 120, 122.

41. In fact, Sartre writes (1962, p. 23): "To the anti-Semite, intelligence is Jewish." For instances of intellectual anti-Semitism see, for example, Margolis and Marx (1969), p. 695; and Snyder (1967), p. 254.

42. Glock and Stark (1966), p. 120.

43. C. P. Snow in the introduction to Rogow (1961), pp. xvi-xvii.

44. Dimont (1973), pp. 276-77.

45. Quoted in Graetz (1895), vol. 5, p. 433.

46. Church (1895), p. 399.

47. Hobsbawm (1962), p. 38.

48. Pulzer (1969), p. 5.

49. Blalock (1967), p. 41.

50. This was the case, for example, in Hungary. See Dubnov (1973), vol. 5, pp. 289-314; and A. L. Sachar (1965), p. 293.

51. Again, it must be remembered that Jews were not usually admitted to the assemblies where their emancipation was being considered.

52. Hertzberg (1968), p. 323.

53. Nor can one argue that intellectual consistency was the key here; consider Voltaire.

54. See, for example, Bronowski and Mazlish (1962), p. 99; and Pulzer (1969), p. 275.

55. See, for example, Katz (1973), p. 43; and Rose (1974), p. 139.

56. Quoted in Graetz (1895), vol. 5, p. 27. Cromwell also commented (Church, 1895, p. 399): "I desire from all my heart,—I have prayed for it,—I have waited for the day to see union and right understanding between the Godly people—sects, English, Jews, Gentiles, Presbyterians, Independents, Anabaptists, and all." See also Graetz (1895), vol. 5, p. 46.

57. Bronowski and Mazlish (1962), p. 62.

58. Katz (1973), p. 74. He notes (ibid., p. 58) that the initial statements supporting Jewish emancipation "appeared occasionally in the 1770's, prompted by humanitarian or charitable Christian motives."

59. Quoted in Rogow (1961), p. 159. Emphasis added.

60. Quoted in Rosenberg (1960), p. 328.

61. Quoted in Graetz (1895), vol. 5, p. 656.

62. Of particular significance were the literary salons conducted by Henrietta Herz and Rachel Varnhagen in Berlin and by Fanny von Arnstein in Vienna. Many influential Christians, such as Alexander von Humboldt and Friedrich Schleiermacher, were regular participants in meetings held at the homes of these women. It is not accidental that many of the Christians who attended the meetings were fighters for Jewish emancipation. Of course it is also true that some Christians supported Jewish rights yet refused to interact with Jews on a personal level. There are, after all, individuals who love mankind but dislike people. However, it is the efficacy of one's support and not one's personal social predilections that is at issue here.

63. H. M. Sachar (1958), p. 116. See also Graetz (1895), vol. 5, p. 506.

64. It is possible that animosity may develop should competition exist for the fruits of the value. Anti-Semitism may be and often is a result of value competition.

# CONCLUSIONS                                   8

## ON JEWISH SURVIVAL

In dealing with European philo-Semitism, perhaps it is best to take as a point of departure the following facts: (a) Jews suffered numerous massacres and forced conversions; (b) There is not a land in Europe from which Jews were not expelled or barred from entering at one time or another; (c) Jews were almost everywhere a recognizable minority; (d) Jews were everywhere and always defenseless; (e) Jews were subjected to constant social, political, and economic restrictions; and (f) Jews were the particular target of the most intense, full-scale attempt at genocide in modern European history. Yet, though millions died, European Jewry has existed for over two thousand years.

As Freud points out, the Jews are the only people from the Mediterranean Basin "that still exists in name and probably also in nature."[1] Not surprisingly, a multitude of scholars have wondered at the Jews' tenacious ethnic-religious survival. Indeed, it is not incautious to state that virtually every student of Jewish history has considered it. The problem is not easy to solve. Parkes, among others, agrees: "Their [Jews'] survival, or rather the survival of their identity, has been an enigma."[2]

Frederick M. Schweitzer states the historians' problem this way:

> By all the ordinary historical canons, the Jews as a people should have
> disintegrated and disappeared over the historical horizon as of A.D. 70,
> just as the numerous people of the ancient Near East disappeared, e.g.,
> the Assyrians and Lydians, and the medieval invaders of Europe, e.g.,
> the Avars and Goths.[3]

Not only in history, but in other fields as well, the continued existence of Jews has apparently defied the rules. Social scientists are also puzzled by this: Carl Mayer points out that "according to sociological laws the Jews should have perished long ago."[4]

A variety of causes for the Jews' survival have been offered. Some give it a supernatural aura. Werner Keller suggests that "the continued existence of the Jews after eras of the most terrible persecutions is the greatest of miracles."[5] Walter Burghardt, noting that "by every calculation [the Jews] should have perished," considers their continued existence as proof of God's presence in the state of Israel.[6] Others offer less miraculous explanations. Mayer, for example, as well as James Parkes, suggests that their religion was the foundation of Jews' continued existence, while Sigmund Freud has it that their survival was fundamentally because of the Jews' aloofness.[7] And Martin Buber, in viewing the problem, remarks that "the Jewish people has become the eternal people not because it was allowed to live, but because it was not allowed to live. Because it was asked to give more than life, it won life."[8]

Buber intimates what would apparently be voted the main cause of Jewish survival: anti-Semitism. Leon Poliakov, for example, considers anti-Semitism to have been a source of Jewish strength, although he limits this to the era of the crusades.[9] Others are less restrictive in their analyses. J. O. Hertzler comments that "it is just likely, as Israel Zangwill stated in this famous dictum, that it is anti-Semitism which preserves the Jew as a Jew."[10] Abraham Leon Sachar suggests that anti-Semitism "stimulated Jewish unity just when the ancient solidarity was being threatened,"[11] and Sartre suggests that anti-Semitism prevents Jews from being assimilated into the larger society and thus logically has preserved their culture and identity.[12] It should be noted that this position is by no means new. Three centuries ago Spinoza argued the same point, "that the hatred of other nations tends to assure the survival of the Jews has . . . been demonstrated by experience."[13]

The reasoning behind these arguments is succinctly given by George Friedman:

Without the persecutions, without the ghetto and its various forms and surrogates, the Jews, dispersed through the nations but taking part in the evolution toward political liberties and "enlightenment" would have been assimilated more rapidly and completely, as they tended to be in the West since the end of the eighteenth century.[14]

This hypothesis is not without supportive, if superficial, evidence. Italy has a relatively ambivalent, that is, a-Semitic, attitude toward Jews and a strong tendency to eschew anti-Semitism.[15] It would seem that assimilation is one consequence of this. Hertzler points out that for over eight hundred years there has been a relatively large migration of Jews into Italy and a relatively small migration of Jews out of Italy. Despite this, the number of Jews in Italy is small, certainly smaller than the migration would suggest. He argues that these limited numbers can only be caused by "wholesale absorption during the centuries."[16] If anti-Semitism has not forced Jews out of the larger society, then given the Catholic tenor of Italy and the numerical differences between Christians and Jews, it cannot be surprising that the number of Jews has declined by attrition, by gradual absorption into the larger, Catholic society.

Another, perhaps more interesting, phase of Jewish history apparently offers even greater support for the thesis of anti-Semitism as a preservative of Jewry: the saga of the progeny of those Jews who migrated to China two millennia ago. There are indications that Jews "penetrated" China about 206 B.C. and in A.D. 1163 reached K'ai-feng Fu, the capital of Honan. As late as the sixteenth century, K'ai-feng Fu had "many families who observed Hebrew religious practices which centered in a synagogue."[17] Yet three hundred years later, according to one scholar, "the Jews of K'ai-feng had been completely assimilated into Chinese society."[18] Other scholars confirm this. One notes that before the twentieth century "the few remaining Jews [in China] had no religious bond, and even their historical relationships are almost forgotten."[19] That anti-Semitism was not the cause of the secession of the community of Chinese Jews is fairly well accepted.[20]

More than this, however, it is argued that a "lack" of anti-Semitism, exacerbated by Jews' participation in the civil service system of imperial China, was the *cause* of their absorption into Chinese society and the concomitant erosion of their loyalty to Judaism.[21] Without anti-Semitism there was no mechanism by which Jews in China (or anywhere else, one assumes) could sustain their ethnic-religious identity. It follows that Jewish survival is, at least in part, contingent upon the continuance of anti-Semitism. Anti-Semitism is a "Jewish glue" that not only contributes to group solidarity but perpetuates, through intimidation, hatred, and real or potential violence, the necessity of adherence to the Jewish community.

It would be well to delay such judgments, however; they are not without serious problems. This reasoning fails to explain, for example, the continuance of the Bene Israel (the Jews of Bombay) or the Cochin Jews of India. The ancestors of these groups arrived in the great Subcontinent in about A.D. 200, about the same time as Jews arrived in China.[22] Yet in the twentieth century there was still a small but flourishing Jewish community in India—about twenty-six thousand people—despite the fact that there was virtually no anti-Semitism there.[23] It is necessary to seek another explanation for the continuance of Jews in India, for it is clear from this example that anti-Semitism is *not* a universal "Jewish glue"; it is not anti-Semitism alone that ensures the survival of the Jewish people.

It is probable that at least one reason for the survival of Indian Jewry and, concomitantly, for the withering away of Chinese Jewry was not a lack of anti-Semitism but the relative degree of isolation of each community. Jews in China were isolated from other Jews and therefore could be and were absorbed into the society around them. Jews in India were in constant contact with Jews who continued to migrate to the Subcontinent.[24]

The "lack" of anti-Semitism permitted and perhaps facilitated the absorption of Chinese Jewry into the larger society, but in and of itself, the "lack" of anti-Semitism is only one aspect of the puzzle. To assert that Jewish absorption into a larger society can happen is not the same thing as asserting that it must or will happen. Thus, even if Chinese a-Semitism permitted and facilitated the dissolution of the Chinese Jewish community, it is not sufficient explanation for that dissolution. As Indian a-Semitism did not dissolve the small Indian Jewish community, Chinese a-Semitism cannot be taken as *the* cause of the dissolution of the Chinese Jewish community.

Further, one can question whether the "lack" of anti-Semitism in China was a factor in the absorption of Chinese Jewry. Indeed, if Chinese Jewry had been subjected to anti-Semitism, its traditions never could have been maintained for over fifteen hundred years; neither could Indian Jewry have survived anti-Semitic pressures for an even longer period of time. These communities were too small and isolated from other Jewish communities (anti-Semitism in India would probably have halted migration there) to withstand even relatively minor anti-Semitic restrictions such as economic, social, or political prohibitions. They most certainly would have been crushed by forced conversions or pogroms.

Hannah Arendt's assertion that assimilation is never a real threat to the survival of Jews must be qualified:[25] it is never a real threat to a Jewish community with (a) a sizable number of Jews or (b) contact with other Jews in or from other countries. One or both of these conditions existed in Europe and India; neither did in China.[26]

It is not disputed here that in the west anti-Semitism has been and is an *internal* preservative of Jewry; that is, it does bind Jews together, although it might be argued that anti-Semitism has caused as many people to abandon Judaism as it kept within Judaism.[27] In general, any in-group will collect itself when threatened by an out-group. But if an out-group is capable of destroying the in-group and is determined to do so, one cannot assume that such a threat is a "preservative" of the in-group. If an in-group is so vulnerable that it can be destroyed by an out-group bent on doing so, attacks on the in-group, if sustained, will lead to annihilation, not preservation. That internal cohesion will prevent ethnic-religious desertions is true to a limited degree, but that internal preservation will sustain a group during cataclysmic attack is logically and empirically absurd. Consider the Albigensians; consider the Jews under Hitler.

Given the number of European Jews and the degree of contact between Jewish communities, one must conclude that these, and not anti-Semitism, were the major mechanisms for Jewish survival in Europe. Anti-Semitism is at best a weak preservative of Jewish ethnicity or religiosity; in no sense is anti-Semitism a blessing in disguise. European Jewry did not survive because of anti-Semitism, it survived despite it.[28]

However, other suggestions have been made to explain why European Jews, unlike other minorities, did not fade into the larger societies. With his usual good sense, Poliakov points out that the reason is not religion, anti-Semitism, or miracles. The fact that Jews "have been an exception to the rule is doubtless due to the extraordinarily complex attitude of the Christians toward them in a situation that was virtually unique."[29] One aspect of this complexity is the prejudice of philo-Semitism.

While anti-Semitism provided internal cohesion, philo-Semitism combatted anti-Semitism and prevented it from reaching its full, noxious potential. There can be no doubt, given the vulnerability of European Jews, that their existence was continually in jeopardy. Philo-Semitism lessened this danger. More than simply countering anti-Semitism, however, philo-Semitism actually contributed to Jewish survival in ways that some ascribe to the effects of anti-Semitism. Philo-Semitism keeps Jews aware of their heritage more than anti-Semitism; philo-Semitism encourages Jewish pride more than anti-Semitism; and philo-Semitism provides a basis for Jewish resistance to conversion and assimilation more than anti-Semitism.

In limited instances self-awareness and self-pride may not be contingent upon outside attitudes (e.g., among street gang members or in artistic communities). Among ethnic groups, however, self-awareness and self-pride are largely rooted or validated in or against outsiders' attitudes. This is especially true when the ethnic group is numerically small in comparison with the larger society and when the group is viewed with opprobrium. Thus, for example, as a reaction to prejudice, that is, not only discrimination, there are regular instances of ethnic self-hatred, name changing, denial of racial or ethnic origins, refusal to associate with group members, and so on in contemporary America.[30] And, as noted, numerous European Jews converted to Christianity because of anti-Semitism.

As a reaction to the negativism of the larger society, internal cohesion is often generated among ethnic groups, and group members close ranks for protection. This closing of ranks is the reason anti-Semitism is of some consequence in terms of Jewish resistance to conversion and assimilation. Further, prejudice against an ethnic group will generate positive prejudice for that group among the group's members. As Gordon Allport notes, "to be prejudiced in favor of one's kind is a natural reflex of out-group prejudice against one's kind."[31]

Yet how much more will one be prejudiced in favor of one's kind if some members of the out-group are also prejudiced in favor of one's group? If some members of the larger society regard the ethnic group favorably, the "natural reflex" will be strengthened. This can be a powerful factor for ethnic awareness, ethnic pride, and ethnic survival.

Christian anti-Semitism holds Jews together through fear and provides the negative glue of contempt and opprobrium; anti-Semitism and voluntary isolation by Jews, which minimized intermarriage with Christians, prevented conversions to some degree, and reduced assimilation, helped sustain Jewish culture. Christian philo-Semitism holds Jews together through confirming pride and self respect, and provides the positive glue of affection and approbation; philo-Semitism helped prevent the Jews' destruction. One basis of the "miracle" of Jewish survival, of continued ethnic and religious Jewish existence, and of Jewish identity, is the regard, respect, and affection Jews have received from philo-Semites for over two thousand years and the manifestations of that regard, respect, and affection. And by no means is this a minor factor in Jewish survival. Quite the contrary; it is a major reason—possibly *the* major reason—why Jews are the only ancient people that survives today. The protection and sanctuaries offered Jews by philo-Semites, the abrogation of forced conversions, and the attempts to halt massacres all contributed to the physical survival of Jews in Europe.[32] The respect, admiration, and affection Jews received from philo-Semites contributed to Jews' awareness of their own heritage and their worth as Jews. Assimilation poses threats to Jewish survival, but unchecked anti-Semitism poses a more immediate threat.

Almost without exception, studies of the history of European Jewry have emphasized the negative aspects of that history. There is, unfortunately, much that is negative to emphasize. However, the comparatively small number of Jews in Europe did continue to exist despite numerous and powerful efforts to consign them to history. There can be no question that intense philo-Semitism, manifested at select and propitious moments, saved European Jewry from extinction. At barest minimum, it is obvious that without their defenders the history of Jews in Europe would have been considerably worse. Throughout the essentially bleak history of European Jewry, and the generally atrocious actions by Christians, rays of light appeared and genuinely Christian acts occurred.

## ON JEWISH EMANCIPATION

It was argued earlier that there is no such thing as pure philo-Semitism—or pure, asocially derived, or innate anti-Semitism, for that matter. Prejudice, both favorable and unfavorable, is rooted in society. The prevalent ideologies and universalisms of any society will determine to a substantial degree the ways in which the citizens of that society perceive the surrounding world and, of course, the individuals and groups within it. Changes in ideologies and universalisms will result in changes in prejudices, among other things. This is clearly illustrated by the various ways in which Christians have regarded Jews. Changing situations in European society, from ecclesiastic to secularistic, from monarchial to democratic, from feudal to industrial, and so on, altered perceptions of Jews and, consequently, the expressions and forms of both anti-Semitism and philo-Semitism. The most general philo-Semitic changes, but not the only ones, were from a religious to a sociopolitical pro-Jewish prejudice, or in other words, from a theological to a liberal-democratic humanism.

One must disagree, then, with Jacob Katz's assertion that the pattern of Jewish-Christian relations does not vary;[33] it does. Arnold A. Rogow correctly points out that "while, for most Gentiles, the Jews have always been 'different', the 'difference' imputed to Jews has changed over time."[34] Christian perceptions of Jews vary; these perceptions depend upon numerous changing conditions in the environment in which Jews live—varying social, economic, and political situations and, most important, current ideologies and styles of universalism. Jewish-Christian relations have never been static or inflexible.

Perhaps the best illustration of this is the ideological process that took place in the changing status of Jews from "permanent aliens" to citizens, from "resident foreigners" to members of European society.

It has already been noted that the right of residence that Jews enjoyed in the Middle Ages began to be questioned in the late eighteenth century. By the nineteenth century the issue was in full debate. The problem, the "Jewish Question," was no longer one of simply tolerating or granting residence to a different religious group or not doing so, but of accepting that different religious group as full members of society. The reason for this change was the rise of nationalism.

Jews in the Middle Ages were usually perceived religiously. Even in instances when they were not so perceived, that is, when they were considered a national entity, few problems arose thereby. The dominant medieval universalism was theological; perception of Jews as a religious group thus took precedence over perception of Jews as a nationality. Further, it mattered relatively little whether Jews were a nation as well. They were not thereby traitorous, nor were they a threat to the host nation. With the exception of a small number of court Jews and Jewish physicians, religious differences generally ensured that most Jews would be separated from the mainstream of Christian society. In addition, medieval Europeans usually thought of themselves as being a part of Christendom on a larger scale or, more narrowly, as belonging to a local area.[35] The nation-state itself was barely conceivable.

In the late eighteenth century, however, with the coming of the nation-state and its concomitant ideology of nationalism, Christian perceptions of Jews changed. National distinctions increasingly took precedence over religious ones, and Jews began to be regarded as a national entity whose loyalty to the "adopted" home must be demonstrated. Nationalistic ideology could not and would not tolerate a "state within a state." That ideology demanded homogeneity: everyone must be *of* the state and not merely within the state. If residence continued, membership must follow. Thus the medieval right of residence was again brought into question and then superseded by a new issue, the right of citizenship.

Initially the issue involving Jewish citizenship—membership in the state—was that of Jews' willingness to be citizens. Would Jews accept a new status if it meant abandoning many Jewish traditions? Would Jews, in a word, become assimilated? There arose a second issue, more volatile than the first and replacing volition with ability as the most important condition: *could* Jews become members of the state? Willingness by Jews to become assimilated did not ensure that the necessary adjustments could be made. This was the battleground for Jewish emancipation in the eighteenth and nineteenth centuries.

It must be understood that the ideology of nationalism did not come to pass in and of itself. There were other ideologies that grew at the same time or close enough in time to nationalism to have an effect on its development. Partially in response to the ideology of nationalism and partially as a cause of that ideology, and most noticeably in the west, the concepts of the rights of man and freedom of religion developed. Parallel with these, however, and generally in eastern and central Europe, ideologies of racism, historical purity, and nationalistic romanticism grew.[36] Nationalism as an ideology thus took a bifurcated path.

Those who accepted the coupling of nationalism with the rights of man usually accepted the possibility of Jews as members of the state; they argued that Jews could become citizens and would if given the opportunity. This was most noticeable in France, where supporters of the Revolution generally endorsed human and religious rights and thus were supporters of Jewish emancipation. Most of those who opposed the Revolution opposed all aspects of it, including Jewish emancipation. In the west, then, with the successful conclusion of the Revolution, the problem of what to do with the Jews was resolved.

However, in the rest of Europe the problem of Jewish inclusion in the state was in full debate and would be throughout the nineteenth century. Moreover, the issue no longer revolved around the Jews' volition or ability to become citizens; rather the willingness of Christians to accept them as citizens dominated the debates.

Generally, as A. L. Sachar notes, the Napoleonic Wars "aroused an intolerant nationalism which brought suspicion upon every alien group."[37] More specifically, the years 1814-19 saw the growth of a "new wave of anti-Jewish propaganda and animosity, ideologically nurtured by the awakening of nationalism and historical romanticism."[38] This "new wave" was the first stage of political (or nationalistic) anti-Semitism.

Anti-Semitism did not exist solely because of nationalistic ideologies, however. During the nineteenth century, religious anti-Semitism was on the wane, but it had not vanished. Quite the contrary; according to Arthur

Hertzberg, "the Christian idea that the religion of the Jews and their rejection of Christianity made them an alien element was still strong in Europe."[39] Hertzberg is speaking here of the post-1848 era; however, religious anti-Semitism, if diminishing in intensity, was still clearly discernible throughout the nineteenth century.

This older form of anti-Semitism, coupled with the growth of nationalism, divided European thought vis-à-vis Jews into two broad camps. Those who based nationalism on a liberal interpretation of human, religious, and state rights were supportive of Jewish emancipation and membership in the nation. Those who viewed nationalism as restrictive, whereby loyalty to the nation was enmeshed with Christianity, romantic nationalism, and nationalistic particularism (that is, everyone must be as one with, in, and for the nation), were opposed to Jewish emancipation.

The struggles for and against acceptance of Jews as members of society, then, were clearly tied to the new ideologies and ideological interpretations. Throughout Europe, liberals tried to assure the populace that their perception of nationalistic ideology—the union of nationalism with liberalism, human rights, and tolerance—was in the interests of that populace. Christian supporters of Jewish emancipation had the additional task of applying that position to Jews, of ensuring that liberalism, human rights, and tolerance would be applied to Jews and Christians alike. Their problem was not simply one of propagating a specific ideological position, but one of ensuring that the ideological particularism was universally applied. They had to combat an opposing ideology and shatter the two-thousand-year-old tradition of Jewish exclusion.

One other point must be considered in conjunction with the changing ideologies: the rise and development of capitalism. It has already been noted that there were instances when the merchant class was opposed to the admission of Jews into their countries or states. Because of pressures from their economic competitors, Jews in medieval cities and states were often expelled, denied admission, or subjected to restrictions that would limit their economic activity.[40] The purpose, of course, was to reduce the competition for Christian merchants. Rulers were generally in favor of admission of Jews if that admission would prove financially beneficial to them; but for a price they, too, would bar or expel Jews.

The growth of capitalism created a new perspective. Most clearly stated in the writings of Adam Smith, new theories of economic universalism extolled the virtues of an unrestricted, free market. This system would provide the greatest possible economic benefits for the nation. The earlier arguments of prohibition, by which Jews were excluded from certain businesses and refused admission to guilds, were increasingly discarded. The intent, of course, was not to help Jews; the purpose, consistent with nationalistic ideology, was to enhance the economic well-being of the state. Yet Jews did benefit. The inclusion of Jews into the free market system reduced their social isolation and allowed them to enter the mainstream of society. Jewish membership in the new economic life of the nation almost necessarily meant Jewish membership in the nation itself.[41]

Societal change, brought about by the new ideologies of nationalism, human rights, and freedom of religion, along with the growth and development of capitalism, was of no small consequence for the acceptance of Jews as members of European society. Yet the efforts of individuals to have these changes include Jews were of equal significance. It is crucial to recognize that the ideologies and societal changes would not have been applied to Jews without Christian support, that is, without the efforts of philo-Semites.

To demonstrate this, it is important to consider what the philo-Semites were struggling against. In addition to the older, still effective—if now somewhat attenuated—religious anti-Semitism, two new forms of anti-Semitism arose: political anti-Semitism and pseudoscientific racial or biological anti-Semitism. These were formidable barriers to Jewish emancipation. Ideology alone could not shatter them, for these anti-Semitisms were also founded on an ideology. Like democratic-liberal philo-Semitism, these were ultimately founded on the ideology of nationalism, albeit differently interpreted.

As noted, a new form of anti-Semitism, based on the denial of Jewish membership in society, began to grow in France during the first stages of Jewish emancipation. This anti-Semitism rapidly spread throughout Europe wherever the issue of Jewish membership in the state was discussed. By the 1870s it was ubiquitous. This is why Arendt can regard modern anti-Semitism as beginning "everywhere" during the last third of the nineteenth century.[42] Modern anti-Semitism is essentially political anti-Semitism.

The first phase of political anti-Semitism was directed against the unwillingness of Jews to surrender their ancient traditions in favor of assimilation. This is at the heart of the claim that Jews constitute a "state within a state."[43] Jews, that is, will not mix with Christians. The "refusal" of Jews to mix with Christians is one basis of Peter G. J. Pulzer's argument that "modern political anti-Semitism is different from any earlier sporadic outbursts of Jewbaiting."[44] Separation of Jews and Christians was not merely accepted but assiduously worked for in the Middle Ages. Indeed, medieval European authorities were afraid that Jews wanted to mix with Christians socially. Authorities in the nineteenth century were concerned with the opposite problem.

Another aspect of political anti-Semitism began to develop in the late Napoleonic period. As nationalistic ideologies moved eastward from France, they became increasingly coupled with historical romanticism and, gradually, with Christian symbolism. Thus, for example, in Germany Christianity and nationalism were not regarded as separate belief systems. Quite the contrary, the two had an intertwined identity to most Germans, based on a "Weltanschauung and a spiritual force." The intertwining of Christianity with national-ism necessarily resulted in the exclusion of Jews from "any social unit."[45] Nor was this conjunction of nationalistic ideology and Christianity limited to Germany. Indeed, it was fairly well accepted by many people throughout central and eastern Europe.

It should be understood that, initially, nationalistic anti-Semitism arose from a reactionary response to liberalism and liberal ideologies that was not especially anti-Semitic or, indeed, nationalistic. Opposed to nationalism because of the west European coupling of that ideology with liberalism, the reactionary, anti-Revolutionary forces in Europe were only peripherally con-cerned with Jews. A new, anti-liberal nationalism developed rather quickly, however, and with it political anti-Semitism. In part because of the liberals' support of Jewish emancipation, conservative nationalists, especially in cen-tral and eastern Europe, became increasingly anti-Semitic and to a substan-tial degree nationalism became equated with anti-Semitism. In an age of intense nationalism, anti-Semitism intensified correspondingly.

With the move eastward, the underlying basis of political anti-Semitism changed. Anti-Semites were no longer worried that Jews would not join the nation, would not abandon their long-cherished separatism, or would not be loyal to the state. The argument now was that Jews *could not* join the nation. Protests by Jews and their Christian allies notwithstanding, Jews were not of the state nor could they ever be of the state. More, this had little to do with religion or Judaism's adaptation to the new social structure. The cause was genetic. The anti-Semitism of earlier times "had now been reinforced by the pagan cultural argument that the Jews were by the very nature of their own culture and even by their *biological* inheritance an unassimilable element."[46] Thus began the first use of an extremely powerful tool of the anti-Semites: racial anti-Semitism.

It is important to recognize that some of the ideologies of liberalism, including the concept of freedom of religion, were fairly well accepted in the nineteenth century. It is undoubtedly true that acceptance of religious free-dom was not brought about by a general willingness to tolerate Jews but was an effect of Europe's Protestant/Catholic dichotomy. Nonetheless, the preju-dice of religious anti-Semitism became increasingly unacceptable as a basis of Jewish exclusion, and racial anti-Semitism became an effective tool. It pro-vided a new basis for anti-Semitism and, with the increasing development of science and, more importantly, of pseudoscience, it apparently achieved sound footing.[47]

Pulzer suggests that racial anti-Semitism has a long history.[48] This is true; to some degree the actions taken against the Marranos in Spain were racially based. Nonetheless, racial anti-Semitism can reasonably be taken to have begun during the period following the French Revolution and to have reached full maturity in the last half of the nineteenth century. This, of course, was the period when most nations in Europe were emancipating their Jews.

The significance of racial anti-Semitism is obvious. Jews were not different merely because of religion; they were biologically different, something other—usually less—than Christians. Supporters of national homogeneity denied citizenship to Jews because of ideology; that is, the desire for national homogeneity prohibited the acceptance of a racially distinct people as members of society.[49] More than this, biological and cultural variations were supposed to be causally connected. To include Jews in the state would not only be inconsistent with this interpretation of nationalistic ideology, but it would eventually result in a distortion of national ideals and, if Jews and Christians were allowed to mix, in racial impurities. This was an enormously effective weapon with which to battle both liberalism and Jewish emancipation.

This discussion of Jewish emancipation points to two specific issues. First, it is clear that bases of prejudice change in content. These changes are based on ideological shifts as well as on variations in interpretation of religious, nationalistic, and democratic ideals and, in the case of anti-Semitism, on the growth of racial and pseudoscientific theories. Shifts in historical and cultural conditions affect the rationales for both anti-Semitism and philo-Semitism and also affect the meaning given to historically specific ideas of particularism and universalism. That is, neither anti-Semitism nor philo-Semitism have universal content; the forms in which they appear depend upon the social conditions at any given time.

Second, in and of themselves the newly developed liberal ideologies could not have and did not emancipate Jews. Christians were needed to develop those ideologies and to argue that Jews as well as Christians should benefit from the changes those ideologies proposed. Liberal Christians were needed to argue against the reactionary anti-Semitic forces in Europe and to do battle with the newer "scientific" forms of anti-Semitism. This, it should be pointed out, is not the usual interpretation of the causes of Jewish emancipation. For instance, Hertzberg writes that Jewish emancipation "was an inevitable corollary of the emerging liberal-secular political order to which the future belonged,"[50] and Katz agrees: Jewish emancipation "was the result of a struggle that merged with the process of social and political changes leading these countries to a greater measure of modernization and constitutionalism."[51]

Yet these statements must be regarded as incomplete. Without disregarding the "liberal-secular political order" of the future or the merging of the "Jewish Question" with "the process of social and political changes," one should question how it is that there were processes of social and political change, how it is that a liberal-secular political order came about, and most important, how it is that Jews were included in this change. The efforts of philo-Semites in every country where there were changes and where emancipation came about must be taken into account.

It was not simply changes in France's sociopolitical structure, for example, that emancipated Jews there. Rather, it was men such as Mirabeau, arguing that Jews should and could be a part of that new structure, that provided the catalyst for Jewish emancipation. "If you wish the Jews to become better men and useful citizens, then banish every humiliating distinction, open to them every avenue of gaining a livelihood; instead of forbidding them agriculture, handicrafts, and the mechanical arts, encourage them to devote themselves to these occupations."[52] Hertzberg's suggestion that the political meaning of the French Revolution was that the state now dealt with individuals rather than with hereditary groups did not mean that Jews would automatically be included within the state. A second alternative, the expulsion of French Jewry, was discussed with the same intensity as the possibility of citizenship.[53]

The efforts of philo-Semites contributed significantly to the willingness of the citizenry to accept Jews as members of the state. Variations in the effectiveness of the philo-Semites explain the variations in time of Jewish emancipation. Thus Herbert I. Bloom notes that in Holland "it was not without a struggle [that] in 1796 emancipation was officially accorded to the Jews." Yet even though "the friends and opponents of emancipation attacked one another violently" during the debate on this issue, the debate only lasted *eight days*.[54] On the other hand, initial discussion of emancipation of German Jewry began before the French Revolution, but that emancipation was not put into effect until nearly *one hundred years* later. To suggest, then, that "emancipation, in Germany as elsewhere, can be said to have been achieved more by the general trend of public sentiment in these countries than by the victory of its champions or the weight of their arguments in favor of the Jews"[55] does not explain the variation in time. The "trend of public sentiment" was divided, and political and racial anti-Semitism had numerous and powerful proponents. To a large degree it was Christian "champions" who shaped that "general trend" in favor of emancipation.

The universalisms of the market (capitalism), of the nation (nationalism), and of humanity (human rights) combined into the universalism of citizenship. To a large degree Jews were included as citizens because of these universalisms; yet it cannot be forgotten that everywhere the Jews had and needed supporters, philo-Semites, to fight for them. It was the philo-Semites who argued that Jews as well as Christians warranted consideration within these universalisms and who demanded Jewish inclusion in the emerging sociopolitical order. This was crucial; without those supporters Jewish emancipation would have been delayed at best. At worst it would have remained a dream. This clearly was the case in Russia and, but for international pressure, would also have been the case in Switzerland.

It cannot be ignored that, in accomplishing this, liberals strengthened their own position. This was especially true in the central and eastern European states, where liberals needed as much support as possible. Liberal support for Jews meant Jewish support for liberals. As noted earlier, there is no doubt that some liberals also included Jews as members of the new social structure because of a natural extension of their ideology; freedom of religion and the rights of man could not arbitrarily halt before Jews. Others, however, saw no contradiction between their ideologies and such an arbitrary distinction.

There is, however, another side to this argument that philo-Semitism was a political exchange. Liberals also weakened their position by arguing in favor of the inclusion of Jews in society. Antiliberals regularly used anti-Semitic propaganda to bolster their position and to plead the cause of romanticized, historical, and pure-Christian nationalism. And nationalism, not toleration, was the dominant ideology of the nineteenth century. Liberals had to convince the Christian populace that liberalism and the inclusion of Jews were part of the new political order.

The position that liberals took vis-à-vis Jews, then, may be said to have been more of a liability to their overall position than an asset. Moreover, the length and depth of the struggles they undertook because of Jews far outweighed the benefits they received by having the relatively small Jewish population side with them. Until they were successful, Jews had no voice in the social and political change and could not aid them in effecting the liberalization of society.

## ON INTERGROUP RELATIONS

It is not at all unusual for social theorists to acknowledge that intergroup harmony is possible within a heterogeneous society. One theorist notes, for example, that "ethnocentrism in itself need not lead to either interethnic conflict or ethnic stratification."[56] Others "recognize that there are instances of harmonious relationships between ethnic groups."[57] Another, in speaking specifically of religious particularism, that is, of viewing only one's own religion as legitimate, suggests that while "particularism is very likely to result in religious hostility, it need not, and indeed does not, always do so."[58]

Some scholars cite individuals who contributed to harmonious intergroup relations and, more impressively, societies in which interethnic harmony flourishes. Hunt and Walker, for example, regard Switzerland as "a successful example of cultural pluralism," and speak of Mexico as a country in which there is "some degree of harmonious [intergroup] adjustment." Others suggest that a similar situation obtains in Brazil.[59] Scholars even note occasions when Jews and Christians not only tolerated one another, but lived together on excellent terms.[60] Beneath these testimonies to interethnic benevolence and tranquillity, however—and not very far beneath them—one can detect a different perspective. Even while paying lip service to the positive instances of intergroup harmony, most social theorists who have written on the subject appear to have come to the conclusion that there is a nearly inevitable hostile aspect to intergroup relations.

There is, the argument usually goes, an almost necessary antipathy between different groups. It can vary in intensity and manifestation, and it may be overt or covert at any given time, but everywhere and at all times the in-group views the out-group with contempt and the out-group views the in-group with resentment.[61] Further, this mutual enmity is not contingent upon specific conditions, although its intensity and manifestations are. The enmity itself always exists.

The reasonableness of Robert K. Merton's arguments in rejecting this position appear to have had little effect; yet he is clearly correct in suggesting that "inner-cohesion and inter-hostility is only *one of several* patterns exhibited by membership groups in their relations with other groups." Moreover, "common observation bears this out." Social theorists, Merton continues, perhaps because of "conceptual fixity and the connotations of the in-group concept have tended to obscure this readily observable fact."[62]

That social theorists regard intergroup hostility as mysteriously universal is determinable from even a cursory examination of discussions of ethnic group relations. The more one examines the literature, the more it becomes apparent that virtually "on every side" it is accepted that "solidarity within the group promotes hostility toward those outside the group, and conversely, in a cumulative spiral of inner-cohesion-and-outer-hostility."[63] Merton is not exaggerating here. Scholars have apparently rejected the idea that ethnic awareness and intergroup harmony can coexist.

For example, while offering an (apparently reluctant) nod to the idea of interethnic peace, tolerance, and even respect, one theorist remarks that "group antagonisms seem to be inevitable when two peoples in contact with each other may be distinguished by differentiating characteristics, inborn, cultural, or fabricated, and are actual or potential competitors."[64] Others note that "even in the most stable situations minority groups are viewed as potentially threatening to the position of the dominant group."[65] In terms of interreligious relations Katz remarks: "The acceptance of an alien religion always involves the overcoming of inhibitions naturally caused by the visible symbols of a religion to which one has not been reared from early childhood."[66] Hertzberg suggests the universality of "the hatred that any people have for aliens in their midst."[67] The Jew, of course, has always been the classical example of the stranger.[68]

These and similar views have a long and respected history. More than seventy years ago William Graham Sumner noted that "the relation of comradeship and peace in the we-group and that of hostility and war towards others-group are correlative to each other."[69] Intergroup hostility, then, has been taken to be a necessary aspect of intragroup harmony. As many scholars and not a few students of Jewish history suggest, one clear indication of this is Christian anti-Semitism, to which, in various forms, Jews have been subjected for two thousand years.

These overstatements and this acceptance of "a cumulative spiral of inner-cohesion-and-outer-hostility" deserves repudiation. Enmity and tranquillity may exist between ethnic groups at the same time; one does not preclude the other. Indeed, simultaneity of interethnic hostility and harmony is the norm, sometimes within the same person.

Moreover, if inter-group hostility between Jews and Christians were natural, it would follow that, simply because Jews are Jews, it is natural and therefore acceptable for Christians to attack and reject them. Arendt points out the speciousness of such a position and the dangers in its acceptance and denies the existence of such an "internal anti-Semitism." She correctly notes that to argue for a natural, eternal anti-Semitism is not to explain anti-Semitism, it is to offer an excuse for it. With such an excuse, anti-Semitic outbursts would "need no special explanation because they are natural consequences of an eternal problem." She adds: "If it is true that mankind has insisted on murdering Jews for more than two thousand years, then Jew-killing is a normal, and even human, occupation and Jew-hatred is justified beyond the need of argument."[70]

Interethnic friction and Christian anti-Semitism do exist. Nor is it the intent of this work to discount or apologize for that friction or for anti-Semitism in any way. But it is one thing to recognize the existence of intergroup conflict and quite another to project its exclusive sway as a sociological axiom. It is not unreasonable to suggest the possibility of another perspective.[71] It should be understood that most intergroup disharmony is diffused, unfocused, and coexistent with intergroup harmony. Further, as illustrated throughout this book, when anti-Semitism was at its worst, there were significant and frequent instances of philo-Semitism. The position that many scholars appear to endorse seems excessively narrow and in conflict with empirical evidence.

Moreover, from a theoretical point of view, that position leaves numerous questions unanswered; worse, it leaves the questions unasked. If, for example, inter-group hostility were universal, it would be difficult to explain the continued existence of heterogeneous societies. How are subcultures to be regarded? How, to paraphrase Thomas Hobbes, is an intergroup society possible? Speaking of Jews specifically, how could Jews have survived, become emancipated, or entered society? If hostility were basic to Jewish-

Christian relations, why is it that Jews were not expelled from Christendom completely? This would have been especially likely when the nation-state was being formed. That the possibility existed has already been shown; expulsion was considered not only in France, but everywhere in Europe as a viable alternative to acceptance of Jews within the nation-state.

Further, if social theorists wish to endorse a theory of "natural" group hostility, then they have been examining the wrong phenomena. If intergroup hostility is ubiquitous and all-powerful, then instances of tolerance, not bigotry, are to be explained. And if anti-Semitism has everywhere and always existed, then the continued existence of Jews within Christendom, not the expulsions and massacres, has to be examined.

Clearly one must acknowledge the existence and effects of inter-group harmony as well as the existence and effects of intergroup hostility. One must also recognize that while anti-Semitism exists and has extracted a monstrous cost from Jews, it has not been ubiquitous, all-powerful, or without Christian opponents. Without denying that intergroup hostility has and still does exist, without denying that anti-Semitism has been and is omnipresent in Christian Europe, and without denying that analyses of group relations in general and Jewish-Christian relations in particular must examine the all-too-frequent antipathies, it is still necessary to acknowledge and scrutinize the positive aspects of these relations. It might also be suggested that by recognizing and examining intergroup harmony, the task of examining intergroup hostility will be facilitated; the latter ought not to be studied without considering the former.

There also exists a vast area between enmity and sympathy that is neither hostile nor benevolent but tolerant, in the sense that groups simply accept and respect the existence of other groups. In addition to overt or covert hostility, there may be a disquieting uneasiness in one group regarding another; there may also be curiosity, admiration, and affection. There may even be a total disregard of differences. This, for example, was the case of the Jews in China, who suffered no discrimination, were accepted into the community, and lived their lives uneventfully.

Intergroup relations, as a field of study, is complex and warrants a broader focus than merely the study of groups in conflict. Numerous other aspects must also be considered, some of which are indicated in the discussion of the forms of philo-Semitism. Even when concentrating on the negative side of intergroup relations, as many sociologists and others seem determined to do, variations within that negativism must be examined. There are varying degrees of conflict and of hostility, which explain in part the continuance of European Jewry during the annihilation of the Albigensians, the burning of heretics, and the religious wars. Scholars acknowledge such variations but rarely analyze them.

A useful beginning for such a project might be to examine *all* the forms of intergroup relations, *all* the variations in attitudes. Intergroup attitudes (everything else follows from these) range not only from hostility to tolerance, but past tolerance and neutrality to positive, accepting, and friendly perspectives.

## NOTES

1. Freud (1967), pp. 133-34.
2. Parkes (1962), p. 238. See also Freud (1967), p. 176. Simpson and Yinger (1972, pp. 254-55) put it this way: "One of the most puzzling problems is that the Jews survived at all as a distinct group, rather than disappearing into the ranks of the dominant society or changing too much to be recognized."
3. Schweitzer (1971), p. 299.
4. Mayer, in Graeber and Britt (1942), p. 315.
5. Keller (1969), p. xx. Teller (1968, p. 242) also regards the survival of the Jewish people as something of a miracle.
6. See *The Village Voice*, June 20, 1974.
7. Mayer, in Graeber and Britt (1942), p. 316; Parkes (1962), p. vii; Freud (1967), p. 158.
8. Quoted in Mayer, in Graeber and Britt (1942), p. 317.
9. Poliakov (1965), p. 46. He also suggests (ibid., p. 82) a variation of this: Taxes on Jews in Germany were placed on the Jewish community, not on individual Jews. This contributed to communal strength.
10. Hertzler, in Graeber and Britt (1942), p. 83.
11. A. L. Sachar (1965), p. 347.
12. Sartre (1962), p. 144.
13. Baruch Spinoza, "Of the Vocation of the Hebrews," *Tractatus Theologia-Politicus*.
14. George Friedman, "Jews as the Product of History," in Gelfand and Lee (1973), p. 134. Friedman continues (ibid., p. 134): "Anti-Semitism produces Jewish feeling and is responsible for Jewish survival, but Jewish separation has helped it and (to the extent that it is prolonged by anti-Semitism) still helps it at the present day."
15. This a-Semitism of Italians is determinable from their actions during World War II as well as from the fact that Jews in Italy have historically suffered relatively little discrimination. The lives of Italian Jews have not generally been complicated because of their Jewishness, particularly since the unification of Italy. See Roth (1946), passim.
16. Hertzler, in Graeber and Britt (1942), p. 84.
17. White (1966), pp. 10-12, 66-67. Originally the Jews of K'ai-feng Fu were called T'iao-chin Chiao, literally, "the sect or religion which plucks out the sinew." Chinese Jews did not like this, and the name of the religion was changed to Chiao Ching Chiao, "the religion that teaches the scriptures."
18. Rhee (1973), p. 118.
19. White (1966), pp. 17-20.

20. See White (1966), p. 175; Rhee (1973), pp. 118-19; and Schweitzer (1971), p. 274. Poliakov (1965, p. 15) agrees and suggests: "Other conditions, it appears, are essential in order to assure the persistence and multiplication of the Jewish people among the nations."

21. Rhee (1973), p. 119. See also Poliakov (1965), p. 15.

22. See Strizower (1971), p. 5.

23. At least this was the case until the 1930s, when Hitler's anti-Semitic propaganda machine directed its attention to the great Subcontinent. Mohandas Gandhi, it should be noted, was not only unreceptive to Germany's arguments but was a forceful anti-anti-Semite.

24. Grayzel (1968, p. 642) agrees: "The Chinese Jews disappeared because of their isolation."

25. Arendt (1958), p. 64. She suggests (ibid., p. 62) that assimilation as a group phenomenon existed among Jewish intellectuals.

26. The assimilation of Italian Jews apparently supports the argument that in a generally a-Semitic society there may be a loss to the Jewish community. The continued existence of Jews in Italy indicates that the threat of assimilation has been somewhat exaggerated by scholars, however. Moreover, regarding the comparative dangers of anti-Semitism and assimilation, it should be considered that there are fewer Jews in Germany today than in Italy.

27. If anti-Semitism is a mechanism for internal Jewish preservation, it is also a mechanism for internal Jewish destruction. It is mainly anti-Semitism, not its lack, that causes conversions, and it is anti-Semitism that brings about the psychological counterpart of conversion, Jewish self-hatred. Whether or not these compensate for whatever degree of Jewish cohesion anti-Semitism brings is, of course, open to debate. It is the opinion of the writer, however, that the damages brought by anti-Semitism far exceed its real or imagined benefits.

28. Not surprisingly Arendt (1958, p. 8) accurately and succinctly points to this obvious fact: "Antisemitism, far from being a mysterious guarantee of the survival of the Jewish people, has been clearly revealed as a threat of its extermination." Arendt is speaking here of modern anti-Semitism; yet one can and should extend this to the entire history of the Jews.

29. Poliakov (1965), p. 46.

30. Rose (1974), pp. 173-74. Weber disagrees with this analysis. See Max Weber, "Class, Status, and Party," in Bendix and Lipset (1966), p. 25, on pariah dignity.

31. Allport (1958), p. 146. Emphasis in the original.

32. It may be argued that the political unity of the Middle Ages was so incomplete that concentrated action against Jews was almost impossible. This did not prevent the Christian Albigensians from being slaughtered, however.

33. Katz (1962), p. xi.

34. Rogow (1961), p. viii.

35. Kohn (1967), p. 6.

36. Kohn (1965), pp. 30, 34.

37. A. L. Sachar (1965), p. 285.

38. Katz (1973), p. 193.

39. Hertzberg (1968), p. 11.

40. For example, Jewish merchants were prohibited from dealing in the City of London until 1831. See Bermant (1971), p. 60.

41. Thus H. M. Sachar writes (1958, pp. 19-20), "Modern European capitalism, mercantilism, and rationalism were directly responsible for battering down the walls of the ghetto, emancipating the Jews physically, politically, and intellectually, and enabling them to move into the bright sunlight of nineteenth-century civilization." Still, Sachar somewhat overstates the case. Even if capitalism, mercantilism, and rationalism were necessary conditions for Jewish emancipation, they were not sufficient conditions.

42. Arendt (1958), p. 35. Also see Hertzberg (1968), p. 5.

43. This phrase was first applied to the Huguenots, not the Jews.

44. Pulzer (1964), p. vii.

45. Katz (1973), p. 199.

46. Hertzberg (1968), p. 11. Emphasis in original.

47. It is crucial to recall here that Jews often were different in appearance and speech from their Christian neighbors. See Katz (1973), p. 80.

48. Pulzer (1964), p. 49.

49. Thus Hitler wrote (Mein Kampf, translated by Ralph Manheim, Boston: Houghton Mifflin Co., 1943, p. 307) that the statement "that the Jews are not a race but a religion" is the "first and greatest lie. . . . The Jew," he argued (ibid., p. 306), "has always been a people with definite racial characteristics and never a religion." Hitler's intellectual predecessors were writers such as Joseph DeMaistre, Joseph DeGobineau, and, at the end of the nineteenth century, Houston Stewart Chamberlain. They set the tone for the new nationalistic, reactionary, and pseudoscientific racial anti-Semitism.

50. Hertzberg (1968), p. 2.

51. Katz (1973), p. 198.

52. Quoted in Graetz (1895), vol. 5, p. 433.

53. Hertzberg (1968), p. 338.

54. Bloom (1969), p. 31; Universal Jewish Encyclopedia, 5, p. 436.

55. Katz (1973), p. 198.

56. Donald L. Noel, "A Theory of Ethnic Stratification," in Gelfand and Lee (1973), p. 21.

57. Gelfand and Lee (1973), p. 4.

58. Glock and Stark (1966), p. 21.

59. Hunt and Walter (1974), pp. 41, 128. They add that there is a movement toward a common culture and sociological classification that seems to suggest assimilationist trends and, consequently, the loss of ethnicity. See also studies by T. Lynn Smith (1972). Smith may be exaggerating the case, however.

60. See, for example, Poliakov (1965), p. 246. A. L. Sachar (1965, p. 194) points out that in southern France during the time of Innocent III, Jews, Moslems, and Christians lived together in harmony—a harmony that was eventually destroyed by Innocent.

61. James G. Martin and Frank R. Westie, "The Tolerant Personality," in Alan R. Brown (1972, p. 131), argue that "the degree to which rejection of particular outgroups is approved varies from one subculture to another and from religion to religion."

Referring to the United States, however, they suggest that "prejudice towards out-groups is part of the normative order of American society" (ibid., p. 131).

62. Merton (1968), p. 352. Emphasis added.

63. Merton (1968), p. 352.

64. Hertzler, in Graeber and Britt (1942), pp. 80-81.

65. Yetman and Steele (1971), p. 5. To Yetman and Steele power relations are the key to in-group/out-group relations (ibid., p. 3).

66. Katz (1962), p. 22. See also Poliakov (1965), pp. 158, 161. If this were the case, various attempts to de-alienize Jews would become extremely relevant, making it possible to reinterpret the actions of Napoleon and Joseph II, for example.

67. Hertzberg (1968), p. 5.

68. Simmel (1950), p. 403. Also see TeSelle (1973), p. 49; and Rose (1974), p. 175. Erdman B. Palmore, in "Ethnophaulisms and Ethnocentrism," in Barron (1967, p. 205), suggests: "It seems to be universal for racial and ethnic groups to coin derogatory terms and sayings to refer to other groups."

69. Quoted from *Folkways* by Merton (1968), p. 351.

70. Arendt (1958), p. 7.

71. Consider, for example, Merton's argument: "What can be questioned, ... and indeed is being questioned here, is whether this is the *only* pattern that connects up the inner cohesion of groups and their external relations, whether, in effect, all membership groups operate in the fashions described by Sumner" (1958, p. 352). Emphasis in the original.

# BIBLIOGRAPHY

To cite every source consulted in the course of writing this book would result in a bibliography almost as long as the study itself. Listed below are books and articles that were particularly valuable or that have been quoted or referred to in the text. Five general references proved invaluable and are noted here separately: *The Universal Jewish Encyclopedia*. 10 vols. New York: KTAV Publishing House, 1969. *Encyclopedia Judaica*. 16 vols. New York: Macmillan Co., 1971. *The International Encyclopedia of the Social Sciences*. 17 vols. New York: Macmillan Co. and the Free Press, 1968. *The Encyclopedia of Philosophy*. 8 vols. New York: Macmillan Co. and the Free Press, 1967. *Cambridge Medieval History*. 8 vols. London: Cambridge University Press, 1936.

Abbott, Wilbur Cortez. *The Writings and Speeches of Oliver Cromwell*. 4 vols. London: Oxford University Press, 1937-47.

Agar, Herbert. *The Saving Remnant*. New York: Viking Press, 1960.

Agus, Irving. *The Heroic Age of Franco-German Jewry*. New York: Yeshiva University Press, 1969.

Agus, Jacob B., ed. *Judaism and Christianity: Selected Accounts, 1892-1962*. New York: Arno Press, 1973.

Allport, Gordon. *The Nature of Prejudice*. New York: Anchor Books, 1958.

Arendt, Hannah. *Origins of Totalitarianism*. 2d ed. New York: Meridian, 1958.

Artz, Frederick B. *The Enlightenment in France*. Kent, Ohio: Kent State University Press, 1968.

Atchildi, Asaf. "Rescue of Jews of Bukharan, Iranian, and Afghan Origin in Occupied France." *Yad Vashem Publications*, Book 6, Jerusalem, 1967.

Bainton, Roland H. *The Reformation of the Sixteenth Century*. Boston: Beacon Press, 1956.

_____ . *Christendom*. 2 vols. New York: Harper and Row, 1966.

Baron, Salo W. *European Jewry before and after Hitler*. Philadelphia: Jewish Publication Society of America, 1962.

_____ . *A Social and Religious History of the Jews*. 2d (enlarged) ed., 12 vols. New York: Columbia University Press, 1965a.

_____ "John Calvin and the Jews." In *Harry Austryn Wolfson Jubilee Volume*. English section, vol. 1. Jerusalem: American Academy for Jewish Research, 1965b.

———— . *Ancient and Medieval Jewish History*. New Brunswick, N.J.: Rutgers University Press, 1972.

Barron, Milton, ed. *Minorities in a Changing World*. New York: Alfred A. Knopf, 1967.

Becker, Carl L. *The Heavenly City of the Eighteenth-Century Philosophers*. New Haven, Conn.: Yale University Press, 1970.

Bendix, Reinhard, and Lipset, Seymour Martin, eds. *Class Status and Power*. 3d ed. New York: Free Press, 1966.

Bensman, Joseph, and Lilienfeld, Robert. *Craft and Consciousness*. New York: John Wiley & Sons, 1973.

Ben-Zvi, Itzhak. *The Exiled and the Redeemed*. Philadelphia: Jewish Publication Society of America, 1961.

Berenstein, Tatiana, and Rutkowski, Adam. "The Rescue of Jews by Poles under Nazi Occupation." *Zydowskiego Instytutu Historycznego* (BZIH), English summary, No. 35, 1960, pp. 129-30.

Bermant, Chaim. *The Cousinhood*. New York: Macmillan Co., 1971.

Bettleheim, Bruno, and Janowitz, Morris. *Social Change and Prejudice*. New York: Free Press, 1964.

Birmingham, Steven. *Our Crowd*. New York: Dell Publishers, 1967.

———— . *The Grandees*. New York: Dell Publishers, 1972.

Bishop, Clair Huchet. *How Catholics Look at Jews*. New York: Paulist Press, 1974.

Blake, Robert. *Disraeli*. New York: St. Martin's Press, 1967.

Blalock, Hubert M. *Toward a Theory of Minority-Group Relations*. New York: John Wiley & Sons, 1967.

Bloom, Herbert I. *The Economic Activities of the Jews of Amsterdam in the Seventeenth and Eighteenth Century*. Port Washington, N.Y.: Kennikat Press, 1969.

Bonacich, Edna. "A Theory of Middleman Minorities." *American Sociological Review* 38 (October 1973).

Brandon, S.G.F. *Jesus and the Zealots*. New York: Charles Scribner's Sons, 1967.

Bronowski, J., and Mazlish, Bruce. *The Western Intellectual Tradition*. New York: Harper and Row, 1962.

Brown, Alan R., ed. *Prejudice in Children*. Springfield, Ill.: Charles C. Thomas, 1972.

Brown, Roger. *Social Psychology*. New York: Free Press, 1965.

Bruun, Geoffrey. *Revolution and Reaction*. Princeton, N.J.: Anvil Books, 1958.

Byrnes, Robert F. *Anti-Semitism in Modern France: The Prologue to the Dreyfus Affair*. Vol. 1. New York: Howard Fertig, 1969.

Calish, Edward N. *The Jews in English Literature*. Port Washington, N.Y.: Kennikat Press, 1969 (orginally published in 1909).

Cannon, William Ragsdale. *History of Christianity in the Middle Ages*. Nashville, Tenn.: Abingdon Press, 1960.

Carlyle, Thomas. *Oliver Cromwell's Letters and Speeches*. 2 vols. New York: Wiley and Putnam, 1845.

Carsten, Francis Ludwig. "The Court Jews: A Prelude to Emancipation." *Leo Baeck Institute Yearbook* 3, 1958.

Chapman, Guy. *The Dreyfus Case*. London: Rupert Hart-Davis, 1955.

Church, Samuel Harden. *Oliver Cromwell: A History*. New York: G. P. Putnam's Sons, 1895.

Clough, Shepard B.; Pflanze, Otto; and Payne, Stanley G. *A History of the Western World*. 3 vols. Boston: D. C. Heath and Co., 1964.

Coser, Lewis A. *The Functions of Social Conflict*. New York: Free Press, 1956.

_____ . *Masters of Sociological Thought*. New York: Harcourt Brace Jovanovich, 1971.

_____ . "The Alien as a Servant of Power: Court Jews and Christian Renegades." *American Sociological Review* 37 (October 1972).

Cuddihy, John Murray. *The Ordeal of Civility*. New York: Delta, 1976.

Davies, Alan T. *Anti-Semitism and the Christian Mind*. New York: Herder and Herder, 1969.

Dawidowicz, Lucy S. *The War Against the Jews 1933-1945*. New York: Holt, Rinehart, Winston, 1975.

Dawson, Christopher. "The Making of Modern Europe." In B. Tierny, D. Kagan, and L. P. Williams, eds., *Christianity in the Roman Empire: Why Did It Succeed?* New York: Random House, 1967.

Dimont, Max I. *Jews, God and History*. New York: Signet, 1962.

_____ . *The Indestructible Jews*. Rev. ed. New York: Signet, 1973.

Dubnov, Simon. *History of the Jews*. 5 vols. Translated from the 4th Russian edition by Moshe Spiegel. South Brunswick, New York, 1969-1973.

_____. *History of the Jews in Russia and Poland from the Earliest Times until the Present Day*. 3 vols. Translated from the Russian by I. Friedlander. Philadelphia: Jewish Publication Society of America, 1916.

Durant, Will. *Caesar and Christ*. New York: Simon and Schuster, 1944.

Dvornik, Francis. *Byzantium and the Roman Primacy*. New York: Fordham University Press, 1966.

Eckhardt, A. Roy. *Elder and Younger Brothers*. New York: Schocken Books, 1973.

Eligulashvili, Levi. "How the Jews of Gruzia in Occupied France Were Saved." *Yad Vashem Publications*, Book 6, Jerusalem, 1967.

Ettinger, Shmuel. "The Beginnings of the Change in the Attitude of European Society towards the Jews." *Scripta Hierocolymitana* 7, 1961.

Falconi, Carlo. *The Silence of Pius XII*. Translated by Bernard Wall. Boston: Little, Brown and Little, 1970.

Faulkner, Joseph E., ed. *Religion's Influence in Contemporary Society*. Columbus, Ohio: Charles E. Merrill, 1972.

Finkelstein, Louis, ed. *The Jews: Their History, Culture and Religion*. 2 vols., 3d ed. New York: Harper and Row, 1960.

_____ , ed. *The Jews: Their History*. 4th ed. New York: Schocken, 1974.

Fitzmyer, Joseph A. *Pauline Theology*. Englewood Cliffs, N.J.: Prentice-Hall, 1967.

Flannery, Edward H. *The Anguish of the Jews*. New York: Macmillan Co., 1965.

Flender, Harold. *Rescue in Denmark*. New York: Simon and Schuster, 1963.

Frend, W.H.C. *The Rise of the Monophysite Movement*. London: Cambridge University Press, 1972.

Freud, Sigmund. *Moses and Monotheism*. New York: Vintage, 1967 (originally published in 1939).

Friedlaender, Saul. *Kurt Gerstein: The Ambiguity of Good*. Translated by Charles Fullman. New York: Alfred A. Knopf, 1969.

Friedman, Philip. *Their Brothers' Keepers*. New York: Crown Publishers, 1957.

Gay, Peter, and Webb, R. K. *Modern Europe*. New York: Harper and Row, 1973.

Gelfand, Donald E., and Lee, Russell D., eds. *Ethnic Conflicts and Power: A Cross-National Prospective*. New York: John Wiley & Sons, 1973.

Gershoy, Leo. *The French Revolution and Napoleon*. New York: Appleton-Century-Crofts, 1964.

Gibb, H.A.R., and Bowen, Harold. *Islamic Society and the West*. London: Oxford University Press, 1957.

Gibbon, Edward. *The Triumph of Christianity in the Roman Empire*. New York: Harper and Brothers, 1958 (orginally published in 1909 as Chapters 15-20 in *The Decline and Fall of the Roman Empire*).

Gilbert, Felix, et al. *The Norton History of Modern Europe*. New York: W. W. Norton and Co., 1971.

Glazer, Nathan. *American Judaism*. Chicago: University of Chicago Press, 1957.

Glock, Charles Y., and Stark, Rodney. *Christian Beliefs and Anti-Semitism*. New York: Harper and Row, 1966.

Godechot, Jacques. *The Counter-Revolution: Doctrine and Action 1789-1804*. Translated by Salvator Attanasio. New York: Howard Fertig, 1971.

Goiten, S. D. *Jews and Arabs*. 3d ed. New York: Schocken, 1974.

Gordon, Milton. *Assimilation in American Life*. New York: Oxford University Press, 1964.

Gottschalk, Louis R. *The Era of the French Revolution*. Cambridge, Mass.: Houghton Mifflin Co., 1929.

Graeber, Isacque, and Britt, Steuart Henderson, eds. *Jews in a Gentile World*. New York: Macmillan Co., 1942.

Graetz, Heinrich. *History of the Jews*. 6 vols. Philadelphia: Jewish Publication Society of America, 1891-1898.

Grant, Michael. *The Jews in the Roman World*. New York: Charles Scribner's Sons, 1973.

Grayzel, Solomon. *The Church and the Jews in the XIIIth Century*. Rev. ed. New York: Hermon Press, 1966.

————. *A History of the Jews*. Rev. ed. New York: Mentor, 1968.

Gregorovius, Ferdinand. *The Ghetto and the Jews of Rome*. New York: Schocken, 1966 (originally published in 1853).

Gutteridge, Richard. *The German Evangelical Church and the Jews 1879-1950*. New York: Barnes and Noble, 1976.

Halasz, Nicholas. *Captain Dreyfus: The Story of Mass Hysteria*. New York: Simon and Schuster, 1955.

Halpern, Ben. *The Idea of the Jewish State*. 2d. ed. Cambridge, Mass.: Harvard University Press, 1969.

Hay, Malcolm. *Europe and the Jews*. Boston: Beacon Press, 1961.

Hayes, Carlton J. H. *Modern Europe to 1870*. New York: Macmillan Co., 1953.

Heer, Friedrich. *The Medieval World*. Translated by Janet Sondheimer. New York: Mentor, 1962.

Heiman, Leo. "They Saved Jews: Ukrainian Patriots Defied Nazis." *The Ukrainian Quarterly* 17 (4), winter 1961.

Helmreich, Ernst Christian. *The German States under Hitler*. Detroit: Wayne State University Press, 1979.

Hertzberg, Arthur. *The French Enlightenment and the Jews.* New York: Columbia University Press, 1968.

Higham, John. *Strangers in the Land.* New York: Atheneum, 1973.

Himmelfarb, Milton. "The Greeks, the Romans, and Captain Dreyfus." *Commentary* 55 (2), February 1973.

Hitti, Philip K. *The Arabs: A Short History.* Rev. ed. Chicago: Gateway, 1947.

Hobsbawm, E. J. *The Age of Revolution 1789-1848.* New York: Mentor, 1962.

Höffding, Harald. *A History of Modern Philosophy.* 2 vols. Translated by B. E. Meyer. New York: Dover Publishers, 1955 (orginally published in 1888).

Hoffmann, Peter. *The History of the German Resistance 1933-1945.* Translated by Richard Barry. Cambridge, Mass.: M.I.T. Press, 1977.

Holt, P. M.; Lambton, Ann K. S.; and Lewis, Bernard, eds. *The Cambridge History of Islam.* 2 vols. London: Cambridge University Press, 1970.

Hughes, Philip. *A Popular History of the Catholic Church.* New York: Macmillan Co., 1947.

Hunt, Chester L., and Walker, Lewis. *Ethnic Dynamics: Patterns of Inter-group Relations in Various Societies.* Homewood, Ill.: The Dorsey Press, 1974.

Insko, Chester. *Theories of Attitude Change.* New York: Appleton-Century-Crofts, 1967.

Janowsky, Oscar I. *Jews and Minority Rights.* New York: AMS Press, 1966.

Johnson, Edgar. *Sir Walter Scott, The Great Unknown.* 2 vols. New York: Macmillan Co., 1970.

Katz, Jacob. *Exclusiveness and Tolerance.* New York: Schocken Books, 1962.

_____ ."Freemasons and Jews." *Jewish Journal of Sociology* 9 (2), December 1967.

_____ . *Out of the Ghetto.* Cambridge, Mass.: Harvard University Press, 1973.

_____ . "Emancipation and Jewish Studies." *Commentary* 57 (4), April 1974.

Keller, Werner. *Diaspora: The Post Biblical History of the Jews.* New York: Harcourt, Brace and World, 1969.

Kirchen, Livin Roth. "Hungary—An Asylum for the Refugees of Europe." *Yad Vashem Publications,* Book 7, Jerusalem, 1968.

Kohn, Hans. *Nationalism: Its Meaning and History.* Rev. ed. New York: Van Nostrand, 1965.

_____ . *The Idea of Nationalism.* New York: Collier Books, 1967 (originally published in 1944).

Kuhn, Arthur. "Hugo Grotius and the Emancipation of the Jews in Holland." *Publication of the American-Jewish Historical Society* 31, 1928.

Küng, Hans. *On Being a Christian.* Translated by Edward Quinn. Garden City, N.Y.: Doubleday, 1976.

Lewis, David L. *Prisoners of Honor: The Dreyfus Affair.* New York: William Morrow and Co., 1973.

Lewy, Guenter. "Pius XII, the Jews, and the German Catholic Church." *Commentary* 37 (2), February 1964a.

_____ . *The Roman Catholic Church and the Third Reich.* New York: McGraw-Hill, 1964b.

Little, Franklin H., ed. *The German Church Struggle and the Holocaust.* Detroit: Wayne State University Press, 1974.

Loewenstein, R. M. *Christians and Jews*. New York: International Universities Press, 1951.

Lot, Ferdinand. *The End of the Ancient World and the Beginnings of the Middle Ages*. Translated by Philip and Mariette Leon. New York: Harper and Brothers, 1961 (first published in 1931).

Macaulay, Thomas Babington. *Critical and Historical Essays*. Arranged by A. J. Grieve. London: J. M. Dent and Sons, 1967 (originally published in 1907).

McCagg, William O., Jr. *Jewish Nobles and Geniuses in Modern Hungary*. East European Quarterly, Boulder, Colo., distributed by Columbia University Press, 1972.

McGarry, Daniel D. *Medieval History and Civilization*. New York: Macmillan Co., 1976.

Mannheim, Karl. *Ideology and Utopia*. New York: Harcourt, Brace and World, 1936.

Marcus, Jacob. *The Jews in the Medieval World: A Source Book 315-1791*. New York: Atheneum, 1965 (originally published in 1938).

Margolis, Max L., and Marx, Alexander. *A History of the Jewish People*. New York: Atheneum, 1969 (originally published in 1927).

Marrus, Michael R. *The Politics of Assimilation: A Study of the French Jewish Community at the Time of the Dreyfus Affair*. London: Oxford, 1971.

Merton, Robert K. *Social Theory and Social Structure*. Enlarged ed. New York: Free Press, 1968.

Millar, Fergus, ed. *The Roman Empire and Its Neighbors*. New York: Delacorte Press, 1966.

Miller, Merle. *Plain Speaking*. New York: Berkley Publishing Corp., 1974.

Morse, Arthur. *While Six Million Died*. New York: Ace Publishing Co., 1967.

Mosse, George L. *Germans and Jews*. New York: Howard Fertig, 1970.

Necheles, Ruth F. "The Abbé Grégoire and the Jews." *Jewish Social Studies* 33 (203), April-July 1971, pp. 120-40.

Niebuhr, Reinhold. "The Revelations of Christians and Jews in Western Civilization." *Central Conference of American Rabbis Journal*, April 1958.

Oren, Nissan. "The Bulgarian Exception. A Reassessment of the Salvation of the Jewish Community." *Yad Vashem Publications*, Book 7, Jerusalem, 1968.

Palmer, R. R., and Colton, Joel. *A History of the Modern World*. 3d ed. New York: Alfred A. Knopf, 1965.

Parkes, James. *A History of the Jewish People*. Chicago: Quadrangle, 1962.

———. *The Conflict of the Church and the Synagogue*. New York: Atheneum, 1969a.

———. *Prelude to Dialogue: Jewish-Christian Relationships*. New York: Schocken, 1969b.

Pearlman, Moshe. *The Maccabees*. New York: Macmillan Co., 1973.

Petit, Paul. *Pax Romana*. Translated by James Willis. Berkeley: University of California Press, 1976.

Polanyi, Karl. *The Great Transformation*. Boston: Beacon Press, 1957.

Poliakov, Leon. *The History of Anti-Semitism from the Time of Christ to the Court Jews*. Translated from the French by Richard Howard. New York: Schocken Books, 1965.

Postal, Bernard, and Levy, Henry W. *And the Hills Shouted For Joy*. New York: David McKay Co., 1973.

Presser, Jacob. "Dutch Defiance, The Great Strike of 1941." *Weiner Library Bulletin* 8, London, 1954.

Prinz, Joachim. *Popes from the Ghetto*. New York: Schocken Books, 1968.

Pulzer, Peter G. J. *The Rise of Political Anti-Semitism in Germany and Austria*. New York: John Wiley & Sons, 1969.

Radin, Max. *The Jews among the Greeks and the Romans*. Philadelphia: Jewish Publication Society of America, 1973 (originally published in 1915).

Ray, John J. "Is Anti-Semitism a Cognitive Simplification? Some Observations on Australian Neo-Nazis." *Jewish Journal of Sociology* 14 (2), December 1972.

Rhee, Song Nai. "Jewish Assimilation: The Case of Chinese Jews." *Comparative Studies in Society and History* 15 (1), June 1973.

Ritter, Gerhard. *The German Resistance*. Translated by R. T. Clark. London: George Allen and Unwin, Ltd., 1958.

Rivkin, Ellis. *The Shaping of Jewish History: A Radical New Interpretation*. New York: Charles Scribner's Sons, 1971.

Robb, James H. *Working Class Anti-Semite*. London: Tavistock Publications, Ltd., 1954.

Rogow, Arnold A., ed. *The Jew in a Gentile World*. New York: Macmillan Co., 1961.

Rokeach, Milton. *The Open and Closed Mind*. New York: Basic Books, 1960.

Rose, Peter I. *They and We*. 2d ed. New York: Random House, 1974.

Rosenberg, Edgar. *From Shylock to Svengali, Jewish Stereotypes in English Fiction*. Stanford, Calif.: Stanford University Press, 1960.

Rossi, Mario. "Emancipation of Jews in Italy." *Jewish Journal of Sociology*, April 1953.

Roth, Cecil. *The History of the Jews in Italy*. Philadelphia: Jewish Publication Society of America, 1946.

_____. *A History of the Marranos*. New York: Meridian, 1959a.

_____. *The Jews in the Renaissance*. New York: Harper and Row, 1959b.

_____. *Essays and Portraits in Anglo-Jewish History*. Philadelphia: Jewish Publication Society of America, 1962.

_____. *A History of the Jews in England*. 3d ed. London: Oxford University Press, 1964.

_____. *A History of the Jews from the Earliest Times through the Six Day War*. Rev. ed. New York: Schocken Books, 1970.

Rude, George. *Revolutionary Europe 1783-1815*. New York: Harper and Row, 1964.

Runciman, Steven. *A History of the Crusades*. 2 vols. London: Cambridge University Press, 1953.

Sachar, Abraham Leon. *A History of the Jews*. 5th ed. New York: Alfred A. Knopf, 1965.

Sachar, Howard Morley. *The Course of Modern Jewish History*. New York: Delta, 1958.

Sartre, Jean-Paul. *Anti-Semite and Jew*. New York: Grove Press, 1962.

Schnee, Heinrich. *Die Hoffinanz und der Modern Statt*. 3 vols. Berlin: Duncker and Humbolt, 1953-55.

Schneider, Peter. *The Dialogue of Christians and Jews*. New York: Seabury Press, 1967.

Schoeps, H. J. *Paul: The Theology of the Apostle in the Light of Jewish Religious History*. Translated by Harold Knight. Philadelphia: Westminster Press, 1961.

Schulweis, Harold. "The Bias against Man." *The Rabbinical Assembly*, 1962.

Schweitzer, Frederick M. *A History of the Jews Since the First Century A. D.* New York: Macmillan Co., 1971.

Secord, Paul F., and Backman, Carl W. *Social Psychology.* New York: McGraw-Hill, 1964.

Selznick, Gertrude J., and Steinberg, Stephen. *The Tenacity of Prejudice.* New York: Harper and Row, 1969.

Shirer, William L. *The Rise and Fall of the Third Reich.* New York: Simon and Schuster, 1960.

Simmel, Georg. *The Sociology of Georg Simmel.* Translated, edited, and with an introduction by Kurt H. Wolf. New York: Free Press, 1950.

Simpson, George E., and Yinger, J. Milton. *Racial and Cultural Minorities.* 4th ed. New York: Harper and Row, 1972.

Slater, Leonard. *The Pledge.* New York: Pocket Books, 1971.

Smallwood, E. Mary. *The Jews under Roman Rule.* Leiden, The Netherlands: E. J. Brill, 1976.

Smith, T. Lynn. *Brazil: People and Institutions.* 4th ed. Baton Rouge: Louisiana State University Press, 1972.

Snyder, Louis, ed. *Documents in German History.* New Brunswick, N. J.: Rutgers University Press, 1958.

————. *The Blood and Iron Chancellor: A Documentary-Biography of Otto von Bismarck.* Princeton, N. J.: Van Nostrand, 1967.

Sombart, Werner. *The Jews and Modern Capitalism.* New York: Free Press, 1951 (originally published in 1913).

Spotts, Frederic. *The Churches and Politics in Germany.* Middletown, Conn.: Wesleyan University Press, 1973.

Stark, Rodney, and Steinberg, Stephen. "It Did Happen Here—An Investigation of Political Anti-Semitism: Wayne, New Jersey." *Anti-Defamation League of B'nai B'rith,* 1967.

Stember, Charles H., et al. *Jews in the Mind of America.* New York: Basic Books, 1961.

Stern, Selma. *The Court Jew.* Philadelphia: Jewish Publication Society of America, 1950.

Stoppleman, Joseph W. F. "The Dutch Defy Hitler." *Congress Weekly,* New York, July 10, 1942.

Strayer, Joseph R. *The Albigensian Crusade.* New York: Dial Press, 1971.

Strizower, Schifra. *The Bene Israel of Bombay.* New York: Schocken Books, 1971.

Suhl, Yuri. *They Fought Back: The Story of Jewish Resistance in Nazi Europe.* New York: Schocken Books, 1975.

Talmage, Frank. "Christianity and the Jewish People." *Commentary* 59 (2), February 1975.

Tawney, R. H. *Religion and the Rise of Capitalism.* New York: Mentor, 1954 (originally published in 1926).

Teller, Judd L. *Strangers and Natives.* New York: Delta, 1968.

TeSelle, S., ed. *The Rediscovery of Ethnicity.* New York: Harper and Row, 1973.

Thompson, J. M. *The French Revolution.* New York: Oxford University Press, 1966.

Tierney, B.; Kagan, D.; and Williams, L. P., eds. *Christianity in the Roman Empire— Why Did It Succeed?* New York: Random House, 1967.

Tovey, De Blossiers. *Anglia Judaica: History and Antiquities of the Jews in England.* New York: Burt Franklin, 1967 (originally published in 1738).

Trachtenberg, Joshua. *The Devil and the Jews.* New Haven, Conn.: Yale University Press, 1943.

Tumin, Melvin. "An Inventory and Appraisal of Research on American Anti-Semitism." New York, 1961.

_____. "Anti-Semitism and Status Anxiety." *Jewish Social Studies*, October 1971.

van den Haag, Ernest. *The Jewish Mystique.* New York: Stein and Day, 1969.

Veblen, Thorstein. "The Intellectual Pre-Eminence of Jews in Modern Europe." *Political Science Quarterly*, March 1919.

Waagenaar, Sam. *The Pope's Jews.* New York: Library Press, 1974.

Weber, Max. *The Protestant Ethic and the Spirit of Capitalism.* New York: Charles Scribner's Sons, 1958a.

_____. *From Max Weber.* Edited by H. H. Gerth and C. W. Mills. New York: Oxford University Press, 1958b.

Weiner, Joel H., ed. *Great Britain, Lion at Home: A Documentary History of Domestic Policy of 1689-1973.* 4 vols. New York: Chelsea House, 1974.

White, William Charles. *Chinese Jews.* 2d ed. New York: Paragon Book Reprint Corp., 1966.

Williams, Robin M., Jr. *Strangers Next Door.* Englewood Cliffs, N. J.: Prentice-Hall, 1964.

Wirth, Louis. *On Cities and Social Life.* Chicago: Phoenix Books, 1964.

Yetman, Norman R., and Steele, C. Hoy, eds. *Majority and Minority.* Boston: Allyn and Bacon, 1971.

# INDEX

Württemberg, 154
Wyclif, John, 33-34

Yad Vashem, 161, 162
Yaghello, Alexander (King of Poland), 89
York (city), 49, 79

Yugoslavia: and the Holocaust, 166

Zionism, 19, 24 n.28, 104, 112, 126 n.9,
    170 n.97, 191 n.8
Zola, Émile, 141, 168 n.36

## About the Author

**ALAN EDELSTEIN** is an Instructor of Sociology at Towson State University in Towson, Maryland. He is currently working on a study of philo-Semitism and anti-Semitism in the United States.